PILGRIMAGE TOURISM
MARKETING STRATEGY

PILGRIMAGE TOURISM MARKETING STRATEGY

With special reference to

Shri Mata Vaishno Devi Shrine

Sushma Mawa

2004

Kaveri Books

New Delhi - 110002

© Sushma Mawa (b. 1972-)

First Published in 2004

ISBN 81-7479-066-7

Published by   : **Rakesh Goel**
                         Kaveri Books
                         4697/5-21A, Ansari Road
                         New Delhi-110002 (India)

                         Tel.: 2328 8140, 2324 5799
                         E-mail: kaveribooks@vsnl.com

Laser Typesetting by : Aarati Computers, Delhi-110 009

Printed at   : Chawla Offset Printers, Delhi-110 052

PRINTED IN INDIA

PREFACE

Travel for religious purposes, i.e, pilgrimages, has significantly increased manifold during recent times. It is the pilgrimages that have caused people to travel since long for regeneration of spirit and quick cultural exchange. During such visits, pilgrims require some services at, and en route, the pilgrimage destination. The availability of such services depend upon the socio-economic demography of the pilgrims and the nature of the destination visited. Shri Mata Vaishno Devi Shrine is a pilgrimage destination of immense religious importance, attracting more than 50 lakh visitors every year, thus generating ample business potential for the pilgrimage tourism services. Every pilgrim visiting the Shrine requires some services at and en route the destination, which is provided by private agencies, Government bodies and Shri Mata Vaishno Devi Shrine Board. This study has tried to evaluate/measure the extent of marketing effectiveness of four important pilgrimage tourism services, viz., hotel services, transportation services, retail services and supervisory vis-à-vis some basic pilgrimage services of the Shrine Board at Vaishno Devi Shrine on a five point Likert scale. The present study, thereby, has been undertaken to evolve a suitable and effective marketing strategy for each pilgrimage tourism services and also for the whole package of these services. The application of such a marketing strategy in actual practice at such destinations will be of much help to achieve a higher level of customer satisfaction, customer retention and continuous growth of the business in the pilgrimage tourism services.

ACKNOWLEDGEMENT

I express my gratitude and indebtedness to Prof. R.D. Sharma, Head & Dean, Department of Commerce, University of Jammu and Prof. Desh Bandhu, Directorate of Distance Education, University of Jammu whose constant guidance, encouragement and support enabled me to complete this task.

I would be failing if I do not acknowledge my gratitude to my parents, my in-laws, brother, sister and brother-in-law, whose affection and encouragement remained the constant source of inspiration in completing my work.

I have no words to express my feelings regarding the injustice caused by me to my son, Aryan, whose time I encroached upon during the completion of this work.

Last but not least I express my sincere thanks to my husband, Mr. Raj Kumar Sharma, who always remained with me and encouraged me at different and difficult times.

Sushma Mawa

CONTENTS

Contents

NOTES

1. **Demography of Respondants**

Age Group-1	Youngsters	Up to 25 years of age
Age Group-2	Middle-aged	25 years to 50 years of age
Age Group-3	Old-aged	50 years and above
Inc-1	Below average	Up to Rs 5000/- p.m.
Inc-2	Average	Rs 5000/- to Rs 10000/- p.m.
Inc-3	Above average	Rs 10000/- & above
E-1	Low educated	Up to graduation
E-2	High education	Graduation and above

2. **Abbreviations used**

SMVDSB	Shri Mata Vaishno Devi Shrine Board
Trpt.	Transport
Lux. Bus	Luxury Bus
Ord. Bus	Ordinary Bus
JKTDC	Jammu & Kashmir Tourism Development Corporation
SRTC	State Road Transport Corporation
D.G. Set	Diesel Generator Set
Acc.	Accommodation
X	Mean

LIST OF TABLES

LIST OF EXHIBITS

(xvii)

INTRODUCTION

Background

Tourism marketing is a systematic, interconnected and coordinated execution of efforts by different independent business organizations like tour operators, transporters, hoteliering companies, retailing institutions and related service organizations at, and enroute to, the destination (Greenlay et al.1983, Ronkainen & Woodside 1978) to deliver optimum satisfaction to identical or different consumer groups with institutional goals (Krippendorf 1971). In some broader context, the tourism network includes potential clients in a number of places on the way to the destination, travel agencies, airlines, investors, food and other service providers and the like (Nash 1992). It is a study of travel motivations focusing on the type of travel, type of destination, needed tourism services and the type of tourists (Ronkainen & Woodside 1978). An important feature of tourism marketing is selling a destination as a product to a tourist involving quantitative and qualitative assessment of consumer profiles and needs (Page 1995) which is instrumental in the choice of a particular destination (Lailajainen 1981). Arising out of journeys to a destination and temporary stays of people there, tourism market has another inherent feature of spatial interaction involving the transaction between different people (Smith 1992). This tourism process originates with the generation of tourists in some society or sub-society and goes on with the frequent encounters between host and visitors belonging to different cultures. This ends up as 'the give and take of the encounter,' and affects both the tourists and those who serve them with the required services (Smith 1992, Pearce 1981). The tourism of today is a voluntary, temporary and short term movement of people outside their routine life for various purposes like pleasure from novelty and change (Chopra 1991, McIntosh 1972) causing different societies to become gradually inter-linked in an economic, social and cultural network (Nash 1992). In its conventional sense, tourism was considered as a luxury and a private affair of the affluent sections of a society (Singh 1991). It has witnessed a phenomenal growth in general since 1950 and particularly its concept of marketing developed since 1980 after the appellation of the term industry to tourism (Tewari 1994, Shaw & Williams 1989). This industry being highly fragmented and diversified (Meiden 1985) includes different areas of its operation viz., domestic tourism, international tourism, historical tourism, ethnic tourism, cultural tourism, environmental tourism, recreational tourism, educational tourism, religious tourism-pilgrimages, etc. It has a single market for all the aforesaid service providers (Middleton 1994) with a consumer himself visiting the destination area and purchasing these services at the seller's place unlike the markets where exchange takes place at the buyer's location (Papadopolous 1989).

Concept of Pilgrimage Tourism

The tourism traffic both domestic and international for various purposes like ethnic and socio-cultural understanding or for pleasure, environmental change and religious purpose, has significantly increased manifold during recent times. It is only the pilgrimage or tirth yatra or tourism for religious purpose, that has caused people to travel for regeneration of spirit and quick cultural exchange (Mathieson & Walls 1982, Gandhi 1980). The earliest motivators for travelling was visiting shrines and holy places as pilgrimage to Mecca, Kairouan in Tunisia, Jerusalem, St. David's in Whales, small Pyrenean town of Lourdes, which drew a large number of tourists for over a hundred years (Robinson 1976). Indian soil dotted with places of pilgrimages is conducive to divine inspiration and there is hardly any place in India, which is not held sacred for one reason or the other. It has been the birth place of many religions like Hinduism, Jainism, Buddhism, etc., leading to the devotion of Gurus, Mahatmas, Pirs and visiting far-off places of religious importance with great hardships (Stanley 1991). Modern pilgrimages have blended ancient ethics with modern ideas and beliefs. It has extended the conventional concept from the limited aspect of an act of devotion with a 'the harder the journey, the better the reward', to a wider concept of a desire for a change, relief from the dull daily life and enthusiasm for a common man.

Marketing Strategy for Pilgrimage Tourism

Modern pilgrims' social background, the specific time for pilgrimage and their economic constraints determine the need for transport, accommodation, food, catering, shopping etc. (Sievers 1987) during their journey to the pilgrimage destination. Thus a pilgrimage destination and religious centre ought to have all such facilities and religious requirements which not only meet the pilgrim's religious and spiritual needs but keep generating a desire in them to visit the destinations time and again with an increase in the average length of their stay (Tewari 1994, Mathieson & Walls 1982). Such a pilgrimage destination generates immense market potential for the aforesaid tourism service related businesses. The marketing strategy for pilgrimage tourism is a continuous process of planned action for the development, improvement, maintenance, diversification, monitoring and promotion of the business in such goods and services as are required by the pilgrims during the whole of their pilgrimage (Hartley & Hooper 1992) so that the pilgrims' word of mouth prove to be a sound channel of marketing communication and feedback for ensuring further time and cost effective tourism services to them (Mathieson & Walls 1982, Baker 1978). Such a marketing strategy has become very challenging, competitive and forward-looking due to fast improvement in the services by the industry in the light of fast changes in the nature and extent of pilgrim requirements backed up by ongoing substantial increase in their purchasing power and conceptual reinterpretation of the pilgrimage tourism. A correct strategy well in time and adjustable to the aforesaid turbulent and changing external and internal environment is essential for excelling in this pilgrimage tourism market and ideal for staying ahead of the game (Doyle 1995). The marketing of goods and services in and around the pilgrimage destination focuses on the customer, environmental sensitivity and relative competition in the pilgrimage tourism market (Brooksbank1991). Therefore every pilgrim being different in socio-cultural background needs to be served with tailor-made services, which ought to be regularly evaluated and improved upon in terms of customer feed-back (Moutinho 1987). Problems relating to the internal and external environment of the tourism market are carefully addressed and present marketing tools are adjusted according to the new concepts of marketing for having effective management (Ruston & Carson 1989) of such market. Adapting to competition in the market, the strategy aims at image evolution of the marketers, their product/service planning, positioning, presentation and promotion (Luck & Ferrell 1979, Baker 1978). These are central issues for a greater market share, customer satisfaction and over-all marketing effectiveness, which have become vital for the success and survival of the pilgrimage tourism industry (Carmichael 1992, Chang & Campco 1980). The marketers of such tourism industry need to pay more attention to understand and satisfy consumer because today's consumer has more information about products and services, more alternatives to choose from, than ever before (McKenna 1995).

In the light of the aforesaid discussion, the major focus in pilgrimage tourism marketing strategy is on customer satisfaction (Poon 1993, Bonoma 1984, Mathieson & Walls 1982) with respect to pilgrimage related products and services like accommodation, food services, transportation, recreation and the delivery of resident-oriented products and services like infrastructure facilities (Jafari 1982). A great deal of tourist influx is affected by provision of accommodation and hospitality to the visitors (Pope 1979, Rai & Kumar 1988). In order to retain the present customers and attract potential visitors, the marketers at such destination work upon the objectives like—how important a visitor/ pilgrim is? what are the main services regarding the pilgrimage?, what are the changing expectations in the pilgrimage tourism market? and thereby, assessing and developing the required strategy of customer relationship (Middleton 1994, Nicolaud 1989, McCarthy 1985). Therefore, 'Pilgrim' and 'pilgrim services' like accommodation, transportation, retailing, etc. (Gronross 1989), are the major aspects for developing the pilgrimage tourism market.

Strategic Profile of Shri Mata Vaishno Devi Pilgrimage

Shri Mata Vaishno Devi Shrine is a prominent pilgrimage destination in northern India attracting approximately 50 lakh pilgrims/visitors every year at an average of 10,000 to 13,000 visitors every day (Table-1.1). These visitors like other tourists require the basic tourist services, viz., transport, accommodation, food and catering, retail services and other basic infrastructural services during their pilgrimage to the Shrine. For understanding the requirement of these pilgrims/visitors to the Shrine, the profile of the destination, the nature of the pilgrimage traffic and various services available are summarized as under:

The Destination in Brief

Situated at a distance of approximately 39 miles to the north of Jammu city and at an altitude of 5200 feet (Exhibit-1.1) on Trikuta Hills, this Shrine is of immense religious sanctity. The pilgrims reach the worship spot inside the Shrine through a 30-metre long narrow tunnel, wading knee deep through the shallow stream. Inside the cave of Trikuta Bhagwati are the images of *Mata Vaishno Devi*, *Mata Saraswati*, *Mahakali* and *Maha Lakshmi* (Pic-2).

Exhibit–1.1

**Distance with Altitude in ft above Sea Level of
Different Pilgrim Spots from Katra to Bhavan**

S.No	From	To (spot)	Distance (in Kms.)	Alt (in ft.)
1	Katra	Darshani Darwaza	1	2700
2	Darshani Darwaza	Ban-Ganga	1	2800
3	Ban Ganga	Charan-Paduka	1.5	3380
4	Charan-Paduka	Adhkumari	4.5	4280
5	Adhkumari	Hathi-Matha	2.5	6500
6	Hathi-Matha	Sanjichatt	2	6200
7	Sanjichatt	Bhairon-Mandir	1.5	6583
8	Sanjichatt	Bhawan	2.5	5200

Source : Mata Vaishno Devi Yatri Guide, J&K Reporter (ed.) June, 2000, pp. 4-5

Katra, the base camp of the Shrine is the only bus terminus for the visitors. From Katra onwards, one has to pass through 'Darshani Darwaza' for starting the actual pilgrimage. About one mile ahead is the 'Ban Ganga' (Pic-3), a stream believed to be associated with the Goddess. A mile ahead is 'Charan Paduka' (Pic-4) where there is an image of the footprints of the Goddess. Two miles above is the most important spot of 'Adhkumari' (Pic-5). It is a beautiful plateau on the hills having a small tunnel-shaped temple named 'Garbjoon' (Pic-6) which pilgrims pass through and it is considered that those who cannot pass through are labeled sinners. This tunnel begins horizontally and ends vertically. At this spot most of the pilgrims prefer to break the journey for a night. A few yards from Adhkumari is the most difficult part of the ascent called 'Hathi Matha' i.e. elephant's forehead (Pic-7) and then one reaches 'Sanjichatt' (Pic-8). Afterwards visitors have to climb down passing through a dense forest named 'Mata Ka Bagh' (Pic-9). After about a mile and a half distance visitors reach the cave site or *'Bhavan'* (Pic-10). Returning from the cave, visitors have to climb up a steep hillside to 'Bhaironghati' (Pic-11) and then these hills join at Sanjichatt and back downwards along the same path to Katra.

Pilgrimage Traffic Trend

The pilgrim traffic to the destination belongs to a varied demographic background. About 87% visitors come from outside J&K state (Table-1.2) and most of them come from Uttar Pradesh, Delhi and Maharashtra (Table-1.3). Though the Shrine has become a place of importance for both pilgrimage and non-pilgrimage, yet nearly 75% of the visitors go to the Shrine exclusively for pilgrimage purposes (Exhibit-1.2). The months of 'May ', 'June' and 'October' show a higher pilgrim influx (Table-1.4) as compared to the rest of the year, due to holidays in educational institutions and 'Navratras' during these months respectively. Among weekdays it is 'Saturday' (Table-1.5) when most of the visitors reach the destination due to weekend, and 'Sunday' being a holiday instead of 'Tuesday' which is considered the Goddess's worship day earlier. Here pilgrim traffic trend shows an inclination towards vacations and weekend holidays for visiting the pilgrimage destination leaving behind religious motives.

Exhibit–1.2
Demographic Classification of Respondents
(500)Respondents

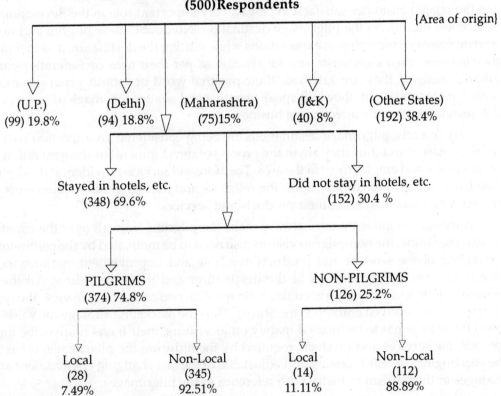

{Area of origin}

(U.P.)	(Delhi)	(Maharashtra)	(J&K)	(Other States)
(99) 19.8%	(94) 18.8%	(75)15%	(40) 8%	(192) 38.4%

Stayed in hotels, etc.
(348) 69.6%

Did not stay in hotels, etc.
(152) 30.4 %

PILGRIMS
(374) 74.8%

NON-PILGRIMS
(126) 25.2%

Local	Non-Local	Local	Non-Local
(28)	(345)	(14)	(112)
7.49%	92.51%	11.11%	88.89%

Availability of Services to Visitors/ Pilgrims

Besides the religious requirements, the visitors to such destinations need many other services. Enroute to the Shrine different services like those of hotels, guest houses, lodges, food and catering in restaurants, dhabas, etc., transportation facilities, souvenir shopping and general retailing are available. Shri Mata Vaishno Devi Shrine Board— an autonomous body incorporated in 1986—governs different operations enroute to the Shrine like provision of sanitation and hygiene, medical facility, telecom facility, shelter sheds, dharmashalas, view points, retailing outlets, guest houses, restaurants, dhabas, cafeterias, etc. It also provides other non-payment facilities like maintenance of temples, roads, stairs, lighting arrangements, provision of clean drinking water, cloak rooms, blankets, etc. Besides the various facilities extended by the Shrine Board, a large number of hoteliers and retailers are doing their business between Katra and *Bhavan*. The transportation services between Jammu and Katra have been made available both by the State Road Transport Corporation and private transporters.

Marketing Strategy for Vaishno Devi Pilgrimage

The nature of pilgrims and their pilgrimage to Shri Mata Vaishno Devi Shrine reveals that this destination not only attracts purely pilgrim visitors but also non-pilgrim visitors who have different requirements, tastes and preferences with respect to different services provided enroute to the pilgrimage. The marketing of such services and the related customer satisfaction plays a very important role in the development of business enroute to the pilgrimage destination. No doubt, these pilgrim and non-pilgrim visitors have different expectations while visiting the destination and in return they interpret their experience and satisfaction as per their own considerations and visualizations. If they are satisfied, their positive word of mouth generates more potential visitors; if not, they will speak negative and shatter the image of services at the destination thereby affecting its business.

Very recently, pilgrimage destinations are being considered an important part of tourism market and thus they are in the process of development for the generation of more income and employment in the area. The aforesaid service-providers at the Shrine also have to take into consideration the religious and non-religious requirements of the visitors while marketing their products and services.

Although religious motives always make the pilgrims from all over the country to visit the Shrine, the non-pilgrim visitors also need to be motivated by the continuous marketing of the services and products available and improvement, maintenance, diversification and promotion of the destination and its surrounding. All these developments and marketing exercises have to be carried on keeping in view the type of traffic trend received enroute to the Shrine. Thus the marketing strategy for Vaishno Devi Pilgrimage has to be focused mainly on its visitors, their travel motive, the time of visit, the services and products required by them during the pilgrimage. It has to be challenging, forward-looking and adjustable to the fast changing environment and changes in the tourism industry with reference to the pilgrimages.

It is in this context that this study has been undertaken for formulating a marketing strategy on the basis of the present experience of the pilgrims about the various goods and services they buy during their pilgrimage so that the pilgrims continue to enjoy better services commensurating with the prices charged by the service-providers.

Table–1.1
Year-wise Pilgrim Traffic Since 1980

S.No	Year	No. of Tourists	Per Month	Per day
1	1980	1212958	101079.83	3323.17
2	1981	1213482	101123.50	3324.61
3	1982	1188855	99071.25	3257.14
4	1983	1283340	106945.00	3516.00
5	1984	1008470	84039.17	2762.93
6	1985	1485982	123831.83	4071.18
7	1986	1395832	116319.33	3824.20
8	1987	1857935	154827.91	5090.23
9	1988	1992605	166050.41	5459.00
10	1989	2312011	192667.58	6334.28
11	1990	2169093	180757.75	5942.72
12	1991	3115447	259620.58	8535.47
13	1992	3516267	293022.25	9633.61
14	1993	3368665	280722.08	9229.22
15	1994	3704944	308745.33	10150.53
16	1995	4011627	334302.25	10990.76
17	1996	4335432	361286.00	11877.90
18	1997	4434233	369519.41	12148.58
19	1998	4622297	385191.41	12663.83
20	1999	4670454	389204.50	12795.76
21	2000	5191915	432659.58	14224.43
22	2001	5056919	421409.91	13854.57
23	2002	4432178	369348.16	12142.95
24	2003	5400296	450024.66	14795.33

Source : (i) SMVDSB, Development Report, 2000

(ii) JKTDC Reports

Table–1.2

Growth of Local and Non-Local Pilgrims
to Shri Mata Vaishno Devi Shrine

S.No	Year	Total	Locals	Non-Locals	Ratio
1	1981	1213482	205105	1008377	17:83
2	1982	1188855	129250	1059607	11:89
3	1983	1283340	143208	1140132	11:89
4	1984	1008470	152358	856122	15:85
5	1985	1485982	179517	1305467	12:88
6	1986	1395832	193604	1203132	14:86
7	1987	1857935	222426	1635182	12:88
8	1988	1992605	259831	1732764	13:87
9	1989	2312011	262691	2049310	11:89
10	1990	2169093	396502	1780758	18:82
11	1991	3115447	444523	2689808	14:86
12	1992	3516267	470450	3254719	13:87
13	1993	3368665	461433	2907302	14:86
14	1994	3704944	471101	3234844	13:87
15	1995	4011627	549278	3462349	14:86
16	1996	4335432	-NA-	-NA-	
17	1997	4434233	487750	3946483	11:89
18	1998	4622297	519458	4102839	11:89
19	1999	4670454	635342	4035112	13:87
20	2000	5191915	700240	4491675	13:87

Source: Shrine Board Central Office, Katra

Table–1.3

Proportion of Pilgrims from Different States of India as per the Survey Conducted

S.No	Name of the State	No of visitors	% of Pilgrims
1	Uttar Pradesh	99	19.80
2	Delhi	94	18.80
3	Maharashtra	75	15.00
4	Jammu & Kashmir	40	8.00
5	Karanataka	28	5.60
6	Punjab	28	5.60
7	Madhya Pradesh	27	5.40
8	West Bengal	26	5.20
9	Bihar	15	3.00
10	Rajasthan	14	2.80
11	Andra Pradesh	13	2.60
12	Haryana	13	2.60
13	Gujarat	8	1.60
14	Assam	7	1.40
15	Himachal Pradesh	3	0.60
16	Manipur	2	0.40
17	Sikkim	2	0.40
18	Orissa	2	0.40
19	Tamil Nadu	2	0.40
20	Goa	2	0.40
	Total	**500**	**100.00**

Table–1.4

Month-wise Pilgrim Traffic Trend to Shrine Since 1988

Month	1988	1989	1990	1991	1992	1993	1994	1995	1996	1997	1998	1999	2000	2001	2002	2003
January	70989	45850	75340	69467	119336	106236	159293	107563	166958	161515	159456	180723	191870	222836	171558	175320
February	72590	56964	71845	90380	68328	97956	92649	89840	126209	126705	153551	176700	147003	174481	136597	161737
March	156453	162093	168756	213884	245120	239519	263053	283962	378326	361928	316678	419580	278452	436844	327223	389687
April	213464	225857	212610	315013	327690	343186	354573	408610	431689	473706	422739	443017	379604	511081	418393	472299
May	227675	226105	212939	279413	400724	364948	415323	421048	465033	471650	486250	521593	629357	570885	407950	573170
June	233920	271601	311561	347570	527684	520146	519278	602198	658538	603805	552672	510210	667655	704657	466899	741605
July	170577	233889	255573	294956	351678	253769	327294	401718	415325	443089	488675	292094	554769	623154	442955	586908
August	193482	249165	229013	326351	365492	263602	328993	379936	396492	429224	469961	427062	561332	382668	517371	541015
September	173591	211617	195048	326168	308067	294431	291999	314651	298788	349899	427984	403781	416945	347934	379714	485572
October	176272	262727	143080	360654	356618	387861	377394	414055	419933	437972	486898	525161	558817	443153	448069	522923
November	171044	214908	148345	262722	247815	238242	324027	290374	323835	342296	363350	418832	419628	312253	361868	380272
December	132548	151235	144983	228869	197715	258769	251068	297672	254306	232444	294083	351701	386483	326973	353581	369788
Total	11992605	2312011	2169093	3115447	3516267	3368665	3704944	4011627	4335432	4434233	4622297	4670454	5191915	5056919	4432178	5400296

Source: JKTDC, Jammu

Table-1.5

Month-wise Average Pilgrim Traffic on Each Day of the Week During First Six Months in 1997

Week Days	January	February	March	April	May	June	Total	Average
Monday	17328	16046	52173	64134	57176	96068	302925	43275
Tuesday	16067	15930	37645	68526	61169	81250	280587	40084
Wednesday	27685	14285	40613	61862	51361	77167	272973	38996
Thursday	20885	14521	43342	61532	69381	80225	289886	41412
Friday	24876	21731	49772	62152	77846	79397	315774	45111
Saturday	31181	25235	74909	85788	90408	83389	390910	55844
Sunday	23493	18957	63474	69712	64310	106309	346255	49465
Total	161515	126705	361928	473706	471651	603805	2199310	314187

Source: JKTDC, Jammu

Table–1.6

Number and Percentage of Visitors with Pilgrim and Non-Pilgrim Travel Motive as per Survey Conducted

S.No	Purpose of visit	No of Pilgrims	% of Pilgrims
(A)	**Pilgrimage Motive**		
1	Darshan	205	51.00
2	Yearly Yatra	108	26.87
3	Faith in Mata Vaishno Devi	32	7.96
4	For fulfilling one's wishes	20	4.98
5	Mundan Ceremony	11	2.74
6	Success of Married Life	11	2.74
7	Just to see the Cave	6	1.49
8	Seek peace	9	2.22
	Total (A)	402	100.00
(B)	**Non-Pilgrimage Motive**		
1	Trekking & Hiking	22	22.45
2	Tour & Travelling	27	27.55
3	Rest, Recreation & Holiday	29	29.59
4	Availing of LTC	5	5.10
5	Picinic	7	7.14
6	Watching snowfall at hills	5	5.10
7	To show place to children	3	3.07
	Total (B)	98	100.00
	Total (A+B)	500	

References

Baker, M.J. (1978), " Limited Options for Marketing Strategists", *Marketing*, June 1978, 23-27.

Bonoma T.V (1984), " Making your Marketing Strategy work," *Harvard Business Review*, March-April 69-76.

Brooksbank , Roger W. (1991), "Successful Marketing Practice—A Literature Review and Checklist for Marketing Practitioners", *European Journal of Marketing*, Vol. 25 (5), 20-29.

Carmichael, B. (1992) "Using Conjoint Modeling Choice and Demand in Tourism", Mansell Publishing, England, 93-98.

Chang,Y.N. & Campo, Flores F. (1980), "Business Policy & Strategy", Good Year Publishing, 15-30

Chopra, Suhita (1991), Tourism & Development in India, Ashish Publications; New Delhi. 2-27.

Doyle, Peter (1995), "Marketing in the New Millenium", *European Journal of Marketing*, Vol. 29 (13), 23-41.

Gandhi, Indira (1980), Eternal India, B.I. Publications; India, 20-25.

Greenlay, Gordon E. & Allan, S. Matcham (1983), "Problems in Marketing Services: The Case of Incoming Tourism", *European Journal of Marketing*, Vol .17, No.(6), 57-64.

Gronross, Christian, (1989), "Defining Marketing, A Market Oriented Approach", *European Journal of Marketing*, Vol. 23 (1) 52-59.

Hartley, Keith & Nicholas Hooper (1992), "Tourism Policy: Market Failure and Public Choice" in Peter Johnson & Barry Thomas (ed.), Perspective on Tourism Policy, Durham 15-27.

Jafari, Jafar, (1982), "The Tourism Market-Basket of Goods and Services" in Tej Vir Singh (ed.), Studies in Tourism and Wild life, Parks and Conservations, Metropolitan, India, 1-3.

Kotler, Philip (1989), Principles of Marketing, Prentice-Hall of India (P) Ltd., New Delhi, 15-40.

Krippendorf, J. (1971), Marketing of Tourism, Berne, Lag., 46 - 50.

Lailajainen, Risto (1981), "The Unfamiliar Tourist Destination—A Marketing Challenge", *European Journal of Marketing*, Vol. 15, No.(7), 69-79.

Luck, D.J. & Ferrell, O.C., (1979), Marketing Strategy and Plans, Prentice-Hall, 5-15.

Mathieson, Alister & Geofery Walls (1982). Tourism—Economic, Physical and Social Impacts, Longman Publisher; London, 1-49, 88-91.

McCarthy, E.J. & William, D. Perreautt,Jr.,(1985). Essentials of Marketing, 3rd ed., Richard, O, Irwin, USA, 116-119, 475-480.

McIntosh, R. W. (1972), Tourism Principles, Practices, Philosophies, Grid. Inc, Columbus, 20-40.

McKenna, Regis (1995), " Real Time Marketing" Harvard Business Review, Vol.73, July-Aug.,1995, 87-95.

Meiden, Arthur, (1985), "The Marketing of Tourism, ' in Gordon Foxall's (ed), Marketing in Service Industry, Frank Cass Publishers, England, 166-185.

Middleton, Victor T.C (1994). Marketing In Travel and Tourism, Butterworth Heinemann, London 4-20.

Moutinho, Luiz (1987), "Consumer Behaviour in Tourism", *European Journal of Marketing*, Vol. 21 (10), 5-44.

Nash, Dannison (1992), "A Research Agenda on Variability of Tourism", in Valence, L. Smith (ed.), Tourism Alternatives, 216-225.

Nicolaud, B (1989), "Problems and Strategies in the International Marketing of Services", *European Journal of Marketing*, Vol. 23 (6), 55-65.

Page, Stephen (1995), Urban Tourism, Routledge; London, 194-231.

Papadopoulos, Socrates, I (1989), "A Conceptual Tourism Marketing Planning Models: Part 1", *European Journal of Marketing*, Vol 23 (1), 31-40.

Pearce, D.G. (1981), Tourism Development—Topics in Applied Geography, Longman, U.K., 6-13.

Poon, Auliana, (1993), Tourism Technology and Competitive Strategies, C.A.B., International, U.K., 53-58.

Pope, N.W. (1979), "More Micky Mouse Marketing", American Banker, Sept.12.

Rai, Lajipathi, H. & J.S. Kumar (1988), "Poverty to Prosperity Through Tourism in Third World", Southern Economist.

Robinson, H. (1976), A Geography of Tourism, McDonald & Evans Publishing; London, 3-18.

Ronkainen, I.A. & A.G. Woodside (1978). " Cross Cultural Analysis of Market Profiles of Domestic & Foreign Travellers", *European Journal of Marketing*, Vol 12 (8), 579-87.

Rusten, M. Angela & David J. Carson (1989). " The Marketing of Services; Managing the Intangibles", *European Journal of Marketing*, Vol. 23 (8), 23-44.

Shaw Gerath & Allan, M. William (1989). Tourism & Economic Development—Western European Experience, London, 2-8.

Seievers, Angelika (1987), "The Significance of Pilgrimage Tourism in Sri Lanka (Ceylon)", *National Geographical Journal of India*, Vol 33 (4), 430-45.

Singh, L.P. (1991), "Tourism Marketing in India—Problems & Prospectus", *Southern Economist*, January 1991, 1-3.

Smith, L.J.S. (1992), Tourism Analysis—A Handbook , Longman Scientific & Technical, Harlow; U.K., 5-13.

Stanley, Wolpart (1991), An Introduction to India, Viking Penguin, India, 70-78.

Tewari, S.P. (1994), Tourism Dimensions, Atma Ram & Sons; New Delhi, 181-205.

Plate 1 : Raghunath Temple, Jammu

Plate 2 : Holy Sight of the PINDIES

Plate 3 : Main Gate – Banganga

Plate 4 : Charan–Paduka

Plate 5 : A view of Adkumari

Plate 6 : Garbh-June Cave

Plate 7 : Heights of Hathi-Matha

Plate 8 : A View of Sanjhi-Chhat

Plate 9 : A Sight of Trikuta-Hills

Plate 10 : Bhawan, Vaishno Devi Shrine

Plate 11 : A View of Bhairon-Ghati

Plate 12 : A View of Vaishno Devi Shrine at Night

Plate 13 : Kaul-Kandholi, Nagrota

Plate 14 : Kaul-Kandholi, Bhandara

Plate 15 : Bhumika-Temple

Plate 16 : Chintamani-Temple

REVIEW OF LITERATURE

The relevant literature on the topic of research reviewed while the formulation of research objectives, hypothesis (Chapter-3) and thus identifying the research gap to be filled up in the form of the present study, has been classified under the following three broad headings:

1) Service Marketing
2) Tourism Marketing
3) Pilgrimage Tourism Marketing

Service Marketing

The literature reviewed on service marketing covered the core and peripheral aspects of the services, their classification on the basis of the nature of the services, their relationship with the customers, their buying behavior, their supply and demand and the over-all delivering process. The studies reviewed have invariably covered measurement of service quality on the basis of 'SERVPREF', 'SERVQUAL', and 'Missing Service Quality Concept' models for establishing a relationship between the customers and the marketers, thereby analyzing the customer's purchase intention etc.

1. Vieira (1994) examined the distinguishing features of service marketing and recommended a continuous process of building relationship between the customers and the marketers for delivering need based services.

2. Kandampully (1993) suggested a dynamic model for quality improvement in all service sectors. The model has three key dimensions, viz. Service delivery, Customer & market and strategists requiring continuous and reliable information about customer/market perceptions and expectations to be translated into service quality standards.

3. Cronin & Taylor (1992) investigated the concept and measurement of service quality and the relationship between service quality, consumer satisfaction and

purchase intentions, and concluded that the evaluation of service quality on the performance basis (SERVPREF) is an improvement over service quality construct (SERVQUAL) as this customer evaluative opinion regarding the service quality indicates his purchase and re-purchase intention.

4.   Ruston & Carson (1989) feel that the service marketing practitioners are uncertain and unsure about certain aspects of marketing operations because the customer's evaluative opinion regarding the service quality is not available in advance before its conception. Therefore, a regular survey of service quality has been suggested for updating the service.

5.   Nicoulaud (1989) stated that given the rapid growth of the service sector, there always exists a need for research due to the characteristic difference in services and the needed changes are always planned in the light of changing market expectation and buying behaviour.

6.   Leppard, et al. (1986) studied the service customer' buying behaviour, the internal and external pressures of service firms affecting the buying decision of customers and accordingly suggested a sales strategy in the light of the relevance of the services to customer needs.

7.   Parasuraman, Zeithamal & Berry (1985) developed 'SERVQUAL' a model of service quality, which claims that the consumer evaluates the quality of a service experience as the outcome of the differences (5 gaps) between the expected and perceived services. These gaps indicate unsuccessful service delivery and, therefore, reducing these gaps in the perceived and expected service quality leads to a higher customer satisfaction.

8.   Norman (1984) suggests that most service offerings or packages consist of a ' core service, i.e. centre piece of service offering, the primary benefit sought by customer and 'peripheral services' i.e. supplementary to primary benefit. Peripherals provide leverage and support the total package. Thus the concept of core and peripheral service provides a framework for thinking systematically about a delivery system while formulating a definite strategy.

9.   Lovelock (1983) Studied in detail the various dimensions of service marketing like competitive sophisticated customer expectations and proposes five schemes for classifying services on the basis of the nature of service relationship with the customer, relative demand and supply and delivery process. He recommended formulating a separate marketing action plan in the form of strategies for each set and developing an on-going relationship with the customers in order to ensure repeat business vis-à-vis customer satisfaction.

10.   Gronoss (1982) developed, the 'Missing Service Quality", concept model focusing on the construct of service image, representing the point at which a gap can occur between an expected and a perceived service. It argues that the function and range of service activities include; what are customers looking for?, what are they evaluating?, how is service quality perceived?, and in what ways is service quality influenced? The out-come of this evaluation is provided by the difference between experienced services and perceived services. It also analyses

the technical and functional quality component of service delivery. He further (1978) discussed in his study marketing problems in service companies and suggested a hypothetical framework of marketing mix planning where the consumer has been focused as an active participant in shopping and developing service offerings.

11. Shostack (1977) stated that services cannot be stored on a shelf, touched, tasted or tried on for size, like shirts and shoes, etc., because of their intangibility character. The more intangible elements there are, the more marketers must endeavour to stand in the consumer's shoes, thinking through and gaining control of all the inputs to the consumer's mind and formulating related tactics and strategies.

Tourism Marketing

The literature on tourism marketing invariably analysed the psychographic and demographic profile of tourists, their perception about the performance of various tourism services like hotel and hospitality, airlines, tour, and attraction, transportation, information and consumer services on the basis of data collected, through group discussions, oral interviews and structured questionnaire on Likert scale. The studies recommended active cooperation between suppliers of different services according to the changing tourism needs through the formulation of creative strategies by putting the customer first. The studies bring forth various loop holes in tourism marketing viz. an acute shortage of satisfactory accommodation, inadequate transport, unsatisfactory infrastructure, adulterated food, unhygienic drinking water and insanitary conditions, which lead to dissatisfaction among tourists. Therefore, these studies have indicated the necessity of primary data based research duly counter-checked through secondary information and with tested validity and reliability coefficients.

1. Baker & Crompton (2000) assessed the relative impact and inter-relationship of performance quality and general satisfaction on a nine point Likert scale by using factor analysis. The results confirmed that satisfaction is generally enhanced by higher perceptions of performances quality, encouraging more loyal customers, positive word of mouth, repeat visits and willingness of consumer to pay more for the opportunity. The study suggests that since performance quality is under the control of service providers, their attainment of goal would lead to better inter-relationship.

2. McVey & King (2000) discussed tourism trends in India with reference to hotel accommodation, viz. category-wise hotel services ranging from 'five star' and "deluxe' to average hotels, state-wise distribution of hotels, their occupancy rates, operational characteristics and development of hotel infrastructure, etc. The study discussed only the supply side of hotel accommodation and ignored the demand side of such accommodation.

3. Reichael et al (2000) conducted an exploratory study of perceived services quality in rural tourism in Israel on the basis of the data collected from service providers on a convenient sampling basis. The study discussed management and marketing

implications for service quality improvement and recommended customers needs based focus in services as the key success factor for tourism marketing.

4.   Upchurch & Teivan (2000) evaluated the positive and negative impact of tourism development on its services and products using a convenience sampling process on a five point Likert scale and recommended a proper analysis of the economic & social environment variables from a longitudinal view with appropriate experimental methodology.

5.   Alavi & Yasin (2000) analyse the growth in tourist arrival to Middle East countries and provide a systematic approach towards managing tourism efforts and activities. This approach starts with creating an environment conducive to tourism by training human resources, improving related infrastructure, encouraging tourism related investments, integrating tourism related strategies to ensure consistency and a well coordinated over-all tourism strategy.

6.   Mc Collough (2000) measured service quality to check customer satisfaction in hospitality sector and tourism industry on a seven point Likert scale using the convenience-sampling technique. The findings of the study reveal service failure and recovery relationship depending upon customer satisfaction and accordingly suggested to build customer confidence in the service quality.

7.   Singh (2000) analyses the problems of marketing in tourism due to the uniqueness of tourism market characterized by an intangible service being sold which cannot be inspected prior to purchase. The author stresses customer oriented tourism research for developing a marketing plan focusing upon long-term tourist needs, wants and satisfaction.

8.   Qu & Ping (1999) studied travellers profile, motivational factors, their satisfaction level and repeat visits. A structured five point Likert scale questionnaire was used for personal interview on the basis of a systematic sampling technique to evaluate service performance. The results indicated that major travelling motivation was 'remaining away from normal life'. The travellers under study reported to be highly satisfied with the quality of food and beverages facility and staff performances; they were least satisfied with recreation, shopping and the attractiveness of the destination under study. The study recommended that tourist satisfaction level is greatly related to the needs and purposes for travel and not everyone gets the same satisfaction from given services. An in-depth study is needed to determine tourist motivation and satisfaction which is essential for marketers and provide greater help to upkeep the improvement of the service quality and enhancement of customer satisfaction.

9.   Tribe & Snaith (1998) developed a research instrument viz. 'HOLSAT' to measure tourist satisfaction with holiday service expectations/performance analysis as per procedure adopted in 'SERVQUAL' (Parsuraman, et al 1985). The study recommended development of a research instrument on a five point Likert scale by examining both the independent and dependent satisfaction attitudes of holiday-makers with a reliable and representative sample frame.

10. Bramwell (1998) examined the satisfaction of visitors with respect to sports tourism products and services and analyzed how the greater understanding of satisfaction of users with these products and services may improve their development. The study conducted on a five point Likert scale recommended the development of tourism products and services, examined the user's dissatisfaction and formed strategic objectives for further improvement in these products and services.

11. Middleton & Hawkins (1998) assert that marketing perspectives of tourism services provide optimum energy for achieving sustainability at tourism destination. The success of tourism is measured in terms of service performance experience regarding relaxation, happiness, entertainment, adventure and satisfaction; it imparts to its customers, where each customer measures the attributes differently. It stresses a need for deep and continuous understanding of visitors, their behaviour and the products and services they purchase.

12. Keyser & Vanhove (1997) suggested top priority in building and maintaining service quality as crucial in planning tourism policy. The study based upon group discussions and oral interviews of holiday-makers listed the problem areas and determined priorities for marketers to make tourists satisfied.

13. Walle (1997) examined the importance of 'quantitative v/s qualitative tourism research and recommended the use of statistical tools supplemented with more qualitative methods capable of dealing with vital tourism marketing problems like limited choice, discourteous personnel behaviour, customer dissonance, etc.

14. Briggs (1997) recommends primary research based upon face-to-face interviews through a structured questionnaire covering the main aspects of tourism marketing, viz. tourist profile, effectiveness of tourism services, reasons/ motivation for visiting and the kind of development visitors would like to see next time in the products and services offered.

15. Otto & Ritchie (1996) studied tourist satisfaction through a self-developed six-point Likert scale by determining the basic dimensions of perceptual understanding and experience of tourism service quality with special reference to hotels, airlines, tour and attraction services. However, the study does not lend insight into the dynamics of service as how tourists might trade off or weigh their evaluations of different aspects of the service experience in arriving at overall satisfaction.

16. Seaton & Bennett (1996) differentiates tourism from other services on the grounds that it is more supply led, constituted by dreams and fantasies of its customers, it is a fragile industry with high involvement and high risk product requiring frequent co-operation between different suppliers. It summarizes the marketing process for tourism as a six step sequence, viz. identifying customers, evaluating the organization on the basis of competition and external environment, setting strategic objectives, planning a suitable marketing mix, implementing the marketing programme and evaluating the results.

17   Kotler, Bowen & Makens (1996) expected the marketing professionals to understand the complexities of tourism services, and respond to changing tourist needs through creative strategies as per marketing requirements. This requires understanding a tourism destination and its attraction, identifying target markets, segmenting the market, assessing demand for tourism and formulating relevant strategies.

18.   Kamra (1996) asserted that tourism has increasingly occupied an important place not only in business sector but also in academics. The paper brings forward economic and non-economic criteria affecting domestic tourism and recommended promotion of domestic tourism instead of the present tendency to pamper international tourism for adequate development of tourism industry and economy as a whole.

19.   Jain (1996) suggested studying tourism concept as a marketing challenge focusing especially on middle-income group visitors as they form a major part of the Indian population. A schematic model has been presented by putting tourism services in a series as per their use during a trip. It recommended establishing a strong link within the series through integrated efforts of related agencies.

20.   Page (1995) explained the special feature of tourism marketing as selling a destination as a product to customers/tourists. This process of place marketing and its research is now gaining increased attention in modern tourism marketing. The author recommends the qualitative and quantitative assessment of the tourist's profile and needs for effective place marketing.

21.   Burton (1995) studied the origin of tourism, its relation to motivation and the overall behaviour of tourists. The study describes the spatial process of tourist development model which proceeds with the understanding of the destination area and the potential tourists generating area, economical push factor motivating people to travel, intensity of development in tourist business at destination area, needs of different tourist segments and accordingly integrating the tourist product life cycle for tourism development.

22.   Chacko (1995) discussed the role of 'positioning' in tourism marketing and presented various approaches to position a tourism destination according to the visitor's profile. The study stresses that to position a destination successfully, it requires recognizing tourist perceptions and their travel needs.

23.   Ryan (1995) argued that the attitudes, expectations and perceptions of the tourists are significant variables in setting tourism goals, influencing tourist behavior and finally determining levels of satisfaction. He further stresses that there is a need for significant amount of primary analytical data explaining tourist attitude for a successful tourism research.

24.   Poon (1994) argued that the standard mass tourism of the early sixties gave way to a new tourism driven by greater sensitivity to consumer tastes and preferences and changing competition. For success in this new environment the author suggested that tourism related agencies would have to sharpen their strategies by putting the consumer first.

25. March (1994) examined tourism literature between 1974 and 1986 and suggested that the although marketing discipline offers tourism a variety of strategic tools and conceptual insight, the marketing's contribution to tourism has been undervalued by tourism policy makers and practitioners. This has led to a mis-understanding about the nature and value of marketing for the tourism industry. The study suggests how marketing research can be properly used in tourism especially by meaningfully classifying not only tourists but also tourism products and services, by developing an operational definition of tourism products and services, thereby providing a more useful marketing insight for tourism operators and promoters with reference to both the customers and the product.

26. Dutta (1994) studied three major marketing tools, viz. promotion, participation and prevention and established its relation with modern tourism marketing strategy. The study recommends sustainable development of tourism by developing a marketing strategy.

27. Witt & Moutinho (1994) describe the tourist's satisfaction as an emotional response to the successful quality of services delivered. It is a process of expectations and perceptions whereby a satisfied tourist experiences a positive change in attitude towards the service. The study stresses that in order to target this element of satisfaction, the service process in totality needs to be re-evaluated according to the changing needs and tastes of the tourists.

28. Danahar & Mattsson (1994) studied service delivery process in hotel service by evaluating responses of hotel guests randomly selected on an eleven point Likert scale. The findings revealed five effective service encounters. viz. 'Check In', 'Room', 'Restaurants', 'Breakfast', 'Check-out' and recommended maintaining a satisfaction level of each encounter by improved quality for better over-all satisfaction.

29. Singh (1994) addressed tourism as a service product, where effective and systematic marketing holds the key to bring back the guest as a friend. The findings of the study reveal that these areas, viz. tourism product development and planning, exploring new potential tourist markets, developing user friendly infrastructure and formulating strategic market plans etc. need to be marketed effectively for sustaining competition and changing environment. It recommends a constant gearing-up of tourism infrastructure and implementation of target-market driven strategies.

30. Kandampully (1993) analyze the nature and concept of tourism services and found that the tourists of today are very critical of quality of service and are unwilling to compromise. The study proposed a systematic model viz. 'Process Flow in Dynamic Service Quality' to facilitate effective service quality improvement. The model assists service organizations to effectively gather regular feedback information from customers for redesigning the service process and achieving step by step service excellence.

31. Heath & Wall (1992) identify tourism markets, determine different segments, and means to access these markets, their attractions, promotion and the prevalent

competition. The study argues that tourism should be planned and marketed especially at regional level if development has to occur appropriately. It presented a framework on 'SWOT' analysis for formulating a strategic tourism marketing plan and recommended appropriate management support for its effective implementation.

32. Milne & Whittles (1992) demonstrate the need for the effective implementation of the tourism marketing strategy, which is often lacking, especially in small areas. The effective implementation is essential to realize success of a devised strategy. It studied the importance of tourism in rural and small towns, the type of tourists visited, the market potential, assessment of tourism product and its development, measuring the performance of different agencies to give a satisfying experience to the tourists and the need for effective implementation of marketing strategy devised on these grounds.

33. Laws (1992) studied the role of marketing in the development of tourism products and services according to the changing tastes and style of tourist segments.

34. Singh (1991) analyze the problems related to the marketing of tourism in India and found an acute shortage of accommodation and transportation services, which add to the dismal state of affairs of tourism marketing. He argues that domestic tourism is a neglected area with unsatisfactory infrastructure, inadequate transportation, paucity of hotel accommodation, adulterated food, unhygienic drinking water and insanitary conditions, which need to be developed by forming sound policies.

35. Smith (1989) proposed the Likert scale for measuring satisfaction and dissatisfaction in tourism services on the basis of first hand experiences so that needed improvement can be planned.

36. Papadopoulos (1989) focuses attention on the development of tourism market by identifying the effective variables, viz. market segmentation, marketing audit and marketing information system. The study proposes a conceptual tourism marketing planning model emphasizing upon four core concepts, viz. where is tourism now? how has it grown over a period of time? where is it heading now ? how does the relative organization organize their resources to get there ? The model begins with the client and ends with the client and recommends continuous monitoring of the strengths and weaknesses of tourism market to develop new marketing tactics.

37. Geva & Goldman (1989) on a seven point Likert scale studied the profile of travellers and measured their expectations and satisfaction by applying factor analysis. The findings revealed that the traveller's perception of a tour passes through an evolutionary process as per the set of attributes one goes through and perceives the trip quite differently in the end. It recommended interwoven attributes and constant service quality throughout the trip by developing effective strategies as per consumer segments.

38. Dann, Nash& Pearce (1988) highlighted those areas of tourism research that lacked a proper methodology with respect to data gathering, measurement and

other aspects of data analysis. The study recommended methodological sophistication in terms of its objectivity, consistency and relevance along with theoretical awareness.

39. Moutinho (1987) studied the cross-cultural analysis of consumer behavior, its travel decision process and tourism product evaluation. The study argues that tourist satisfaction is a function of tourist product performance, specific expectations and expectancy confirmation and disconfirmation based upon post-purchase evaluation of vacation and the destination. It recommends a strategy for better service quality to meet changing needs of the tourists by examining their behaviour towards tourist services and the destination.

40. Raaiji (1986) recommends classifying tourists in terms of behavioural constructs for a proper and systematic consumer research, which is less developed and where tourism product is complex and diverse.

41. Doren & Lollar (1985) study the changes and development of travel and tourism by providing the review of five industry components, viz. transportation, attraction, facilities and services, information and consumer, etc. The study recommends that the over-all goal should be to evaluate the tourism industry on the basis of a satisfactory travel experience.

42. Gordon & Mattcham (1983) describe the tourism industry as highly fragmented and diversified where variation in tourism needs requires different marketing strategies for meeting the requirements of different tourists segments. They studied the problems associated with the marketing of incoming tourism through the postal questionnaire methods and revealed the various tourism marketing problems, viz. intangibility, perishability, heterogeneity and demand fluctuation.

43. Mathieson & Walls (1982) evaluate the socio-economic and physical impact of tourism on the destination area and the experiences of the tourists. It found that there is a lack of methodological and conceptual research in tourism and recommended that the main objective of a tourism action plan should be to ensure such opportunities, as provide the tourists with an enjoyable and satisfying experience.

44. Ronkainen & Woodside (1978) surveyed the profile of two sets of travellers with an identical questionnaire on a random and systematic sample basis. The results indicated that knowledge of demographic and psychographic profiles may assist in creative process of positioning and promotion in tourism, designing the product and planning an offer to a certain set of tourist segments whose perceptions on recreation and leisure time keeps on changing.

Pilgrimage Tourism Marketing

A lot of literature on tourism marketing in general is available but most of these studies could not give due weightage to pilgrimage tourism marketing. The various aspects of the pilgrimage tourism marketing covered in these studies are accommodation, transportation, shopping facilities, etc., but most of these lagged behind in one aspect or the other. The literature available on pilgrimage tourism marketing has been reviewed as under:

1. Raghuram & Madhavan (2000) formulate strategies to handle pilgrim flow, improve quality of service, waiting time and smooth pilgrimage throughout at Tirumala Tirupati, Devasthanam. The study is based upon field observations, discussions, secondary data and primary questionnaire survey along with a comparative understanding of pilgrimage at 'Shirdi' 'Vaishno Devi' and 'Sabarimala'. It assesses the projections of pilgrim inflow until 2006, waiting time, darshan time, quality of services and recommends improvement in the framework of the pilgrim flow by an improved queue system, increase in darshan time, availability of appropriate accommodation and systematic computerized future research based upon regular MIS reports on pilgrim profiles.

2. Sharma, et al (2000) measure the satisfaction level among the pilgrims with respect to the hotel services at Katra & *Bhavan* during the Shri Mata Vaishno Devi pilgrimage. The study based upon the five point Likert scale recommends improvement in the hotel services regarding provision of food and catering, sanitation and hygienie and the prices paid for the various services provided.

3. Mishra (2000) studies the motivations, expectations and experiences of the pilgrims of Braj Mandal and the behaviour of their hosts. The study based upon direct and indirect investigations examines the prospects and problems of pilgrimage tourism and suggests a model for the better management of pilgrimage tourism. It suggests a co-ordinated effort of government bodies, private agencies sector, local bodies and NGO's to create the required infrastructure with respect to the increasing inflow of pilgrims.

4. Russell (1999) studies the significance of different types of accommodation, transportation, related infra-strssucture, the changing trends of pilgrimages and explains the pilgrimage tourism as an extremely sensitive area attracting mostly those people that are holidaying for leisure but having different expectations.

5. Vukonic (1996) identifies the essence of religious attributes to tourism and discusses the nature of religious tourists, the motives of their pilgrimage, the problems of transportation, food, catering, accommodation, health care and supervisory staff faced during the pilgrimage. It recommends regular research for appropriate action in updating the pilgrimage destination according to the changing needs of the pilgrims.

6. Deshmukh & Navale (1994) study the attitudinal opinion of the residents, entrepreneurs and public administrators regarding the impact of pilgrimages and recommends that, for the sustainable development of tourism, there is a need to give serious thought towards the positive and negative socio-economic impacts of tourism—the positive impacts are beneficial for growth and the negative ones discourage the pilgrimage.

7. Ahmed (1992) studies the importance of Islamic Pilgrimage (Hajj) in international tourism and recommends separate marketing efforts for different pilgrim segments with modernized pilgrim infrastructure as per their requirements. The

study provides tips for better pilgrimage management, viz. controlling begging, host courtesy, queue management, capacity limits, setting standards of accommodation, need of guides and controlling profiteers.

8. Desh Bandhu (1983) analyzes the income and employment effect of tourism in J&K economy. The study based upon primary and secondary data analyzes the growth of pilgrim traffic in the state and the impact of transportation, accommodation, shopping, catering and entertainment services on the pilgrimage tourism. The study recommends the need for a better tourism policy of government and initiatives from private enterprises to attract more tourists.

Research Gap

The literature covering different phenomenons of service marketing, tourism marketing and pilgrimage marketing has been reviewed to identify the research gap to be bridged up by this study. The studies covered services and tourism marketing in general and pilgrimage tourism marketing in particular. Different tourism services, viz. hotels, food & beverages (McVey & King 2000, Qu & Ping 1999, Otto & Ritchie 1996, Danahar & Mattsson 1994), transportation, hospitality, shopping, airlines, tour and attraction, its infrastructure, etc. (Alavi & Yasin 2000, McCollough 2000, Qu & Ping 1999, Russell 1999, Otto & Ritche 1996, Vukonic 1996, Doren & Lollar 1985) have been studied but no study has taken these services together as a full package for the formulation of both service-wise marketing and the strategy for the whole pilgrimage tourism service package.

Many studies were based upon the Likert scale questionnaire, face-to-face surveys or interviews (Baker & Crompton 2000, Upchurch & Teivane 2000, Sharma, et al. 2000, McCollough 2000, Qu & Ping 1999, Otto & Ritchie 1996, Danhar & Mattsson 1994, Geva & Goldman 1989) but most of them used the convenience sampling method for data collection and applied less of factor analysis for data reduction and scale purification and other statistical tools, mean scores for reliability of the results.

The studies on pilgrimage tourism in particular lack marketing aspect and methodological requirements (Misra 2000, Russell 1999, Vukonic 1996, Deshmukh & Navale 1994, Ahmed 1992, Desh Bandhu 1983).

As per the said research gap, the present study took four important pilgrimage tourism services as per the given destination, viz. hotels—including accommodation & food services, transport, shopping and supervisory effectiveness of apex governing body at the destination, all together to evaluate relative pilgrim satisfaction and accordingly formulated a marketing strategy for the whole package as well as for individual service after applying statistical tools, viz. mean, multiple regression, 'F' test and factor analysis for data reduction, scale purification and convergent validity.

References

Ahmed, Zafar U (1992), "Islamic Pilgrimage (Hajj) to Kaaba in Makkah (Saudi Arabia): An Important International Tourism Activity", *The Journal of Tourism Studies*, Vol. 3(1), 35-43

Alavi, Jafar & Mahmoud M.Yasin (2000), "A Systematic Approach To Tourism Policy" *Journal of Business Research*, Vol. 48,147-156.

Bagri, S.C. (1996) "Domestic Tourism in India; Analyzing Tourist Destinations and Policies for Sustainable Tourism, Article submitted at National Seminar on Domestic Tourism Jan 17-19, 1996. Department of Tourism Management, Kurukshetra University, Kurukshetra.

Baker, A. Dwayne & John L. Crompton (1999)" Quality Satisfaction & Behavioural Intentions", *Annals of Tourism Research*, Vol. 27 (3), 785-803.

Bramwell, Bill (1998), "User Satisfaction and Product Development in Urban Tourism", *Tourism Management* , Vol. 19 (1), 35-47.

Briggs, Susan (1997), "*Successful Tourism Marketing – A Practical Handbook*", Kogan Page Ltd., 43-90.

Burton, Rosemary (1995), *Travel Geography*, IInd ed., Pitman: London, 61-138.

Chacko, Harsha E. (1995), "Positioning a Tourism Destination to Gain a Competitive Edge", *Asia Pacific Journal of Tourism Research*, Vol (2), 69-75.

Cronin, Jr. J. Joseph & S. Taylor, (1994)." SERVPREF versus SERVQUAL, Reconciling Performance—Based and Perceptions minus Expectations Measurement of Service Quality", *Journal of Marketing*, Vol. 58, 125-131.

Cronin, Jr. J. Joseph & A. Taylor (1992), "Marketing Service Quality: A Re-examination & Extension", *Journal of Marketing*, Vol. 56, 55-68.

Danaher, Peter J. & Jan Mattsson (1994), "Customer Satisfaction During the Service Delivery Process", *European Journal of Marketing*, Vol. 28 (5), 5-16.

Deshmukh, S.B. & A.M. Navale (1996), "Impact of Pilgrimage Tourism on Host Population of Pandharpur", *Tourism Recreation Research*, Vol., 166-175.

Doren, Carlton S & Sam A. Lollar (1985), "The Consequences of Forty Years of Tourism Growth", *Annals of Tourism Research*, Vol.12, 467-489.

Dutta, Dev Malya (1994). " Application of Modern Societal Marketing Strategy—Concept for Sustainable Tourism Development in India', *Tourism Recreation Research*, 134-141.

Etzel, M. & R. Wahlers (1985), "The Use of Requested Promotional Material by Pleasure Travellers", *Journal of Travel Research*, Vol. 23 (4), 2-6.

Geya, Aviva & Arieh Goldman (1989), "Changes in the Perception of a Service During its Consumption: A Case of Organized Tours", *European Journal of Marketing*, Vol. 23(12), 44-51.

Gordon, E. Greenlay & Allan S. Mattcham (1983), "Problems in Marketing Services: The case of Incoming Tourism ", *European Journal of Marketing*, Vol. 17 (6), 57-64.

Gronoss, C. (1978), "A Service Oriented Approach to Marketing of Services, *European Journal of Marketing*, Vol. 12 (8) 588-601

Gronoss, C. (1989), "Defining Marketing: A market oriented Approach," *European Journal of Marketing*, Vol.23 (1), 52-59.

Heath, Erine & Geoffrey Wall (1992). Marketing Tourism Destination, John Wiley & Sons, 3-25.

Jain, R.K. (1996), "Tourism Marketing: Issues and Strategies" Article Submitted at National Seminar on Domestic Tourism, Jan 17-19,1996, Department of Tourism Management, Kurukshetra University, Kurukshetra.

Kamra, K.K. (1996), "Domestic Tourism A Force to Reckon with" Article submitted at National Seminar on Domestic Tourism Jan 17-19,1996 Department of Tourism Management, Kurukshetra University, Kurukshetra.

Kandampully, J. (1983), Total Quality Management Through Continuous Improvement in Service Industries, Unpublished Doctoral Thesis, University of Exeter.

Keyser, Rik De & Norbert Vanhove (1997), "Tourism Quality Plan: An Effective Tourism Policy Tool", *The Tourist Review*, Vol. 3, 32-39.

Kotler, Philip, John Bowen & James Makens (1996), Marketing of Hospitality and Tourism, Prentice-Hall 10-18, 635-650.

Lailajainen, Risto (1981), "The Unfamiliar Tourist Destination—A marketing Challenge", *European Journal of Marketing*, Vol. 15 (7), 69-79.

Laws, Eric (1992), Tourism Marketing—Service and Quality Management Perspective, Stanley Thornes Publishers, 76-130.

Leppard, M. John, W. Malcolm HB McDonald (1986), How to Sell a Service—Guidelines for Effective Selling in Service Business, Heinemann, London, 12-35.

Lovelock, C.H. (1983), "Classifying Services to Gain Strategic Marketing Insight", *Journal of Marketing*, Vol. 47, 9-20.

March, Roger (1994), "Tourism Marketing Myopia", *Tourism Management*, Vol. 15 (6), 411-415.

McCollough, Michael A (2000), "The Effect of Perceived Justice and Attributions Regarding Service Failure & Recovery on Post Recovery Customer Satisfaction and Service Quality Attitudes", *Journal of Hospitality and Tourism Research*, Vol. 24 (4), 423-447.

McQueen, J & K Miller (1985), "Target market selection of Tourists: A Comparison of Approaches", *Journal of Travel Research*, Vol. 24 (1), 2-6.

McVey Michael & Brian King (2000), "A Profile of India's Hotel Sector: Is a Giant Finally Awakening?" *Tourism Recreation Research*, Vol. 25 (2), 97-100.

Michie, D (1986), "Family Travel Behaviour & its Importance for Tourism Management", *Tourism Management*, Vol. 7(1), 8-20.

Middleton, Victor T.C. & Rebecca Hawkins (1995), Sustainable Tourism—A Marketing perspective, Butterworth, Heinemann, Oxford, 118-130.

Middleton, Victor T.C. (1994). Marketing in Travel and tourism, IInd ed., Butterworth, Heinemann: Oxford, 4-20.

Mill, Robert Christie & A.M. Morisson (1985) The Tourism System—An Introductory, Prentice-Hall Inc., 356-366.

Miline, David, Frank, M. Go & Lorne J.R. Whittles (1992) "Communities as Destination: A Marketing Taxonomy for the Effective Implementation of the Tourism Action Plan", *Journal of Travel Research*, Spring. 31-37.

Moutinho, Luiz (1987) "Customer Behaviour in Tourism," *European Journal of Marketing*, Vol. 21 (10), 5-44.

Navale A.M. & S.B. Deshmukh (1989) "A view on Pilgrimage Tourism: A Study in Human Geography." *The National Geographical Journal of India*, Vol. 35 (1), March, 23-26.

Nicoulaud, B (1989) "Problems and Strategies in the International Marketing of Services", *European Journal of Marketing*, Vol. 23 (6), 55-65.

Norman, R. (1984) Service Management : Strategy and Leadership in Service Business, John Wiley & Sons; New York.

Otto, Julie E & J.R. Brent Ritchie (1996) "The Service Experience in Tourism", *Tourism Management*, Vol. 17 (3), 165-174.

Page, Stephen (1995). Urban Tourism, Routledge; London, 3-8.

Papadapoulos, Socrates, I. (1989) "A Conceptual Tourism Marketing planning Model: Part 1", *European Journal of Marketing*, Vol. 23 (1), 31-40.

Papadopoulos, S.I. (1989) : Strategy Development and Implementation of Tourism Marketing Plans: Part-2", *European Journal of Marketing*, Vol. 23 (3), 37-47.

Papadopoulos, S.I. (1986) "The Tourism Phenomenon: An Examination of Important Theories & Concepts", *Tourist Review*, Vol. 3, 2-11.

Parasuraman, A. Zeithamal, V, and Berry, L. (1985) "Conceptual Model of Service Quality and its implications for Future Research," *Journal of Marketing* , Vol. 49 (4), 41-50.

Poon, Auliana (1994) "The New Tourism Revolution', *Tourism Management*, Vol. 15 (2), 91-92.

Qu, Hailin & Elsa Wong Yee Ping (1999) "A Service Performance Mode of Hong Kong Cruise travellers Motivation Factors and satisfaction", *Tourism Management*, Vol. 20, 237-244.

Raaiji, W. Fred Van (1986) "Consumer Research on Tourism Mental and Behavioural Constructs", *Annals of Tourism Research*, Vol. 13, 1-9.

Raghuram, G. & T. Madhavan (2000). " Issues in Handling Pilgrim Population at Tirumala", in Delivering service Quality—Managerial Challenges for 21st Century by M. Raghavachari & K.V. Ramani, McMillan India, 541-551.

Reichael, Aric , Oded Lowengart & Ady Milman (2000) "Rural Tourism in Israel: Service Quality and Orientation', *Tourism Management*, Vol. 21, 451-459.

Ronkainen, I.A & A.G. Woodside (1978) "Cross Cultural Analysis of Market Profiles of Domestic & Foreign Travellers", *European Journal of Marketing*, Vol. 12 (8), 579-587.

Russell, Paul (1999) "Religious Travel in the New Millennium", *Travel & Tourist Analyst*,. Vol. (5), 39-68.

Ruston, M. Angela & David J. Carson (1989) "The Marketing of Services; Managing the Intangibles", *European Journal of Marketing*, Vol. 23 (8), 23-44.

Ryan, Chris (1995) Researching Tourist Satisfaction: Issues Concepts & Problems, Routledge London 40-61.

Seaton, A.V. & M. M. Bennett (1996) Marketing Tourism Products Concepts, Issues, Cases, International Thomson Business Press, 23-27.

Shostack, G. Lynn (1977) "Breaking Free From Service Marketing", *Journal of Marketing*, Vol. 41, 73-80.

Singh, L.G. (1991) "Tourism Marketing in India—Problems & Prospectus", *Southern Economist*, January 1991, 17-19.

Singh Rattan Deep (2000) Tourism Marketing Principles, Practices and Strategies, Kanishka Publishers: New Delhi, 114-164,385-450.

Singh, J.D. (1994) Management and Marketing of Tourism in India: The Challenge, in P.K. Sinha & S.C. Sahoo's (ed.), Services Marketing—Text & Reading, Himalayan Publishing: New Delhi, 140-163.

Smith, L.J.S. (1989). Tourism Analysis – A Handbook, Longman London, 2-13.

Tribe, John & Tim Snaith (1998) "From SERVQUAL TO HOLSAT: Holiday Satisfaction in Varadero, Cuba", *Tourism Management*, Vol. 19 (1), 25-34.

Ugur, Yavas (1987) "Foreign Travel Behaviour in a Growing Vacation Market: Implications for Tourism Markets", *European Journal of Marketing*, Vol. 21, (5), 57-68.

Upchurch, Randell S. & Una Teivan (2000) "Resident Perceptions of Tourism Development in Riga Latvia", *Tourism Management*, Vol. 21, 499-507.

Vieira, Walter E. (1994) "Marketing Service—The Challenges in India: in P.K. Sinha & S.C Sahoo's (ed.) Services Marketing—Text Readings, Himalayan Publishing House, N. Delhi, 242-253.

Vukonic, Boris (1996) Tourism and Religion, Pergamon, 53-68, 117-142.

Wahab, S.E. A. (1975) "Wahab on Tourism Management, : Tourism International Press; London, 5-15.

Walle, Alf H. (1996) "Quantitative versus Qualitative Tourism Research", *European Journal of Marketing*, Vol. 24 (3), 524-536.

Witt, S.F. & Luiz Moutinho (1994) Tourism Marketing and Management – A Handbook, Prentice-Hall; London, 279-284.

Witt, S.F. (1992). The Management of International Tourism, Routledge, 23-39.

RESEARCH DESIGN AND METHODOLOGY

Background

The study proposes a marketing strategy for various services drawn basically on the basis of an evaluation of these services the visitors avail themselves of during their pilgrimage to Shri Mata Vaishno Devi particularly between Katra and *Bhavan*. The various levels of pilgrim satisfaction in different services have been taken as a basis for the formulation of the marketing strategies for the pilgrimage tourism. The various aspects of research design and methodology are discussed as under :

Need of the Study

An in-depth examination of the available tourism studies indicate inadequate attention of the researchers towards the marketing efforts in pilgrimage tourism services. More than 400 articles were published in 'Annals of Tourism Research' and 'Journal of Leisure Research' between the early seventies and the late eighties, and marketing was the least represented area with only ten articles, out of which none related to pilgrimage tourism. It is only since late eighties that pilgrimage tourism studies geared up focusing on the impact of the pilgrimages beyond single spiritual benefit, attracting both religious and secular visitors, who demand better facilities (Kaur 1996 and 1982). The earlier cost-driven pilgrimage has given way to an amalgam of religious aspects with sight-seeing, holidaying, culture and relaxation (Russell 1999). This modern pilgrimage tourism requires adequate provision of standard transportation, accommodation, food, entertainment and shopping services for the pilgrims of different demography at a single destination (Deshmukh & Navale 1996, Ahmed 1992).

Accommodation and transportation services are the integral and basic components of tourism product but in spite of rapid growth in hotel business (McVey & King 2000, Ahuja & Sarna 1990, Chakraborty 1981) and transportation service (Kaul 1985), they do not match the needs of target market segments (Middleton & Hawkins 1998). Any decision to build a particular category of these services by different commercial and non-commercial agencies (Ahmed 1992) on marketing grounds require determination of profile and characteristics of pilgrims attracted to it (Middleton & Hawkins 1998, Laws 1992), based on systematic and regular information system (Raghuram & Madhavan 2000). However, the industry requires marketing professionals who understand and can respond to the changing consumer needs through creative strategies based upon solid marketing knowledge (Kotler, et al 1996). It is in this context that the study has been undertaken for the formulation of a marketing strategy for the pilgrimage tourism services.

More than fifty lakh people visiting the Shrine every year provide long term and quite suitable income generating employment opportunities particularly in the pilgrimage tourism services. Though with the inception of the Shrine Board under the Mata Vaishno Devi Shrine Act of 1996, there is sufficient quantitative improvement (Annexure-2 & 3) in the non-commercial services undertaken by the Board itself, yet the various commercial services like hotel services, transportation, food and catering are being rendered without much systematic and planned efforts in the light of pilgrim requirements. The yearly increasing pilgrim traffic to the Cave (Table-3.1) generates both socio-economic significance and business prospects for the pilgrimage tourism services. The yearly contribution of the outside state tourists visiting the Shrine, to the state economy amounts to Rs 24.28 crores with a per capita expenditure of Rs.240 (Desh Bandhu 1983).

Moreover, even after a gap of two decades and with such a high market potential, no research work has yet been completed which could prove to be useful to the marketers of these services as well as for the effective supervisory mechanism by the Shrine Board. However, even the studies available, (Raghuram & Madhavan 2000, Russell 1999, Teye & Leclerc 1998, Vukonic 1996, Kaur 1996, Deshmukh & Navale1996, Ahmed 1992, Desh Bandhu 1983, Kaur 1982), have not duly addressed themselves to the marketing aspect of pilgrimage tourims.

Nature and Scope of the Study

As stated earlier, the study is evaluative in nature and as such the marketing strategy for pilgrimage tourism has stemmed up from the pilgrim judgement about the existing major services required by these pilgrims of different profiles (Exhibit-3.1). The major pilgrimage tourism services classified under various groups like hotel services, transportation services and retailing services have been studied in detail for the formulation of marketing strategy. Besides, the supervisory effectiveness of the Shrine Board has also been studied to make the study complete and meaningful for planned and effective marketing efforts by both commercial and non-commercial providers of these services.

Hypotheses

The review of literature and the pilot study facilitates the following hypotheses:

i)   Characteristics and profile of visitors influence their judgement about satisfaction from different services (Sharma, Desh Bandhu & Sushma 2000, Middleton & Hawkins 1998, Laws 1992).

Exhibit–3.1

Profile of Visitors to the Shrine

Total Respondents contacted

(500)

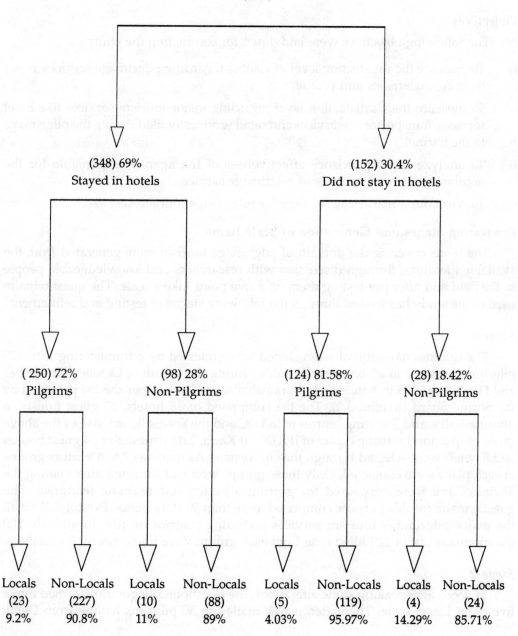

(348) 69%
Stayed in hotels

(152) 30.4%
Did not stay in hotels

(250) 72%
Pilgrims

(98) 28%
Non-Pilgrims

(124) 81.58%
Pilgrims

(28) 18.42%
Non-Pilgrims

Locals
(23)
9.2%

Non-Locals
(227)
90.8%

Locals
(10)
11%

Non-Locals
(88)
89%

Locals
(5)
4.03%

Non-Locals
(119)
95.97%

Locals
(4)
14.29%

Non-Locals
(24)
85.71%

ii) In spite of rapid growth in different tourism services, the pilgrims always experience low level of satisfaction as per their different socio-economic profiles (Sharma, Desh Bandhu & Sushma 2000, Ahuja & Sarna 1990, Kaul 1985, Dash Bandhu 1984, Chakraborty 1981).

iii) Different commercial and non-commercial services provided during the pilgrimage significantly affect the over-all satisfaction level (Sharma, Desh Bandhu & Sushma 2000, Ahmed 1992).

Objectives

The following objectives were laid down for conducting the study :

i) To evaluate the satisfaction level of visitors regarding pilgrimage services as per their characteristics and profile.

ii) To measure their satisfaction level regarding major tourism services like hotel services, transportation services and retail services availed during the pilgrimage to the Shrine.

iii) To analyze the supervisory effectiveness of the agency responsible for the regulation and maintenance of pilgrimage services.

iv) To work out a marketing strategy for pilgrimage tourism services.

Pre-testing Stages and Generation of Scale Items

The items covering the domain of pilgrimage tourism were generated from the available literature, through discussion with researchers and knowledgeable people in the field and after pre-testing them on a five point Likert scale. The questionnaire used in the study has passed through the following stages of testing and refinement :

Stage-1

The questionnaire initially developed was pretested by administering it to 120 pilgrims contacted in all on every 'Sunday' during the month of October, November and December 1995 in hotels and dharamshallas at Katra as per the list provided by the Shrine Board (Exhibit-3.2). The list comprised of 38 hotels, 15 guest houses, 6 dharmashallas and 3 retiring centres of JKTDC and the Shrine Board. As per the above given proportion 1 retiring centre of JKTDC at Katra, 2 dharmashallas, 4 guest houses and 8 hotels were selected through the chit system. As many as 7 to 8 visitors groups at each place were contacted. Only those groups who had returned after visiting the Shrine/Cave were contacted for getting a better and realistic response. The questionnaire for this purpose comprised more than 50 statements (Exhibit-3.3) on all the major pilgrimage tourism services including pilgrim profile. In all only 100 questionnaire out of 120 filled (one from each group) were found useful for analysis.

Stage-2

In 1997, after making some alterations, the questionnaire got transformed into a five point Likert scale. Thereafter, it was mailed to 50 pilgrims hailing from Delhi,

Exhibit–3.2

List of Hotels/ Guest Houses at
Katra Town with Bed Capacity

S.No	Name of Hotel/ Guest House	Total beds
1	Hotel Asia	169
2	Hotel Ambica	124
3	Hotel Basera	38
4	Hotel Durga	81
5	Hotel Holiday	72
6	Hotel Bandhu Palace	60
7	Hotel Mahindra Palace	54
8	Hotel Mayur	63
9	Hotel Rama Palace	38
10	Hotel Natraj	14
11	Hotel Samart	64
12	Shivalik Hotel	62
13	Subash Hotel	36
14	New Subash Hotel	60
15	Swastik Hotel	60
16	Hotel Tridev	74
17	Hotel Trikuta	58
18	Hotel Acika	48
19	Hotel Surya Palace	72
20	Hotel Shivam	96
21	Hotel Kumar	36
22	Prem Guest House	26
23	Vivek Hotel	42
24	Hotel Vasu	21
25	Sunrise Hotel	69
26	Ashoka Hotel	38
27	Durga Huts	6
28	National Guest House	25
29	Vikram Palace	25
30	Hotel Prem	28
31	Sham Guest House	46
32	Kesar Guest House	18

S.No	Name of Hotel/ Guest House	Total beds
33	Subash Guest House	46
34	Krishan Hotel	18
35	Bhuvi Guest House	17
36	Vijay Guest House	28
37	Rohit Guest House	51
38	Lalit Guest House	18
39	Nirmal Guest House	28
40	Prem Yatri Niwas	27
41	Holy Shrine Hotel	22
42	Durga Yatri Niwas	22
43	Lodge Aashiana	20
44	Janta Hotel	36
45	Trikuta Guest House	10
46	Panchvati Guest House	16
47	Shanker Guest House	35
48	Shripati Hotel	134
49	New Natraj Hotel	55
50	Parveen Guest House	80 persons (Floor type)
51	Chinar Guest House	200 "
52	Raju Guest House	130 "
53	Hotel Tara Deluxe	18 "

JKTDC Retiring Rooms

1.	Tourist Bunglow, JKTDC, Katra	80 beds
2.	Tourist Retiring Centre, JKTDC, Katra	206 beds & 75 pax (Floor type)
3.	Yatri Niwas, JKTDC, Katra	316 beds & 360 Common (Floor type)

Dharmashala

1.	Sridhar Sabha	500 person (floor type)
2.	Parshotam Dharmashala	160 "
3.	Chintamani Dharmashala	1088 "
4.	Rawalpindi Dharmashala	230 "
5.	Dharmvit Sabha	400 "
6.	Durga Bhavan	700 "

Source : Shrine Board, Central Board Office, Katra

Exhibit–3.3
Profiling Vaishno Devi Tourists

Particulars of the respondents

1. S.No   _____

2. Relation of respondent with others in the group   _____

3. Age   _____

4. Sex   _____

5. Occupation   _____

6. Religion   _____

7. Marital Status   _____

8. Monthly Income   _____

9. State to which you belong   _____

10. Are you coming for first time?   Yes/No

11. If No, Number of times you have visited   _____

12. Specify the source from which you got information for first time
    about the Shrine.   _____

13. What motivated you to come for Darshan?   _____

14. Would you like to come again?   Yes/No

15. If not, why ?   _____

16. Will you share the experience of pilgrimage with your friends, relatives
    at your hometown?   Yes/No

17. Will you motivate other people to visit?   Yes/No

18. Do you think the aim for which you visited the Shrine is fulfilled?   Yes/No

19. Is any other of your desires fulfilled till now by praying before Mata? Yes/No

20. Did you get mental satisfaction after visiting the cave?   Yes/No

21. Did you come for performing some rites or pooja?   Yes/No

22. Are you any time tempted to visit the cave by seeing it is a vision in your dream? Yes/No

23. Do you come just for a pleasure trip?   Yes/No

24. Are the transport facilities adequate to visit the Shrine   Yes/No

25. Are the fare charges cheap and economical?   Yes/No

26. Have you hired any accommodation in the region?   Yes/No

27. Did you get the accommodation at genuine rates?   Yes/No

28. Did you get the food of your choice?   Yes/No

29. If not, why ?   _____

30. Have you enjoyed the north Indian food?   Yes/No

31. Do you know the old story about this Shrine?   Yes/No

32. You prefer going by Foot _____ Pony _____

33. Are you satisfied by the darshan inside the cave?   Yes/No

34. If not, why ?   _____

35. Have you visited the Bhairon Ghati after darshan at the cave?   Yes/No

36. Do you think that it is one of the best pilgrimages according to
    various facilities provided ?   Yes/No

37. Are the shopping facilities adequate in the region?   Yes/No

38. What items have you purchased in the region?   _____

39. Are the prices fair and reasonable?   Yes/No

40. Was the overall shopping fair and enjoyable?   Yes/No

41. Do you think that the recreational facilities are adequate?   Yes/No

42. Is the behaviour of the people in the region cooperative?   Yes/No

43. Is the condition of region good with respect to hygiene factor?   Yes/No

44. Are the security arrangements adequate for pilgrims?   Yes/No

45. If not, why ?   _____

46. Are you satisfied with the facilities provided in the route ?   Yes/No

47. If not, why ?   _____

48. Have you cancelled any of your earlier trips due to terrorism?   Yes/No

49. Is there any other pilgrimage which you visited better than
    Mata Vaishno Devi Shrine?   Yes/No

50. If yes, name it   _____

51. Do you think the overall publicity and advertisement of pilgrimage
    is satisfactory?   Yes/No

52. Name the problems which you feel while travelling from the base
    camp to the cave   _____ _____

53. Can you suggest something for betterment of the pilgrimage?   _____ _____

U.P. and Punjab at the addresses taken from a travel agent of a chartered bus during 'Puja pilgrimage'. But due to no response, it was administered to 150 pilgrims selected in the same manner as discussed at Stage-1. The questionnaire consisted of queries about the profile of customers, their composition, mode of transport used, satisfaction regarding different services provided in hotels at Katra vis-à-vis the related grievances and suggestions.

Stage- 3

At this stage, the schedule was administered to 750 pilgrims out of which only 500 questionnaires were finally selected for analysis. After passing through the above two stages, it finally comprised of 11 queries regarding profile of visitors, 9 items explaining the composition of visitors and the mode of transport used, 78 items assessing the satisfaction level from different pilgrim services, 14 items relating to judgement of various social aspects grievances and suggestions (Annexure-1). A five point Likert scale (5———1) ranging from 'Strongly agree' (5) to 'Strongly disagree' (1) has been used for the questionnaire. Moreover, the scale values of negatively worded items were reversed before data processing.

Sample Design

The selected sample of 500 respondents of different demographic profile (Exhibit-3.4) was drawn from three major points on the pilgrimage journey viz.- 'Katra'—the base camp, 'Jammu railway station and 'Jammu bus stand'. The respondents were contacted at retiring room of Jammu Railway Station, Jammu Bus Stand and hotels at Katra selected in the same manner as given in stage-1. Every available group on 'Sundays' during August 1997 to July 1998 was contacted. Only one knowledgeable person who happened to be the leader as well and represent the group as a whole, was contacted. At each place invariably 250 groups were contacted scoring a total of 750 questionnaires out of which only 500 (66.67%) were found complete and useful for analysis.

Scale Purification

For determining the various dimensions of scale items generated for pilgrimage tourism services marketing, the SPSS package with special focus on the principal axis procedure of factor analysis was used along with varimax rotation to simplify the data by reducing a large number of variables to a small meaningful number for analysis. This technique was used for scale purification of data in 'hotel services' and in all the pilgrimage services taken together as items covered under the other two services viz. 'transportation' and 'retail services' were not large enough and the variations calculated were quite reasonable. Therefore, the purification of data for these two services was done manually by checking and deleting the conflicting responses. The domain of marketing orientation for hotel services purified through factor analysis after several iterations finally resulted in 15 items under five factors and similarly for all the pilgrimage services taken together it resulted in 31 items under eight factors. The

Exhibit–3.4
Group-wise Seggregation of Respondents
Total Respondents

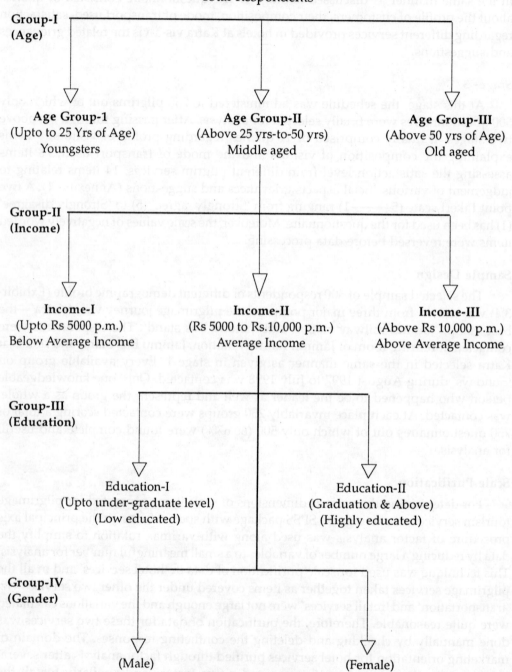

Group-I
(Age)

Age Group-1
(Upto to 25 Yrs of Age)
Youngsters

Age Group-II
(Above 25 yrs-to-50 yrs)
Middle aged

Age Group-III
(Above 50 yrs of Age)
Old aged

Group-II
(Income)

Income-I
(Upto Rs 5000 p.m.)
Below Average Income

Income-II
(Rs 5000 to Rs.10,000 p.m.)
Average Income

Income-III
(Above Rs 10,000 p.m.)
Above Average Income

Group-III
(Education)

Education-I
(Upto under-graduate level)
(Low educated)

Education-II
(Graduation & Above)
(Highly educated)

Group-IV
(Gender)

(Male)

(Female)

items with loading less than 0.5 and loading on more than one factor were discarded. (Lilin & Rangaswamy 1998, Rao & Steckel 1998, Hotelling 1983, Tabachwick & Fidell 1983, Hooley 1980, Crawford & Lomas 1980, Tull & Hawkins 1980).

Measurement of Marketing Effectiveness

The marketing effectiveness for each service has been measured separately and also by taking all the services together in terms of arithmetic mean. The relationship between over-all satisfaction about a particular service (dependent variable) and different marketing mix variables (independant variables) was estimated with the help of 'multiple regression' and subsequently the strength of association between these dependent and independent variables was worked out through 'co-efficient of determination' (Hooley 1980, Crawford & Lomas 1980). Statistically, the estimates of difference of variance and the validity of findings was tested with the help of 'F' test and the variability-wise spread of marketing orientation of visitors under three orientation regions of convergent validity viz.—Below average (<3), average (=3), Above average (>3).

Chapter Design

The study has been divided into eight chapters.

The first chapter, 'Introduction' gives a brief concept of tourism marketing, pilgrimage tourism marketing and strategic profile vis-à-vis pilgrim traffic trend of Shri Mata Vaishno Devi Shrine.

The second chapter focuses the review of related literature on service marketing, tourism marketing and pilgrimage tourism marketing, thereby identifying the common gap for conducting the present study.

The third chapter is devoted to research design and methodology including the need and scope of the study, formulation of hypotheses, objectives, pre-testing, generation of scale items, sample design, scale purification, measurement of marketing effectiveness and limitations of the study. It also gives a geographic and demographic profile of the pilgrims and traffic trend to the Shrine.

The fourth, fifth and sixth chapters on the three basic services of pilgrimage tourism are devoted to the formulation of marketing strategy for pilgrimage tourism with respect to hotel services, transportation services and retail services.

The seventh chapter explains the supervisory effectiveness of Shri Mata Vaishno Devi Shrine Board, the only governing agency of the Shrine. It assesses the marketing effectiveness of both the payment and non-payment services provided by the Board.

The last chapter, 'Marketing strategy for pilgrimage tourism' evaluates the effectiveness of all the pilgrimage services taken together and summarises the findings, problems and suggestions for enhancing marketing culture in the different services of pilgrimage tourism.

Limitations

The present work/study has been carried out under the following limitations:

1.　Only those visitors who returned after having Darshan were contacted.

2.　Only one respondent from one group of pilgrim was selected as the representative of a whole group.

3.　Factor analysis has been applied separately to only one service viz. 'hotel service at Katra and *Bhavan*' and other two services, viz 'transportation' and 'retail services' could not be factorised due to the limited number of items of the scale applied.

Table–3.1

Flow of Pilgrim Traffic to Mata Vaishno Devi Cave before and after establishment of Shrine Board (in lakhs)

S.No	Year	Pilgrims	S.No	Year	Pilgrims
1	1970	3.30	18	1987	18.58
2	1971	3.22	19	1988	19.93
3	1972	3.71	20	1989	23.12
4	1973	4.54	21	1990	21.69
5	1974	5.81	22	1991	31.15
6	1975	6.20	23	1992	35.16
7	1976	7.03	24	1993	33.69
8	1977	8.16	25	1994	37.05
9	1978	8.82	26	1995	40.12
10	1979	11.25	27	1996	43.35
11	1980	12.13	28	1997	44.34
12	1981	12.13	29	1998	46.22
13	1982	11.89	30	1999	46.70
14	1983	12.83	31	2000	51.91
15	1984	10.08	32	2001	50.57
16	1985	14.85	33	2002	44.32
17	1986	13.97	34	2003	54.00

Source: Shrine Board Central Office, Katra

References

Ahmed, Zafar U (1992). "Islamic Pilgrimage (Hajj) to Kaaba in Makkah (Saudi Arabia) : An International Tourism Activity", *The Journal of Tourism Studies*, Vol. 3(1), 35-43.

Ahuja, S.P. & S.R. Sarna (1990). *Tourism in India* – A Perspective to 1990, The Institute of Economic & Market Research; New Delhi, 70-85.

Barbara G. Taba Chnick,Linda, S. Fidell (1983) *Using Multivariate Statistics*, Harper & Row Publisher; New York, 388-411.

Chakraborty, B.K. (1981) *A Technical Guide to Hotel Operations*, A.P.H. Publishing, New Delhi 7-27.

Crawford, I.M. & R.A. Lomas (1980) "Factor Analysis—A Tool for Data Reduction", *European Journal of Marketing*, Vol. 14, (7), 414-421.

Desh Bandhu (1983) "Income and Employment Effect of Tourism—A Case Study of J&K State", A Thesis Submitted at University of Jammu, 142-150, 180-185.

Deshmukh, S.B. & A.M. Navale (1996) "Impact of Pilgrimage Tourism on Host Population of Pandharpur" *Tourism Recreation Research*, Vol. , 134-141.

Hooley, G.J. (1980) "The Multivariate Jungle: The Academics Playground but the Managers Minefield", *European Journal of Marketing*, Vol. 14(7), 379-386.

Hotelling, H. (1983) "Analysis of a Complex of Statistical Variables into Principal Components", *Journal of Education Psychology*, Vol. 24, 417-441 & 498-520.

Kaul, R.N. (1985) Dynamics of Tourism—A Trilogy-Transportation. Sterling Publishers; New Delhi.3-25.

Kaur, Jagdish (1996) "Badrinath—A Study in Himalayan Pilgrimage"In Tej Vir Singh's Tourism Wildlife Parks and Conservation, Metropolitan; New Delhi, 101-114.

Kotler, Philip, John Bowen & James Makens (1996) Marketing of Hospitality and Tourism, Prentice-Hall, 10-18,635-650.

Laws, Eric (1992) Tourism Marketing—Service and Quality Management Perspective, Stanley Thornes Publishers, 76-100.

Lilin, Gary I. & Arvind Rangaswamy (1998) Marketing Engineering Computer Assisted Marketing Analysis & Planning Addition-Wesley, Longman ; New York, 108-112.

March, Roger (1994) "Tourism Marketing Myopia", Tourism Management, Vol. 15 (6), Butterworth, Heinemann; Oxford, 411-415.

McVey Michael & Brian King (2000) "A Profile of India's Hotel Sector: Is a Giant Finally Awakening?" *Tourism Recreation Research*, Vol. 25 (2), 97-100.

Middleton, Victor T.C. & Rebecca Hawkins (1998) Sustainable Tourism—A Marketing perspective, Butterworth, Heinemann, Oxford, 118-130

Raghuram, G. & T. Madhavan (2000) "Issues in Handling Pilgrim Population at Tirumala", in Delivering Service Quality—Managerial Challenges for 21st Century by M Raghavachari & K.V. Ramani, McMillan; India, 541-551

Rao, Vithala, R. & Joel H. Steckel (1998) Analysis for Strategic Marketing, Adission-Wesley, Longman Inc., New York, 67-69.

Russell, Paul (1999) "Religious Travel in the New Millennium", *Travel & Tourist Analyst*, Vol. (5), 39-68

Sharma, R.D., Desh Bandhu & Sushma (2000). " Marketing Strategy for Pilgrimage Tourism— A Case Study of Hotel Services at Katra & Bhavan, " *Co-Operator's Bulletin*, Vol. 43 (9-10), 14-21

Teye, B. Victor & Denis Leclerc (1998) "Product & Service Delivery Satisfaction among North American Cruise Passengers", *Tourism Management*, Vol. 19 (2), 153-160.

Vukonic, Boris (1996) Tourism and Religion, Pergamon, U.K., 110-124.

MARKETING STRATEGY FOR PILGRIMAGE TOURISM WITH REFERENCE TO HOTEL SERVICES

Background

Tourism provides a lot of business opportunities in the form of hotel services, food and catering services and other related and inter-linked services (Smith 1989) to the people during their journey to a destination. In fact, the volume of tourism business with the improved roads and communication services gave way to hotel business (Burkart & Medlik 1981) like motels, guest houses, bed and breakfast services, accommodation, catering, etc. (Witt 1992).

At any destination accommodation, catering and entertainment constitute the primary tourist services, which make hotels and its supportive services of vital concern to the large proportion of tourists (Burkart & Medlik 1981). For spiritual and pilgrimage reasons a large number of people in India desire to visit holy places and different Shrines, but still it is eminently a common activity dealing with human beings moving from place to place and in due course they need some services (Tewari 1994). They need accommodation for stay and if they are offered comfortable, well-furnished accommodation with proper sanitation and hygienic facilities, safety and other services along with good food at fair and reasonable prices, the tourists will not only like the visit (Kaul 1985) but will also repeatedly visit the same place where they enjoy maximum satisfaction. The customers for travel and tourism are more sophisticated and more demanding (Middleton 1994) which fact reflects their different expectations and demands for hotel service due to different socio-economic background, the time of their visit and the duration of their stay (Edris & Meidan 1990, Sivers 1987). While designing hotel services for different segments of visitors, the hoteliers should carefully study their travelling and vacation habits (Negi 1982) as 75% of the problems of tourists/visitors are connected with unsatisfactory hotel accommodation and related services (Kaul 1985). Primarily hotels, which have emerged to satisfy the global demand of mass tourism (Poon 1993), should provide convenient access and attraction to the travellers to come, an enjoyable room and good food services (Gunn 1994). There has been a long-term impact of hotel services on tourist receipts (Bryden 1973), which act as an important agent for delivery of standardized, packaged hotel services for the masses (Poon 1993). These services along with various types of physical facilities at different price ranges (Negi 1982) are so basic as to warrant separate treatment especially from the marketer's stand-point (Robinson 1976) and go beyond the conventional lip service to effective marketing efforts (Brooksbank 1991) for satisfying the customers.

Nature and Scope of the Study

Traditionally the hotel industry accounted for a major proportion of commercial and trade-related accommodation services but, however, it has shifted the focus from the luxurious hotel services to more economically clean and hygienically sound services and facilities (Witt 1992, Bala 1990 & Pearce 1981). All these on-going efforts of hoteliers need to be planned within the framework of marketing orientation, so that the hotel services are suitably designed to meet the requirements of different tourism markets like those of business tourists, adventure tourists, cultural tourists, educational tourists, pilgrimage tourists, etc.

The hotel building is a major aspect of our tourism infrastructure (Bala 1990) and therefore, this chapter critically examines the various hotel services at Katra—the base camp of Shri Mata Vaishno Devi Pilgrimage and at *Bhavan* of the Shrine on the basis of the primary information gathered from the pilgrim within the parameters of customer/pilgrim satisfaction-oriented marketing spread over the important aspects of hotel services.

About 70% of the effective 500 respondents finally selected for the study, who stayed in hotels at Katra and *Bhavan* during their visit to the Shrine, indicate the extent and nature of pilgrimage tourism business available to the hoteliers. These days nearly 50 lakh people visit the Shrine every year which means that 35 lakh (70% of 50 lakh) pilgrims need hotel services and this pilgrim traffic has been increasing for long (Table 4.1). With this increasing rate of growth in pilgrims traffic the number of pilgrims in 2004 & 2009 is estimated as 54.18 and 59.32 lakhs respectively, meaning thereby a lot of market potential for hotel services at Katra & *Bhavan*. The market potential for these hotel services may further be studied from the proportion of respondents presented in Exhibit-4.1. Of the aforesaid hotel customers, the pilgrim-non-pilgrim ratio of 72:28 and local-non-local tourist ratio of 9:91 reveal the nature of the hotel services required. During the pilgrimage, particularly at Katra and *Bhavan*, the pilgrims expect special hotel services. They eat vegetarian food and need simple but clean accommodation with proper sanitation, hygiene & security at reasonable prices. It may not be out of place to mention here that even the routine visitors (non-pilgrims) to the Shrine avoid non-vegetarian food and liquor as a mark of devotion and respect towards the Shrine. Moreover, the hoteliers, dhabas and tea-stall owners have unanimously taken a permanent decision for not selling non-vegetarian food, liquor and eggs around the entire area of the pilgrimage destination right from Katra to *Bhavan*. Similarly 91% of these hotel customers being non-locals hailing from far-off places expect variety in food and cuisines particularly of their own preparation and taste. Table 4.1 & 4.2 indicate the nature of the hotel services required and available at Katra in terms of the fast increasing number of tourists hailing from almost all states of the country (Table 1.3) who have different socio-cultural background with different eating, enjoying, living and spending habits. It is evident from the table that more than 53% of pilgrims come from only three states, viz. U.P., Delhi and Maharashtra whose work style/life style, occupational background, time at their disposal during the visit, do influence their requirements for the hotel services at Katra and *Bhavan*.

All this indicates the type of marketing efforts these hoteliers are expected to put in for developing their basic service package and infrastructure to serve a versatile and fast growing pilgrim traffic. Specialized marketing efforts with respect to food services, accommodation, sanitation, security and other infrastructural services have already been made by the hoteliers keeping in view these segments of pilgrims and non-pilgrims so that every group of visitors enjoys their stay and leave the place with satisfaction.

However, till date no efforts have been ever made either at an individual or institutional level to evaluate and monitor the marketing efforts of these hoteliers for better strategies so that not only the pilgrims get better services but they also speak good of their experience during the pilgrimage, particularly about the hotel services to the people whom they happen to meet and talk to. In this context, the present study has been taken up with the prime objective of formulating an effective marketing strategy for the hotel services catering to the needs of the pilgrims by identifying the gaps in the on-going marketing efforts by the hoteliers within the domain of customer satisfaction.

Measurement of Customer Satisfaction—An Index of Marketing Effectiveness

Since 1950's customer satisfaction has been the corner-stone of marketing thoughts and practices (Rebello 1991, Czepial & Rosenberg 1987, Swan & Combs 1976). The measurement of customer satisfaction in hotel services is the evaluation of marketing efforts through the customer experiences based judgement. In fact, it is a barometer for measuring the success of hotel business (Poon 1993 & Brooksbank 1991) in terms of the quality of marketing efforts by the hoteliers. It being a function of the hotelier's product performance, customer expectations and expectancy confirmation and disconfirmation, influence the attitudinal changes, the purchase intention and determines whether the tourist becomes a repeat user of the services or moves into the non-repeat user group (Moutinho 1987). Pilgrim satisfaction measurement provides an opportunity to the marketers at any pilgrimage destination to exploit the maximum market potential and gain repeat business for their services. Therefore, the hoteliers at Katra and at *Bhavan* have to enhance their marketing efforts because the long term existence of the hotel business depends upon the pilgrims'/tourists' positive response. Here customer satisfaction has been measured by collecting first hand information from randomly selected 348 pilgrims through a five point (1————5) Likert scale with as many as 23 statements selected finally out of nearly 60 statements from the survey of existing literature and originally prepared questionnaire in consultation with other researchers within the domain of marketing orientation, purified through factor analysis which after several iterations finally resulted in 15 items under five factors. (Food at *Bhavan*, over-all facilities in hotels, accommodation at Katra, food at Katra, accommodation at *Bhavan*) of **MKTORIENT** (Table-4.3). The nature and extent of customer satisfaction among different segments of the pilgrims who stayed at different hotels at Katra and *Bhavan* regarding these services during their pilgrimage to the holy Shrine, has been further measured as under:

Satisfaction Among Local Pilgrims

Local pilgrims who require 'bed and breakfast' type services in hotels at Katra and *Bhavan* constitute about 9.2% (Exhibit-4.1) of the total customers i.e. a target market of 3 lakh local pilgrims every year is available to these hoteliers. Their requirements for hotel services during the pilgrimage are quite different as compared to the non-pilgrims due to their socio-economic and local conditions. Moreover, the local people do not seem to synchronize their holiday or pleasure trips with the pilgrimage, as most of them prefer to visit the Shrine on some specific occasions like 'Navratras' and 'Sankrants', etc. Therefore, customer satisfaction regarding the hotel services has been worked out separately for local pilgrims to study the relationship between the different demographic characteristics of the pilgrims and their satisfaction about the hotel services both at Katra and *Bhavan*.

Local Male Pilgrims ·

The over-all low level of satisfaction of 2.52 (Table-4.4) observed by the local male pilgrims pertaining to the food and accommodation services provided by the hoteliers at both the places indicate the ineffective, inadequate and unsatisfactory arrangements made by them. Different segments of the customers show different levels of satisfaction regarding these services. It is the highly educated, middle-aged local males, falling in an average income group who show an above-average score of satisfaction in these services, viz. 3.46 for satisfaction from food and accommodation services provided at Katra and *Bhavan* taken together, 3.50 for such services at Katra and 3.42 at *Bhavan* respectively. They show an above-average score of 3.44 for over-all satisfaction from the hotel services and only an average score of 3 for high quality of the hotel services outside Katra indicating their low preference and high satisfaction with respect to these services at Katra and *Bhavan*. However, they show less satisfaction for the services at *Bhavan* as compared to Katra. Their middle-aged counterparts of high education having a below-average income show a below-average range of satisfaction for all these services, viz. 1.86 for food and accommodation services at *Bhavan*, 2.11 for Katra and 1.99 for these services taken together for *Bhavan* and Katra. They again show a below-average score of 2.67 for over-all satisfaction from all the hotel services. This group shows preference at 4 point for such services available outside Katra. The table further reveals that the accommodation services provided at Katra are more satisfactory than those of *Bhavan*. Especially the charges for accommodation at *Bhavan* are not reasonable. It is worth while to mention here that most of the accommodation provided en-route to the Shrine right from Katra to *Bhavan* operates on a 'No Profit-no Loss' basis under the control of the Shri Mata Vaishno Devi Shrine Board.

Local Female Pilgrims

The local female pilgrims also observed a below-average of 2.94 level of satisfaction for the food and accommodation services taken together in and around Katra town and at *Bhavan* indicating again the ineffective and unsatisfactory state of affairs. The highly educated segment of the middle aged females having an average income, show throughout a below-average level of satisfaction from these services, viz. 2.25 for the food and accommodation services at Katra and 2.75 at *Bhavan*. They show only 2.5 score of satisfaction from these services taken together and a simple average for over-all satisfaction regarding these services. All the segments in this group show an above-average of 4-point satisfaction for provision of such services outside Katra indicating thereby a preference for these services. They also observe an above-average satisfaction from all these services; however, the service-wise below-average score of satisfaction at Katra, viz. 1.67 for reasonable rates, and easy availability respectively brings down the over-all customer satisfaction of hotel service at Katra to 2.48. The accommodation provided at *Bhavan* reflects an above-average score of satisfaction indicating that local female visitors are much satisfied with these services provided at *Bhavan* giving way to their preference for such services outside Katra town. (Table-4.4).

Satisfaction Among Non-Local Pilgrims

About 91% customers of hotel services at both *Bhavan* and Katra come from outside the state of Jammu & Kashmir (Exhibit-4.1) and constitute a target market of about 29 lakh visitors every year. Since they hail from different backgrounds and lifestyles, their requirements of these hotel services are unlike those of the local pilgrims. Moreover, the majorities of them visit the Shrine once every year and as such their stay in these hotels is likely to be of more duration as compared to their local counterparts. Therefore, it is in this context that the extent of customer satisfaction among the non-local pilgrims staying at the hotels in an around Katra has been worked out hereunder, so that an appropriate marketing strategy is suggested for the hotel services catering to the needs of such pilgrims.

Exhibit–4.1

Composition of Visitors Staying as per the Survey
Total Respondents Contacted (500) 100%

No. of Respondents stayed in hotels

(348) 69.6%

Pilgrims		Non-Pilgrims	
(250) 72%		(98) 28%	
Locals	Non-Locals	Locals	Non-Locals
(23) 9.2%	(227) 90.8%	(10) 11%	(88) 89%

Non-Local Male Pilgrims

Similar to their local counter parts, the non-local male pilgrims also acquire a below-average satisfaction from food and accommodation services provided by the hoteliers at both the places indicating the same situation of inadequate and ineffective services. The low educated middle-aged non-locals having an above-average income observe below-average satisfaction of 2.27 for food and accommodation at Katra and *Bhavan* taken together, thereby assigning 2.12 score for such services at *Bhavan* and 2.41 at Katra. The over-all satisfaction from all the hotel services in this case has arrived at 3.22 and a similar above-average of 3.29 for the preference of such services outside Katra. Their old-aged highly educated counterparts having the same income again explain a below-average (2.63) score of satisfaction from these hotelier services and an above-average of 3.05 for preference of these services outside Katra reflecting parity with the local pilgrims. However, all these visitors show a very low level of satisfaction at 2.19 for easy availability of accommodation at *Bhavan* and 2.34 for satisfactory accommodation at *Bhavan*, thereby, bringing down its overall mean score at 2.24. This shows that non-local male pilgrims are not satisfied with the accommodation services provided at *Bhavan*. This not only indicates the lack of responsibility among the hoteliers but also their non-seriousness regarding the needs of non-local pilgrims (Table-4.5).

Non-Local Female Pilgrims

Like their male counterparts, non-local female pilgrims observe a below-average level of over-all satisfaction at 2.33 regarding the food and accommodation services of hoteliers at both Katra and *Bhavan* (Table-4.6). Customers observe a very low level of satisfaction of 2.3 for these service at *Bhavan* especially the accommodation services at *Bhavan* show a very low level of 2.02. Again the same service at Katra also shows a below-average of 2.19 level of satisfaction. It is because of such a state of affairs at both the places that pilgrims show preference for such services outside Katra at an above-average satisfaction score of 3.18. All the segments of non-local female pilgrims show a below-average level of satisfaction regarding the accommodation and food services provided by these hoteliers. The service-wise mean scores reveal that these visitors are not satisfied with such services and there is a need for effective efforts in upgrading them. Out of the total 14 segments under study it is only the low educated old aged female pilgrims having an average income who show a highest score of 3.48 at an above average level of satisfaction regarding food and accommodation service at *Bhavan*. Further, there are only four segments who mark lesser preference for such services outside Katra at a below-average level, all other eleven groups show a considerable level of satisfaction ranging from an average of 3 point to a maximum of 5 point in this regard.

Satisfaction Among Non-Pilgrims

The expectations and requirements of non-pilgrims at a pilgrimage destination are quite different from the pilgrims who visit only out of devotion. The non-pilgrims expect more comforts and better services with sight-seeing and other recreations. The hotel services at Katra have to be evaluated from the non-pilgrim's point of view as they form approximately 29% of the respondents.

Non-Local Non-Pilgrims Males

Table-4.7 shows a below average (2.73) score of over-all satisfaction from the food and accommodation provided at Katra and *Bhavan*. It is again the easy availability of accommodation at *Bhavan*, which shows the lower of 1.96 score of satisfaction. They show an above-average score of 3.03 level only for the taste and delight of the food provided in these hotels at *Bhavan*. Different segments of non-pilgrims show different levels of satisfaction with regard to these services. It is only the highly educated teenager males falling in the above average income group that are fully satisfied at 5 point with respect to accommodation services provided at Katra. No other segment has shown such a high level of satisfaction from these services either at Katra or at *Bhavan*. Food services at both the places show a higher satisfaction at 4.34 and 4.45 level among the highly educated old aged non-local non-pilgrim males having an average income level. Among all these groups it is the highly educated young males having an average income who show a very low level of 1 point satisfaction from these hotel services provided en route to the Shrine and this indicates that all the non-local non-pilgrim males show a below-average satisfaction from such services and an above-average preference for such services outside Katra may be due to the fact that they want to see the nearby places and enjoy these services some where outside the conjested Katra town.

Non-Local Non-Pilgrim Females

Confirming the below average satisfaction by such services derived by their male counter parts, the non-local, non-pilgrim females also show a below-average of 2.55 satisfaction from the accommodation and food services provided by the hoteliers at Katra and *Bhavan* (Table 4.8). All these segments show a very similar response and there are only two segments of these females who show an above-average response from such services, viz. low educated teenagers with a below average income level at 3.19 and highly educated old-aged with an average income level at 3.08. It is the highly educated old-aged non-local pilgrim females having an above average income who show the lowest of 1.33 and 2 point satisfaction with respect to the accommodation services provided by these hoteliers at Katra and *Bhavan* respectively. This indicates scope for improvement in these services. Their preference for such services outside Katra has been evaluated in the form of customer satisfaction at 3 points.

Local Male Non-pilgrims

A below average level of 2.58 satisfaction has been reflected by local male non-pilgrims regarding the food and accommodation services provided at Katra and *Bhavan*. It is the highly educated middle-aged male non-pilgrims having an above-average income who express a much lower of 1.25 level of satisfaction from these services reflecting an ineffective and unsatisfactory trend followed by highly educated old-aged males having the same income at 2.17 score of satisfaction. All these services relating to accommodation and food services show a below average range of satisfaction. The overall satisfaction from these hotel services also reflect a below-average satisfaction at 2.77, it reflects 3.20 of above average for level of satisfaction regarding provision of adequate bedding, a near average over-all satisfaction with respect to other services viz. 2.93 for provision of over-all adequate accommodation followed by 2.53 & 2.40 for clean drinking water and cloak room and security arrangements respectively. The table further shows an above-average preference by all the segments for such services outside Katra, especially the highly educated middle aged non-pilgrim local males with a below-average income level who mark their satisfaction at 5 point (Table 4.9).

The data reduction and scale purification reduced the number of statements from the initial questionnaire but mean scores estimation after and before purification of data does not show much variation. In both the cases a below-average scores of satisfaction from the said services are reflected in most of the cases by most of the pilgrim groups. It is only the preference for such services outside Katra which show an above-average score of satisfaction in both the cases (Table-4.10 — 4.15) The four linear regression equations, viz.

(i) $Y = .429 + .583(ACKX_1) - .423(ACBX_2) + .616(FOKX_3) + .179(FOBX_4)$———Local Pilgrims.

(ii) $Y = 2.460 + .154(ACKX_1) - .206(ACBX_2) + .147(FOKX_3) + .185(FOBX_4)$———Non-Local Pilgrims

(iii) $Y = .012 + .666(ACKX_1) - .151(ACBX_2) + .681(FOKX_3) +. 071(FOBX_4)$———Local Non Pilgrims

(iv) $Y = 2.322 + .30(ACKX_1) + .124(ACBX_2) + .009(FOKX_3) + .244(FOBX_4)$—Non Local Non Pilgrims

Exhibit–4.2

S.No	GROUPS	FOUR LINEAR EQUATIONS
1.	Local Pilgrims	.429+.583(AX1)-.423(BX2)+ 6.16(CX3)+.179(DX4)
2.	Non-Local Pilgrims	2.460+.154(AX1)-.206(BX2)+.147(CX3)+.185(DX4)
3.	Local Non-Pilgrims	0.123+.666(AX1)-.151(BX2)+.681(CX3)-.071(DX4)
4.	Non-local Non-Pilgrims	2.322+.030(AX1)+.124(BX2)+.009(CX3)+.244(DX4)

Note: A= Accommodation at Katra

B= Accommodation at *Bhavan*

C= Food at Katra

D= Food at *Bhavan*

indicate that the pilgrim's satisfaction in all the four groups under study is positively and negatively associated with the variables of hotel services. The results show that variable 'C' i.e. food at Katra has the highest significance in determining customer satisfaction especially among the local pilgrims and non-pilgrims staying at these hotels followed by variable 'A' i.e. 'accommodation at Katra' The least important appears to be the variable 'B' i.e. 'accommodation at *Bhavan*' in terms of assessing the level of significance as it is negatively associated with the satisfaction of three out of four groups. The validity & reliability of these equations is shown by their respective coefficients of multiple determination 'R^2' . The variation in the satisfaction of local pilgrims and non-pilgrims is explained at 72% and 87% respectively, whereas, it explains 19% and 17% variation in case of non-local pilgrim and non-pilgrim visitors, thereby signifying this equation a better fit-in case of local visitors and explaining maximum of variation. The multiple correlation coefficient 'R' also shows a very satisfactory situation of local visitors whereas for non-local visitors it shows a lesser satisfaction (Table-4.17). Since the calculated values of 'F' are greater than the tabulated values at 5 per cent level of significance in all four cases, it shows that these four variables do not have an equal impact on overall customer satisfaction and they are not linearly related (Table-4.18). The over-all customer satisfaction and marketing orientation which arrived at 2.91 (Table-4.16) has been convergently proved valid as the proportion of pilgrims and non-pilgrims falling in the above-average region of over-all satisfaction arrived at 3 points each (Table-4.19) which has been estimated as 48% and 44.9% respectively as against 9.2% and 42.8% of below-average and average region in case of pilgrims and 7.14% and 47.96% of below-average and average region in case of non-pilgrims.

Strategic Action

With reference to the over-all satisfaction and marketing effectiveness, the extent of marketing orientation indicates three types of strategies (Table-4.16 & 4.19) for creating and maintaining a marketing culture in hotel services available to pilgrims at Katra and *Bhavan*.

The first type of strategic action extracted from research findings proposes a marketing plan which not only helps in retaining the present level of marketing orientation regarding these aspects of hotel services where both pilgrim and non-pilgrim groups enjoy an 'above -average' score of satisfaction, but also takes it to the highest possible level on the satisfaction scale.

50.08% of pilgrims and 47.8% non-pilgrims have expressed an above average satisfaction with respect to the accommodation services provided at Katra. Such services at *Bhavan* make 46.93% of pilgrims and 41.1% of non-pilgrims satisfactory to the above average level. This shows that these nearly half of the visitors are highly satisfied with respect to such services especially available at Katra and en route to the

Bhavan. The provision of food services at Katra make 48.39% pilgrims and 43.83% non-pilgrims satisfied at an above average level as compared to such services at *Bhavan* which satisfy 47.68% pilgrims and 46.05% non-pilgrims at an above average level and Table 4.19 reveals that it is the provision of hygienic food at both the places which make nearly half of the visitors satisfied to such an extent.

Other over-all services provided at these hotels make 47% of pilgrims and 44.58% non-pilgrims satisfied at an above average level. It is the preference of such services outside Katra which make nearly 49% of pilgrims more satisfied at an above-average level. Adequacy of accommodation at both these places and the cloak room & security services make more than 47% of pilgrims and 44% of non-pilgrims satisfied at an above-average score.

Thus nearly half of the visitors conclude with an above-average score of satisfaction from these hotel services en route to the pilgrimage.

The second type of strategic action requires further improvement in the present level of marketing culture about all the hotel services where pilgrims and non-pilgrims score an average satisfaction.

41.78% pilgrims and 47.05% non-pilgrims scored an average satisfaction from the accommodation services available at Katra. These services at *Bhavan* make 45.82% pilgrims and 53.42% non-pilgrim satisfied at an average level. More than half of non-pilgrim visitors feel average satisfaction from accommodation services at *Bhavan*.

Food services at both the places satisfy 42% of pilgrims and 46% to 49% of non-pilgrims at an average score. Half of the non-pilgrim visitors show an average satisfaction with respect to hygienic food provided at Katra followed by cheap rates of such services. Over-all satisfaction from other services provided at these hotels make 44.56% pilgrims and 48.59% non-pilgrims satisfied at an average level.

The third type of strategy gives stress upon immediate attention of policy makers, administrators and hoteliers providing such services, towards those aspects of marketing structure, which scored below-average level of satisfaction.

7% to 9% of non-pilgrim and pilgrim visitors express a below-average level of satisfaction from such hotel services en route to the Shrine. These visitors feel less satisfied from these hotel services en route to the pilgrimage. They feel less of satisfaction with respect to the reasonable charges for accommodation services at Katra and satisfaction from the accommodation services provided at *Bhavan*.

These below-average scores of satisfaction reduce the over-all satisfaction to a great extent and deserve much attention for improvement. This needs a sound strategy for improving such services.

Table–4.1
Yearly Growth of Pilgrims to the Shrine
Since 1966 (in lakhs)

S.No	Year	Total Pilgrims	S.No	Year	Total Pilgrims
1	1965	212300	21	1985	1484984
2	1966	Not available	22	1986	1396736
3	1967	212170	23	1987	1857608
4	1968	234422	24	1988	1992595
5	1969	251818	25	1989	2312001
6	1970	330543	26	1990	2177260
7	1971	336935	27	1991	3134331
8	1972	371329	28	1992	3725169
9	1973	535573	29	1993	3368735
10	1974	531202	30	1994	3705495
11	1975	620013	31	1995	4011627
12	1976	703429	32	1996	4335432
13	1977	815517	33	1997	4434233
14	1978	908336	34	1998	4622297
15	1979	1126514	35	1999	4670454
16	1980	1212958	36	2000	5191915
17	1981	1213482	37	2001	5056919
18	1982	1188857	38	2002	4432178
19	1983	1283340	39	2003	5400296
20	1984	1008480			

Source: Shrine Board, Central Office, Katra

Table–4.2

Profile of Hotel Accommodation at Katra

S.No	No.of Hotels	No.of Rooms	Tariff (in Rs.)	Food and Catering Service	Transport Service	D.G.Set	Location
1	4	1 to 10	200-800	No	No	No (3)	Dak Bunglow Road (1)
						Yes (1)	Bus Stand (2)
							Kashmir Road (1)
							Jammu Road
2	10	10 to 20	125-1300	Yes (1)	Yes (1)	Yes (2)	Dak Bunglow (3)
				No (9)	No (9)	No (8)	Kashmir Road (1)
							New Bus Stand (3)
							Main Bazar (1)
							Jammu Road (2)
3	14	20 to 30	175-1050	No	No	No (10)	Dak Bunglow (1)
						Yes (4)	Kashmir Road (5)
							New Bus Stand (1)
							Main Bazar (1)
							Jammu Road (6)
4	11	30 to 40	395-4000	Yes (9)	Yes (9)	Yes (10)	Jammu Road (5)
				No (2)	No (2)	No (1)	Main Bazar (1)
							Bus Stand (1)
							Main Bazar (1)
							Kashmir Road (1)
5	5	40 to 50	250-2500	Yes (3)	Yes (3)	Yes (3)	Jammu Road (4)
				No (1)	No (1)	No (1)	New Bus Stand (1)
6	2	50 to 60	1000-2200	Yes	Yes (3)	Yes	Jammu Road (2)
7	1	60 to 70	650-3500	Yes	Yes (3)	Yes	Dak Bunglow (1)

Source: Hotel Association, Katra

Table–4.3

Summary of Results from Scale Purification—Loading & Variance Explained

FACTORS	DIMESNIONS/ STATEMENTS	FACTOR LOADING	%OF VARIANCE EXPLAINED
FACTOR-1	FOOD AT BHAVAN		28.1
	1. Tasty & delicious food	0.83	
	2. Hygienic food	0.81	
	3. Variety in food available	0.71	
FACTOR-2	OVERALL FACILITIES IN HOTELS		11.2
	1. Cloak room & security	0.84	
	2. Clean drinking water	0.70	
	3. Adequate Bedding	0.66	
	4. Adequate accommodation	0.55	
FACTOR-3	ACCOMMODATION AT KATRA		9.5
	1. Easily available	0.82	
	2. Reasonable charges	0.81	
	3. Satisfactory accommodation	0.78	
FACTOR-4	FOOD AT KATRA		7.8
	1. Cheap food at Katra	0.69	
	2. Hygienic food	0.58	
FACTOR-5	ACCOMMODATION AT BHAVAN		6.4
	1. Easily available	0.76	
	2. Satisfactory accommodation	0.72	
	3. Preference of accommodation Outside Katra	0.60	
Total Variance Explained			63.0

Table-4.4

Mean Score of Marketing Effectiveness Measured through Local Male & Female Pilgrim Judgement in Hotel Services

Variables	Age	Age Group-I (Up to 25 Yrs.)			Age Group-II (25 to 50 Yrs.)			Age Group-III (Above 50 Yrs.)			Age Group-II (25 to 50 yrs.)		Age Group-III (Above 50 yrs.)		
	Income	Inc-1		Inc-2	Inc-1	Inc-2		Inc-2	Inc-3		Inc-1	Inc-2		Inc-2	
	Education	E-1	E-2	E-1	E-2	E-1	E-2	E-2	E-2	X	E-2	E-2	E-1	X	X
(1)	(2)	(3)	(4)	(5)	(6)	(7)	(8)	(9)	(10)	(11)	(12)	(13)	(14)	(15)	(16)
Acc. Services at Katra															
Satisfactory		4.00	4.00	4.00	2.67	3.00	4.00	3.00	3.00	3.33	4.00	4.00	1.00	3.00	3.17
Easily Available		3.00	3.00	2.00	2.33	1.00	3.00	2.33	1.00	2.21	3.00	1.00	1.00	1.67	1.94
Reasonable Charges		3.00	1.00	2.00	1.67	2.00	3.50	3.00	1.00	2.15	3.00	1.00	1.00	1.67	1.91
X1		3.33	2.67	2.67	2.22	2.00	3.50	2.78	1.67	2.56	3.33	2.00	1.00	2.11	2.34
Food Services at Katra															
Hygienic		2.00	1.00	3.00	1.67	3.00	3.25	3.00	4.00	2.62	3.00	1.00	4.00	2.67	2.65
Cheap rates		1.00	1.00	4.00	2.33	2.00	3.75	2.67	3.00	2.47	4.00	4.00	1.00	3.00	2.74
X2		1.50	1.00	3.50	2.00	2.50	3.50	2.84	3.50	2.55	3.50	2.50	2.50	2.84	2.70
X12		2.42	1.84	3.09	2.11	2.25	3.50	2.81	2.59	2.56	3.42	2.25	1.75	2.48	2.52
Acc. Services at Bhavan															
Satisfactory		2.00	1.00	1.00	1.00	3.00	4.00	3.00	4.00	2.38	4.00	4.00	4.00	4.00	3.19

Contd.....

(1)	(2)	(3)	(4)	(5)	(6)	(7)	(8)	(9)	(10)	(11)	(12)	(13)	(14)	(15)	(16)
Easily Available		1.00	3.00	1.00	2.00	2.00	3.00	2.00	3.00	2.13	3.00	1.00	4.00	2.67	2.40
X3		1.50	2.00	1.00	1.50	2.50	3.50	2.50	3.50	2.26	3.50	2.50	4.00	3.34	2.80
Food Services at Bhavan															
Hygienic		3.00	3.00	3.00	2.33	2.00	3.50	3.00	2.00	2.73	3.00	2.00	4.00	3.00	2.87
Tasty & delicious		2.00	3.00	2.00	2.33	2.00	3.50	2.33	3.00	2.52	4.00	4.00	4.00	4.00	3.26
Variety in food served		4.00	1.00	2.00	2.00	4.00	3.00	2.33	2.00	3.00	3.00	3.00	4.00	3.33	3.06
X4		3.00	3.33	2.00	2.22	2.67	3.33	2.55	2.33	2.68	3.33	3.00	4.00	3.44	3.06
X34		2.25	2.67	1.50	1.86	2.59	3.42	2.53	2.92	2.47	3.42	2.75	4.00	3.39	2.93
Overall X		2.34	2.26	2.30	1.99	2.42	3.46	2.67	2.76	2.52	3.42	2.50	2.88	2.94	2.73
Overall services															
Adeq. Accom		4.00	2.00	4.00	2.33	4.00	3.25	4.00	3.00	3.32	4.00	2.00	4.00	3.33	3.33
Clean drinking water		2.00	1.00	4.00	2.33	3.00	3.00	3.67	4.00	2.88	3.00	2.00	4.00	3.00	2.94
Cloak room & security		3.00	4.00	4.00	3.00	3.00	4.00	3.00	5.00	3.63	4.00	4.00	4.00	4.00	3.82
Adeq. bedding		4.00	1.75	4.00	3.00	4.00	3.50	3.67	4.00	3.27	4.00	4.00	4.00	4.00	3.64
X5		3.25	2.00	4.00	2.67	3.50	3.44	3.59	4.00	3.28	3.75	3.00	4.00	3.58	3.43
Pref. of Services outside Katra X6		3.00	2.00	2.00	4.00	3.00	3.00	2.50	5.00	3.06	4.00	4.00	4.00	4.00	3.53

Table–4.5

Mean Score of Marketing Effectiveness Measured through Non-Local Male Pilgrim Judgement in Hotel Services

Variables	Age Income Education	Age Group-I (Up to 25 Yrs.)				Age Group-II (25-50 Yrs.)						Age Group-III (Above 50 Yrs.)					X
		Inc-1	Inc-2		Inc-3	Inc-1		Inc-2		Inc-3		Inc-1	Inc-2		Inc-3		
		E-1	E-1	E-2	E-2	E-1	E-2	E-1	E-2	E-1	E-2	E-1	E-1	E-2	E-1	E-2	X
(1)	(2)	(3)	(4)	(5)	(6)	(7)	(8)	(9)	(10)	(11)	(12)	(13)	(14)	(15)	(16)	(17)	(18)
Acc. Services at Katra																	
Satisfactory		2.63	3.75	3.67	4.00	2.00	3.00	3.08	2.35	2.43	2.92	4.00	1.00	3.73	3.50	2.78	2.99
Easily Available		2.88	2.50	2.33	4.00	3.00	2.20	3.15	2.96	2.71	3.71	4.00	1.00	3.64	3.25	3.12	2.96
Reasonable Charges		2.25	2.75	3.00	4.00	3.00	2.20	2.54	2.27	2.43	2.64	4.00	1.00	2.55	3.25	2.36	2.68
X1		2.59	3.00	3.00	4.00	2.67	2.47	2.92	2.53	2.52	3.09	4.00	1.00	3.31	3.33	2.75	2.88
Food Services at Katra																	
Hygienic		3.00	3.50	3.25	3.00	2.50	3.00	2.67	2.81	2.29	2.67	4.00	3.00	2.23	3.50	2.87	2.95
Cheap rates		2.50	2.75	3.00	3.00	2.00	3.50	2.13	3.19	2.29	2.07	4.00	2.00	2.00	3.25	2.24	2.66
X2		2.75	3.13	3.13	3.00	2.25	3.25	2.40	3.00	2.29	2.37	4.00	2.50	2.12	3.38	2.56	2.81
X12		2.67	3.07	3.07	3.50	2.46	2.86	2.66	2.77	2.41	2.73	4.00	1.75	2.72	3.36	2.66	2.85
Acc. Services at Bhavan																	
Satisfactory		2.29	2.50	2.00	1.00	2.50	3.33	3.23	3.26	2.86	3.09	1.00	1.00	1.00	3.50	2.48	2.34

Contd.....

(1)	(2)	(3)	(4)	(5)	(6)	(7)	(8)	(9)	(10)	(11)	(12)	(13)	(14)	(15)	(16)	(17)	(18)
Easily Available		2.00	2.50	2.00	1.00	3.00	3.33	2.92	2.84	1.14	2.55	1.00	1.00	1.63	3.00	2.22	2.14
X3		2.15	2.50	2.00	1.00	2.75	3.33	3.08	3.05	2.00	2.82	1.00	1.00	1.32	3.25	2.35	2.24
Food Services at *Bhavan*																	
Hygienic		2.75	3.50	3.67	3.00	2.00	3.40	2.87	2.84	2.29	2.89	4.00	3.00	3.07	2.67	3.13	3.01
Tasty & delicious		2.50	3.00	2.67	3.00	2.00	3.40	2.47	2.61	2.14	2.27	4.00	3.00	2.71	2.67	2.84	2.75
Variety in food served		2.50	2.75	3.00	2.00	2.50	3.20	2.53	2.74	2.29	2.55	4.00	3.00	2.64	3.00	2.48	2.75
X4		2.58	3.08	3.11	2.67	2.17	3.33	2.62	2.73	2.24	2.57	4.00	3.00	2.81	2.78	2.82	2.83
X34		2.37	2.79	2.56	1.84	2.46	3.33	2.85	2.89	2.12	2.70	2.50	2.00	2.82	3.02	2.59	2.59
Overall X		2.52	2.93	2.82	2.67	2.46	3.10	2.76	2.83	2.27	2.72	3.25	1.88	2.07	3.19	2.63	2.67
Overall services																	
Adeq. Accom		3.75	3.50	3.50	3.00	1.50	3.80	3.47	3.77	3.14	3.08	4.00	4.00	3.40	4.00	3.08	3.40
Clean drinking water		3.75	3.50	3.75	3.00	2.50	2.60	3.13	3.32	3.43	3.62	4.00	3.00	3.47	4.00	2.60	3.38
Cloak room & security		3.63	2.50	3.75	5.00	5.00	4.00	3.67	3.58	3.00	3.71	4.00	3.00	3.40	4.00	3.00	3.68
Adeq. bedding		3.75	3.50	3.50	5.00	4.50	4.00	3.26	3.71	3.29	3.07	4.00	3.00	3.33	3.75	2.32	3.60
X5		3.72	3.25	3.63	4.00	3.38	3.60	3.38	3.60	3.22	3.37	4.00	3.25	3.40	3.94	2.75	3.52
Pref. of Services																	
outside Katra X6		3.17	4.50	3.00	4.00	3.00	3.33	4.07	3.29	3.29	2.50	4.00	3.00	4.08	3.50	3.05	3.45

Table–4.6

Mean Score of Marketing Effectiveness Measured through Non-Local Female Pilgrim Judgement in Hotel Services

Variables	Age Income Education (2)	Age Group-I (Up to 25 Yrs.)			Age Group-II (25-50 Yrs.)					Age Group-III (Above 50 Yrs.)						X (17)
		Inc-1		Inc-2	Inc-1		Inc-2	Inc-3		Inc-1		Inc-2		Inc-3		
(1)		E-1 (3)	E-2 (4)	E-1 (5)	E-1 (6)	E-2 (7)	E-2 (8)	E-1 (9)	E-2 (10)	E-1 (11)	E-2 (12)	E-1 (13)	E-2 (14)	E-1 (15)	E-2 (16)	
Acc. Services at Katra																
Satisfactory		1.00	4.00	1.00	2.50	2.55	2.60	4.00	3.00	2.00	1.00	2.00	2.50	3.00	2.55	2.41
Easily Available		3.00	2.00	1.00	2.50	2.91	2.00	3.00	4.00	2.33	1.00	2.50	3.00	1.00	2.18	2.32
Reasonable Charges		1.00	2.00	1.00	2.00	2.18	2.40	2.00	3.00	1.00	1.00	1.50	3.50	1.00	2.18	1.84
$X1$		1.67	2.67	1.00	2.33	2.55	2.33	3.00	3.33	1.78	1.00	2.00	3.00	1.67	2.30	2.19
Food Services at Katra																
Hygienic		3.33	3.00	3.00	2.63	2.71	3.00	2.00	1.00	2.60	2.00	3.00	2.50	4.00	2.42	2.66
Cheap rates		2.00	3.00	3.00	2.13	2.38	3.00	3.00	2.00	1.40	2.00	2.00	2.00	3.00	2.08	2.36
$X2$		2.67	3.00	3.00	2.38	2.55	3.00	2.50	1.50	2.00	2.00	2.50	2.25	3.50	2.25	2.51
$X12$		2.17	2.84	2.00	2.36	2.55	2.67	2.75	2.42	1.89	1.50	2.25	2.63	2.59	2.28	2.35
Acc. Services at Bhavan																
Satisfactory		3.00	1.00	1.00	2.38	2.89	2.60	3.00	2.00	3.33	1.00	3.67	1.00	4.00	2.58	2.39

Contd.....

(1)	(2)	(3)	(4)	(5)	(6)	(7)	(8)	(9)	(10)	(11)	(12)	(13)	(14)	(15)	(16)	(17)
Easily Available		1.00	1.00	1.00	2.25	1.78	1.60	2.00	1.00	3.00	1.00	3.33	1.00	1.00	2.08	1.65
X3		2.00	1.00	1.00	2.32	2.34	2.10	2.50	1.50	3.17	1.00	3.50	1.00	2.50	2.33	2.02
Food Services at *Bhavan*																
Hygienic		3.00	4.00	3.00	2.75	2.77	3.00	3.00	3.00	3.20	1.00	3.67	1.50	1.00	2.33	2.66
Tasty & delicious		3.00	4.00	3.00	2.50	2.46	3.20	3.00	3.00	2.20	1.00	3.00	3.00	1.00	2.33	2.62
Variety in food served		2.67	4.00	2.00	2.38	2.15	2.60	3.00	3.00	1.60	1.00	3.67	3.00	1.00	2.42	2.46
X4		2.89	4.00	2.67	2.54	2.46	2.93	3.00	3.00	2.33	1.00	3.45	2.50	1.00	2.36	2.58
X34		2.45	2.50	1.84	2.43	2.40	2.52	2.75	2.25	2.75	1.00	3.48	1.75	1.75	2.35	2.30
Overall X		2.31	2.67	1.92	2.40	2.48	2.60	2.75	2.34	2.32	1.25	2.87	2.19	2.17	2.32	2.33
Overall services																
Adeq. Accom		4.00	3.00	3.00	3.13	3.54	3.60	2.00	3.00	3.00	4.00	3.67	2.50	3.00	2.75	3.16
Clean drinking water		4.00	3.00	4.00	3.50	3.38	3.20	3.00	3.00	3.40	4.00	4.00	4.00	3.00	3.08	3.47
Cloak room & security		4.00	3.00	3.00	3.63	3.54	2.80	4.00	4.00	4.00	4.00	3.67	3.00	3.00	3.42	3.50
Adeq. bedding		4.00	3.00	3.00	3.38	3.31	3.60	3.00	4.00	3.80	4.00	3.67	3.50	3.00	3.42	3.48
X5		4.00	3.00	3.25	3.41	3.44	3.30	3.00	3.50	3.55	4.00	3.75	3.25	3.00	3.17	3.40
Pref. of Services																
Outside Katra X6		1.67	2.00	5.00	2.50	3.69	3.20	3.00	4.00	3.60	3.00	3.33	2.50	4.00	3.00	3.18

Table–4.7

Mean Score of Marketing Effectiveness Measured through Non-Local Male Non-Pilgrim Judgement in Hotel Services

Variables (1)	Age Group-I (Up to 25 Yrs.) Inc-1 E-2 (3)	Inc-2 E-2 (4)	Inc-3 E-2 (5)	Age Group-II (25-50 Yrs.) Inc-1 E-1 (6)	Inc-1 E-2 (7)	Inc-2 E-1 (8)	Inc-2 E-2 (9)	Inc-3 E-1 (10)	Inc-3 E-2 (11)	Age Group-III (Above 50 Yrs.) Inc-1 E-1 (12)	Inc-1 E-2 (13)	Inc-3 E-1 (14)	Inc-3 E-2 (15)	X (16)
Acc. Services at Katra														
Satisfactory	3.00	1.00	5.00	1.00	2.50	2.00	2.73	3.00	3.20	4.00	4.00	2.00	3.33	2.83
Easily Available	3.00	1.00	5.00	2.00	2.00	4.00	3.00	1.00	3.60	4.00	3.33	2.00	3.22	2.86
Reasonable Charges	3.00	1.00	5.00	2.00	3.50	2.00	2.33	2.00	3.20	2.00	2.67	3.00	2.71	2.65
X_1	3.00	1.00	5.00	1.67	2.67	2.67	2.69	2.00	3.33	3.33	3.33	2.33	3.09	2.78
Food Services at Katra														
Hygienic	4.00	1.00	3.00	3.00	1.67	2.00	3.95	2.00	2.80	4.00	4.67	3.00	2.91	2.92
Cheap rates	4.00	1.00	3.00	3.00	1.67	3.00	3.00	3.00	2.80	2.00	4.00	3.00	2.82	2.79
X_2	4.00	1.00	3.00	3.00	1.67	2.50	3.48	2.50	2.80	3.00	4.34	3.00	2.87	2.86
X_{12}	3.50	1.00	4.00	2.34	2.17	2.59	3.09	2.25	3.07	3.17	3.84	2.67	2.98	2.82
Acc. Services at Bhavan														
Satisfactory	3.00	1.00	1.00	1.00	3.50	3.00	3.60	3.00	4.00	4.00	4.00	2.00	2.86	2.77

Contd.....

(1)	(2)	(3)	(4)	(5)	(6)	(7)	(8)	(9)	(10)	(11)	(12)	(13)	(14)	(15)	(16)
Easily Available		3.00	1.00	1.00	1.00	1.00	2.00	3.13	2.00	2.50	2.00	2.00	2.00	2.86	1.96
X3		3.00	1.00	1.00	1.00	2.25	2.50	3.37	2.50	3.25	3.00	3.00	2.00	2.86	2.36
Food Services at Bhavan															
Hygienic		4.00	1.00	3.00	2.00	2.67	2.00	3.21	4.00	2.50	4.00	4.67	3.00	3.00	3.00
Tasty & delicious		4.00	3.00	3.00	3.00	2.67	2.00	2.84	3.00	2.00	4.00	4.67	3.00	2.27	3.03
Variety in food served		1.00	3.00	3.00	2.00	3.67	3.00	3.26	2.00	2.50	2.00	4.00	3.00	2.43	2.68
X4		3.00	2.33	3.00	2.33	3.00	2.33	3.10	3.00	2.33	3.33	4.45	3.00	2.57	2.91
X34		3.00	1.67	2.00	1.67	2.63	2.42	3.24	2.75	2.79	3.17	3.73	2.50	2.72	2.64
Overall X		3.25	1.34	3.00	2.01	2.40	2.51	3.17	2.50	2.93	3.17	3.79	2.59	2.85	2.73
Overall services															
Adeq. Accom		1.00	3.00	4.00	4.00	3.40	4.00	3.89	4.00	2.50	4.00	3.33	3.00	3.55	3.36
Clean drinking water		4.00	1.00	3.00	4.00	3.40	4.00	3.79	2.00	3.00	4.00	3.33	3.00	3.36	3.22
Cloak room & security		4.00	3.00	3.00	4.00	3.40	4.00	3.95	5.00	3.20	4.00	3.33	2.00	3.73	3.59
Adeq. bedding		4.00	3.00	3.00	4.00	3.40	4.00	3.84	4.00	3.80	4.00	3.33	2.00	3.73	3.55
X5		3.25	2.50	3.25	4.00	3.40	4.00	3.87	3.75	3.13	4.00	3.33	2.50	3.59	3.43
Pref. of Services															
Outside Katra X6		4.00	4.00	1.00	2.00	3.40	4.00	3.74	4.00	3.20	4.00	4.67	4.00	3.09	3.47

Table–4.8

Mean Score of Marketing Effectiveness Measured through Non-Local Female Non-Pilgrim Judgement in Hotel Services

Variables	Age Group-I (Up to 25 Yrs.)	Age Group-II (25 to 50 Yrs.)				Age Group-III (Above 50 Yrs.)		
Age								
Income	Inc-1	Inc-1	Inc-2		Inc-3	Inc-2	Inc-3	
Education (2)	E-1 (3)	E-2 (4)	E-1 (5)	E-2 (6)	E-2 (7)	E-2 (8)	E-2 (9)	X (10)
(1)								
Acc. Services at Katra								
Satisfactory	4.00	2.00	2.00	2.00	1.00	2.67	2.00	2.24
Easily Available	4.00	1.60	2.00	2.50	4.00	2.67	1.00	2.54
Reasonable Charges	3.50	1.60	2.00	1.00	4.00	2.67	1.00	2.25
X1	3.83	1.73	2.00	1.83	3.00	2.67	1.33	2.34
Food Services at Katra								
Hygienic	3.00	2.00	3.00	2.00	1.00	3.50	3.00	2.50
Cheap rates	3.00	2.80	3.50	1.50	1.00	3.50	2.50	2.54
X2	3.00	2.40	3.25	1.75	1.00	3.50	2.75	2.52
X12	3.42	2.07	2.63	1.79	2.00	3.09	2.04	2.43
Acc. Services at Bhavan								
Satisfactory	4.00	2.00	2.00	3.00	4.00	3.00	3.00	3.00

Contd......

(1)	(2)	(3)	(4)	(5)	(6)	(7)	(8)	(9)	(10)
Easily Available		2.00	2.00	2.00	2.00	4.00	3.00	1.00	2.29
X3		3.00	2.00	2.00	2.50	4.00	3.00	2.00	2.64
Food Services at *Bhavan*									
Hygienic		3.00	1.60	3.50	2.00	1.00	3.33	2.50	2.42
Tasty & delicious		3.00	2.60	3.00	2.00	3.00	3.00	2.50	2.73
Variety in food served		2.67	3.60	3.50	1.50	3.00	3.00	3.50	2.97
X4		2.89	2.60	3.33	1.83	2.33	3.11	2.83	2.70
X34		2.95	2.30	2.67	2.17	3.17	3.06	2.42	2.68
Overall X		3.19	2.19	2.65	1.98	2.59	3.08	2.23	2.56
Overall services									
Adeq. Accom		3.33	4.00	3.50	2.50	4.00	4.00	3.50	3.55
Clean drinking water		3.33	4.00	2.50	3.00	4.00	3.00	4.00	3.40
Cloak room & security		3.33	3.60	2.50	3.00	4.00	3.00	3.50	3.28
Adeq. bedding		3.67	3.60	3.00	3.50	4.00	4.33	2.00	3.44
X5		3.42	3.80	2.88	3.00	4.00	3.58	3.25	3.42
Pref. of Services									
Outside Katra X6		3.67	2.40	3.00	3.50	4.00	3.67	3.00	2.80

Table–4.9

Mean Score of Marketing Effectiveness Measured through Local Male Non-Pilgrim Judgement in Hotel Services

Variables	Age Income Education	Age Group-II (25 to 50 yrs.)				Age Group-III (Above 50 Yrs.)	
		Inc-1	Inc-2		Inc-3	Inc-3	X
(1)	(2)	E-2 (3)	E-1 (4)	E-2 (5)	E-3 (6)	E-2 (7)	(8)
Acc. Services at Katra							
Satisfactory		5.00	2.67	3.67	4.00	2.00	3.47
Easily Available		4.00	3.33	2.67	1.00	2.00	2.60
Reasonable Charges		4.00	2.67	3.00	1.00	1.00	2.33
X1		4.33	2.89	3.11	2.00	1.67	2.80
Food Services at Katra							
Hygienic		2.00	3.33	3.00	1.00	4.00	2.67
Cheap rates		2.00	2.67	3.00	1.00	4.00	2.53
X2		2.00	3.00	3.00	1.00	4.00	2.60
X12		3.17	2.95	3.06	1.50	2.84	2.70
Acc. Services at Bhavan							
Satisfactory		5.00	3.00	4.00	1.00	1.00	2.80

Contd......

(1)	(2)	(3)	(4)	(5)	(6)	(7)	(8)
Easily Available		5.00	2.33	2.33	1.00	1.00	2.33
X3		5.00	2.67	3.17	1.00	1.00	2.57
Food Services at Bhavan							
Hygienic		2.00	3.00	2.67	1.00	2.00	2.13
Tasty & delicious		4.00	3.00	2.67	1.00	2.00	2.53
Variety in food served		4.00	2.67	2.33	1.00	2.00	2.40
X4		3.33	2.89	2.56	1.00	2.00	2.35
X34		4.17	2.78	2.87	1.00	1.50	2.46
Overall X		3.67	2.87	2.97	1.25	2.17	2.58
Overall services							
Adeq. Accom		2.00	4.00	3.67	1.00	4.00	2.93
Clean drinking water		4.00	4.00	1.67	1.00	2.00	2.53
Cloak room & security		3.00	4.00	2.00	1.00	2.00	2.40
Adeq. bedding		3.00	4.00	4.00	1.00	4.00	3.20
X5		3.00	4.00	2.84	1.00	3.00	2.77
Pref. of Services							
Outside Katra X6		5.00	2.67	4.00	3.00	4.00	3.73

Table-4.10

Mean Score of Marketing Effectiveness Measured through Local Male & Female Pilgrim Judgement in Hotel Services

Variables		Male Pilgrims									Female Pilgrims				
Age		Age Group-I Up to 25 Yrs.				Age Group-II 25-50 Yrs.		Age Group-III Above 50 Yrs.			Age Group-II 25-50 Yrs.		Age Group-III Above 50 Yrs.		
Income		Inc-1		Inc-2		Inc-1	Inc-2	Inc-2	Inc-3		Inc-1	Inc-2	Inc-3		
Education		E-1	E-2	E-1	E-2	E-1	E-2	E-2	E-2	X	E-2	E-2	E-1	X	X
(1)	(2)	(3)	(4)	(5)	(6)	(7)	(8)	(9)	(10)	(11)	(12)	(13)	(14)	(15)	(16)
Acc. Service at Katra															
Satisfactory		4.00	4.00	4.00	2.67	3.00	4.00	3.00	3.00	3.46	4.00	4.00	1.00	3.00	3.00
Easily available		3.00	3.00	2.00	2.33	1.00	3.00	2.33	1.00	2.21	3.00	1.00	1.00	1.67	1.77
Reasonable charges		3.00	1.00	2.00	1.67	2.00	3.50	3.00	1.00	2.15	3.00	1.00	1.00	1.67	1.74
X1		3.33	2.67	2.67	2.22	2.00	3.50	2.78	1.67	2.60	3.33	2.00	1.00	2.11	2.17
Food services at Katra															
Hygienic		2.00	1.00	3.00	1.67	3.00	3.25	3.00	4.00	2.62	3.00	1.00	4.00	2.67	2.65
Tasty & delicious		1.00	1.00	2.00	1.67	3.00	3.50	2.00	4.00	2.27	4.00	3.00	4.00	3.67	2.97
Cheap rates		1.00	1.00	4.00	2.33	2.00	3.75	2.67	3.00	2.47	4.00	4.00	1.00	3.00	2.74
Variety in food served		3.00	4.00	1.00	2.00	3.00	4.00	2.00	4.00	2.88	3.00	4.00	4.00	3.67	3.28
X2		1.75	1.75	2.50	1.92	2.75	3.63	2.42	3.75	2.56	3.50	3.00	3.25	3.25	2.91
X12		2.54	2.21	2.59	2.07	2.38	3.57	2.60	2.71	2.58	3.42	2.50	2.13	2.68	2.54
Acc. Service at Bhavan															
Satisfactory		2.00	1.00	1.00	1.00	3.00	4.00	3.00	4.00	2.38	4.00	4.00	4.00	4.00	3.19
Easily available		1.00	3.00	1.00	2.00	2.00	3.00	2.00	3.00	2.13	3.00	1.00	4.00	2.67	2.40

Contd.....

(1)	(2)	(3)	(4)	(5)	(6)	(7)	(8)	(9)	(10)	(11)	(12)	(13)	(14)	(15)	(16)
Reasonable charges		1.00	1.00	1.00	2.50	2.00	3.25	1.50	3.00	1.91	3.00	1.00	3.00	2.33	2.12
X3		1.33	1.67	1.00	1.83	2.33	3.42	2.17	3.33	2.14	3.33	2.00	3.67	3.00	2.57
Food services at Katra															
Hygienic		3.00	3.00	3.00	2.33	2.00	3.50	3.00	2.00	2.73	3.00	2.00	4.00	3.00	2.87
Tasty & delicious		2.00	3.00	2.00	2.33	2.00	3.50	2.33	3.00	2.52	4.00	4.00	4.00	4.00	3.26
Cheap rates		2.00	3.00	2.00	2.67	3.00	3.50	3.67	2.00	2.73	4.00	4.00	1.00	3.00	2.87
Variety in food served		4.00	4.00	1.00	2.00	4.00	3.00	2.33	2.00	2.79	3.00	3.00	4.00	3.33	3.06
X4		2.75	3.25	2.00	2.33	2.75	3.38	2.83	2.25	2.69	3.50	3.25	3.25	3.33	3.01
X34		2.04	2.46	1.50	2.08	2.54	3.40	2.50	2.79	2.41	3.42	2.63	3.46	3.17	2.80
Overall X		2.29	2.34	2.05	2.08	2.46	3.49	2.55	2.75	2.50	3.42	2.57	2.80	2.93	2.67
Overall Services															
Sanitation & Hygiene		1.00	2.00	4.00	2.33	1.00	3.00	2.33	1.00	2.08	3.00	3.00	4.00	3.33	2.69
Provision of light		4.00	1.00	3.00	3.33	3.00	4.50	3.33	3.00	3.15	3.00	4.00	4.00	3.67	3.41
Adequate accommodation		4.00	1.00	4.00	2.33	4.00	3.25	4.00	3.00	3.20	4.00	2.00	4.00	3.33	3.33
Clean drinking water		2.00	1.00	4.00	2.33	3.00	3.00	3.67	4.00	2.88	3.00	2.00	4.00	3.00	2.94
Cloak room & security		3.00	4.00	4.00	3.00	3.00	4.00	3.00	5.00	3.63	4.00	4.00	4.00	4.00	3.82
Adequate bedding		4.00	1.00	4.00	3.00	4.00	3.50	3.67	4.00	3.40	4.00	4.00	4.00	4.00	3.64
Adequate infrastructure		2.00	4.00	1.00	3.00	4.00	4.25	4.00	3.00	3.16	4.00	1.00	4.00	3.00	2.85
Feeling of safety		3.00	3.00	1.00	3.67	4.00	3.50	4.00	3.00	3.15	4.00	1.00	4.00	3.00	2.85
X5		2.88	2.13	3.13	2.87	3.25	3.63	3.50	3.25	3.08	3.63	2.63	4.00	3.42	3.19
Preference of Service															
Outside Katra X6		3.00	2.00	2.00	4.00	3.00	3.00	2.50	5.00	3.06	4.00	4.00	4.00	4.00	3.53

Table—4.11

Mean Score of Marketing Effectiveness Measured through Non-Local Male Pilgrim Judgement in Hotel Services

Variables	Age	Age Group-I Up to 25 Yrs.				Age Group-II 25-50 Yrs.						Age Group-III Above 50 Yrs.					X
	Income	Inc-1	Inc-2		Inc-3	Inc-1		Inc-2		Inc-3		Inc-1	Inc-2		Inc-3		
(1)	Education (2)	E-1 (3)	E-1 (4)	E-2 (5)	E-2 (6)	E-1 (7)	E-2 (8)	E-1 (9)	E-2 (10)	E-1 (11)	E-2 (12)	E-1 (13)	E-1 (14)	E-2 (15)	E-1 (16)	E-2 (17)	(18)
Acc. Service at Katra																	
Satisfactory		2.63	3.75	3.67	4.00	2.00	3.00	3.08	2.35	2.43	2.92	4.00	1.00	3.73	3.50	2.78	2.99
Easily available		2.88	2.50	2.33	4.00	3.00	2.20	3.15	2.96	2.71	3.71	4.00	1.00	3.64	3.25	3.12	2.96
Reasonable charges		2.25	2.75	3.00	4.00	3.00	2.20	2.54	2.27	2.43	2.64	4.00	1.00	2.55	3.25	2.36	2.68
X1		2.59	3.00	3.00	4.00	2.67	2.47	2.92	2.53	2.52	3.09	4.00	1.00	3.31	3.33	2.75	2.88
Food services at Katra																	
Hygienic		3.00	3.50	3.25	3.00	2.50	3.00	2.67	2.81	2.29	2.67	4.00	3.00	2.23	3.50	2.87	2.95
Tasty & delicious		3.13	3.50	3.25	2.00	2.50	3.40	2.53	2.84	2.86	3.07	4.00	3.00	2.08	3.75	2.88	2.99
Cheap rates		2.50	2.75	3.00	3.00	2.00	3.50	2.13	3.19	2.29	2.07	4.00	2.00	2.00	3.25	2.24	2.66
Variety in food served		2.50	2.75	2.75	1.00	3.00	3.40	2.73	2.68	2.00	2.64	4.00	3.00	2.54	3.25	2.76	2.73
X2		2.78	3.13	3.06	2.25	2.50	3.33	2.52	2.88	2.36	2.61	4.00	2.75	2.21	3.44	2.69	2.83
X12		2.69	3.07	3.03	3.13	2.59	2.90	2.72	2.71	2.44	2.85	4.00	1.88	2.76	3.39	2.72	2.86
Acc. Service at Bhavan																	
Satisfactory		2.29	2.50	2.00	1.00	2.50	3.33	3.23	3.26	2.86	3.09	1.00	1.00	3.25	3.50	2.48	2.49
Easily available		2.00	2.50	2.00	1.00	3.00	3.33	2.92	2.84	1.14	2.55	1.00	1.00	2.38	3.00	2.22	2.19

Contd.....

(1)	(2)	(3)	(4)	(5)	(6)	(7)	(8)	(9)	(10)	(11)	(12)	(13)	(14)	(15)	(16)	(17)	(18)
Reasonable charges		2.00	2.00	2.00	1.00	2.00	3.33	2.54	3.00	2.43	2.82	1.00	1.00	2.50	3.50	1.91	2.20
X3		2.10	2.33	2.00	1.00	2.50	3.33	2.90	3.03	2.14	2.82	1.00	1.00	2.71	3.33	2.20	2.29
Food services at Katra																	
Hygienic		2.75	3.50	3.67	3.00	2.00	3.40	2.87	2.84	2.29	2.89	4.00	3.00	3.07	2.67	3.13	3.01
Tasty & delicious		2.50	3.00	2.67	3.00	2.00	3.40	2.47	2.61	2.14	2.27	4.00	3.00	2.71	2.67	2.84	2.75
Cheap rates		2.38	3.00	3.00	3.00	3.00	4.00	2.53	3.19	2.00	1.45	4.00	2.00	2.07	3.00	2.08	2.71
Variety in food served		2.50	2.75	3.00	2.00	2.50	3.20	2.53	2.74	2.29	2.55	4.00	3.00	2.64	3.00	2.48	2.75
X4		2.53	3.06	3.09	2.75	2.38	3.50	2.60	2.85	2.18	2.29	4.00	2.75	2.62	2.84	2.63	2.80
X34		2.32	2.70	2.55	1.88	2.44	3.42	2.75	2.94	2.16	2.56	2.50	1.88	2.67	3.09	2.42	2.55
Overall X		2.51	2.89	2.79	2.51	2.52	3.16	2.74	2.83	2.30	2.71	3.25	1.88	2.72	3.24	2.57	2.71
Overall Services																	
Sanitation & Hygiene		2.13	2.50	3.67	3.00	1.00	2.80	2.40	2.90	2.00	2.43	4.00	2.00	3.07	3.00	3.26	2.68
Provision of light		3.50	3.75	3.50	4.00	3.50	3.80	3.00	3.48	2.71	3.86	4.00	4.00	3.47	3.75	2.88	3.55
Adequate accommodation		3.75	3.50	3.50	3.00	1.50	3.80	3.47	3.77	3.14	3.08	4.00	4.00	3.40	4.00	3.08	3.40
Clean drinking water		3.75	3.50	3.75	3.00	2.50	2.60	3.13	3.32	3.43	3.62	4.00	3.00	3.47	4.00	2.60	3.31
Cloak room & security		3.63	2.50	3.75	5.00	5.00	4.00	3.67	3.58	3.00	3.71	4.00	3.00	3.40	4.00	3.00	3.68
Adequate bedding		3.75	3.50	3.50	5.00	4.50	4.00	3.26	3.71	3.29	3.07	4.00	3.00	3.33	3.75	2.32	3.60
Adequate infrastructure		3.40	3.75	4.00	3.00	4.00	3.75	3.80	3.41	3.71	3.58	3.00	1.00	3.75	3.33	2.72	3.35
Feeling of safety		2.60	3.25	3.00	3.00	4.00	3.50	3.40	3.14	2.00	2.57	1.00	1.00	3.50	3.00	2.58	2.77
X5		3.31	3.28	3.58	3.63	3.25	3.53	3.27	3.41	2.91	3.24	3.50	2.63	3.42	3.60	2.81	3.29
Preference of Services																	
Outside Katra X6		3.17	4.50	3.00	3.00	3.00	3.33	4.07	3.29	3.29	2.50	2.00	3.00	4.08	3.50	3.05	3.25

Table-4.12

Mean Score of Marketing Effectiveness Measured through Non-Local Female Pilgrim Judgement in Hotel Services

Variables	Age Group-I Upto 25 Yrs.			Age Group-II 25-50 Yrs.					Age Group-III Above 50 Yrs.						X
	Inc-1		Inc-2	Inc-1		Inc-2	Inc-3		Inc-1		Inc-2		Inc-3		
	E-1	E-2	E-1	E-1	E-2	E-2	E-1	E-2	E-1	E-2	E-1	E-2	E-1	E-2	
Education (2)	(3)	(4)	(5)	(6)	(7)	(8)	(9)	(10)	(11)	(12)	(13)	(14)	(15)	(16)	(17)
Acc. Service at Katra															
Satisfactory	1.00	4.00	1.00	2.50	2.55	2.60	4.00	3.00	2.00	1.00	2.00	2.50	3.00	2.55	2.41
Easily available	3.00	2.00	1.00	2.50	2.91	2.00	3.00	4.00	2.33	1.00	2.50	3.00	1.00	2.18	2.32
Reasonable charges	1.00	2.00	1.00	2.00	2.18	2.40	2.00	3.00	1.00	1.00	1.50	3.50	1.00	2.18	1.84
X1	1.67	2.67	1.00	2.33	2.55	2.33	3.00	3.33	1.78	1.00	2.00	3.00	1.67	2.30	2.19
Food services at Katra															
Hygienic	3.33	3.00	3.00	2.63	2.71	3.00	2.00	1.00	2.60	2.00	3.00	2.50	4.00	2.42	2.66
Tasty & delicious	3.33	3.00	3.00	2.88	2.31	3.20	2.00	2.00	2.80	2.00	3.00	2.00	4.00	2.58	2.72
Cheap rates	2.00	3.00	3.00	2.13	2.38	3.00	3.00	2.00	1.40	2.00	2.00	2.00	3.00	2.08	2.36
Variety in food served	2.67	3.00	4.00	2.13	2.08	3.20	3.00	1.00	2.40	2.00	3.00	2.50	3.00	2.42	2.60
X2	2.83	3.00	3.25	2.44	2.37	3.10	2.50	1.50	2.30	2.00	2.75	2.25	3.50	2.38	2.58
X12	2.25	2.84	2.13	2.39	2.46	2.72	2.75	2.42	2.04	1.50	2.38	2.63	2.59	2.34	2.39
Acc. Service at Bhavan															
Satisfactory	3.00	1.00	1.00	2.38	2.89	2.60	3.00	2.00	3.33	1.00	3.67	1.00	4.00	2.58	2.39
Easily available	1.00	1.00	1.00	2.25	1.78	1.60	2.00	1.00	3.00	1.00	3.33	1.00	1.00	2.08	1.65

Contd.....

(1)	(2)	(3)	(4)	(5)	(6)	(7)	(8)	(9)	(10)	(11)	(12)	(13)	(14)	(15)	(16)	(17)
Reasonable charges		1.00	1.00	1.00	2.13	2.56	2.00	2.00	1.00	2.33	1.00	2.00	3.00	1.00	2.17	1.73
X3		1.67	1.00	1.00	2.25	2.41	2.07	2.33	1.33	2.89	1.00	3.00	1.67	2.00	2.28	1.92
Food services at Katra																
Hygienic		3.00	4.00	3.00	2.75	2.77	3.00	3.00	3.00	3.20	1.00	3.67	1.50	1.00	2.33	2.66
Tasty & delicious		3.00	4.00	3.00	2.50	2.46	3.20	3.00	3.00	2.20	1.00	3.00	3.00	1.00	2.33	2.62
Cheap rates		2.00	4.00	1.00	2.63	2.00	2.60	3.00	2.00	2.20	1.00	2.33	1.50	1.00	2.25	2.11
Variety in food served		2.67	4.00	2.00	2.38	2.15	2.60	3.00	3.00	1.60	1.00	3.67	3.00	1.00	2.42	2.46
X4		2.67	4.00	2.25	2.57	2.35	2.85	3.00	2.75	2.30	1.00	3.17	2.25	1.00	2.33	2.46
X34		2.17	2.50	1.63	2.41	2.38	2.46	2.67	2.04	2.60	1.00	3.09	1.96	1.50	2.31	2.19
Overall X		2.21	2.67	1.88	2.33	2.42	2.59	2.71	2.23	2.32	1.25	2.74	2.30	2.05	2.33	2.29
Overall Services																
Sanitation & Hygiene		4.00	4.00	1.00	2.38	2.54	2.40	2.00	2.00	2.20	2.00	2.67	1.50	1.00	2.17	2.28
Provision of light		3.33	4.00	3.00	3.33	3.54	2.60	4.00	3.00	3.40	4.00	3.67	4.00	3.00	3.67	3.47
Adequate accommodation		4.00	3.00	3.00	3.13	3.54	3.60	2.00	3.00	3.00	4.00	3.67	2.50	3.00	2.75	3.16
Clean drinking water		4.00	3.00	4.00	3.50	3.38	3.20	3.00	3.00	3.40	4.00	4.00	4.00	3.00	3.08	3.47
Cloak room & security		4.00	3.00	3.00	3.63	3.54	2.80	4.00	4.00	4.00	4.00	3.67	3.00	3.00	3.42	3.50
Adequate bedding		4.00	3.00	3.00	3.38	3.31	3.60	3.00	4.00	3.80	4.00	3.67	3.50	3.00	3.42	3.48
Adequate infrastructure		4.00	1.00	1.00	3.40	3.29	3.40	3.00	2.00	3.00	1.00	3.67	4.00	4.00	3.58	2.88
Feeling of safety		1.00	1.00	1.00	2.60	2.71	3.20	4.00	4.00	1.33	1.00	3.33	4.00	3.00	2.60	2.48
X5		3.54	2.75	2.38	3.17	3.23	3.10	3.13	3.13	3.02	3.00	3.54	3.31	2.88	3.09	3.09
Preference of Services																
Outside Katra X6		1.67	2.00	5.00	2.50	3.69	3.20	3.00	4.00	3.60	3.00	3.33	2.50	4.00	3.00	3.18

Table-4.13

Mean Score of Marketing Effectiveness Measured through
Non-Local Male Non-Pilgrim Judgement in Hotel Services

Variables (1)	Education (2)	Age Group-I Up to 25 Yrs. Inc-1 E-2 (3)	Inc-2 E-2 (4)	Inc-3 E-2 (5)	Age Group-II 25-50 Yrs. Inc-1 E-1 (6)	Inc-1 E-2 (7)	Inc-2 E-1 (8)	Inc-2 E-2 (9)	Inc-3 E-1 (10)	Inc-3 E-2 (11)	Age Group-III Above 50 Yrs. Inc-1 E-1 (12)	Inc-2 E-2 (13)	Inc-2 E-1 (14)	Inc-3 E-2 (15)	X (16)
Acc. Service at Katra															
Satisfactory		3.00	1.00	5.00	1.00	2.50	2.00	2.73	3.00	3.20	4.00	4.00	2.00	3.33	2.83
Easily available		3.00	1.00	5.00	2.00	2.00	4.00	3.00	1.00	3.60	4.00	3.33	2.00	3.22	2.86
Reasonable charges		3.00	1.00	5.00	2.00	3.50	2.00	2.33	2.00	3.20	2.00	2.67	3.00	2.71	2.65
X1		3.00	1.00	5.00	1.67	2.67	2.67	2.69	2.00	3.33	3.33	3.33	2.33	3.09	2.78
Food services at Katra															
Hygienic		4.00	1.00	3.00	3.00	1.67	2.00	3.95	2.00	2.80	4.00	4.67	3.00	2.91	2.92
Tasty & delicious		4.00	3.00	3.00	3.00	3.00	2.00	3.79	2.00	3.00	4.00	4.67	3.00	3.00	3.19
Cheap rates		4.00	1.00	3.00	3.00	1.67	3.00	3.00	3.00	2.80	2.00	4.00	3.00	2.82	2.79
Variety in food served		1.00	3.00	3.00	2.00	2.33	2.00	3.74	2.00	3.40	2.00	4.00	3.00	3.14	2.66
X2		3.25	2.00	3.00	2.75	2.17	2.25	3.62	2.25	3.00	3.00	4.34	3.00	2.97	2.89
X12		3.13	1.50	4.00	2.21	2.42	2.46	3.16	2.13	3.17	3.17	3.84	2.67	3.03	2.84
Acc. Service at Bhavan															
Satisfactory		3.00	1.00	1.00	1.00	3.50	3.00	3.60	3.00	4.00	4.00	4.00	2.00	2.86	2.77
Easily available		3.00	1.00	1.00	1.00	1.00	2.00	3.13	2.00	2.50	2.00	2.00	2.00	2.86	1.96

Contd.....

(1)	(2)	(3)	(4)	(5)	(6)	(7)	(8)	(9)	(10)	(11)	(12)	(13)	(14)	(15)	(16)
Reasonable charges		3.00	1.00	1.00	1.00	2.50	2.00	3.07	2.00	3.50	2.00	2.67	3.00	2.86	2.28
X3		3.00	1.00	1.00	1.00	2.33	2.33	3.27	2.33	3.33	2.67	2.89	2.33	2.86	2.33
Food services at Katra															
Hygienic		4.00	1.00	3.00	2.00	2.67	2.00	3.21	4.00	2.50	4.00	4.67	3.00	3.00	3.00
Tasty & delicious		4.00	3.00	3.00	3.00	2.67	2.00	2.84	3.00	2.00	4.00	4.67	3.00	2.27	3.03
Cheap rates		1.00	1.00	3.00	2.00	1.33	3.00	2.89	3.00	3.00	2.00	4.00	3.00	2.33	2.43
Variety in food served		1.00	3.00	3.00	2.00	3.67	3.00	3.26	2.00	2.50	2.00	4.00	3.00	2.43	2.68
X4		2.50	2.00	3.00	2.25	2.59	2.50	3.05	3.00	2.50	3.00	4.34	3.00	2.51	2.79
X34		2.75	1.50	2.00	1.63	2.46	2.42	3.16	2.67	2.92	2.84	3.62	2.67	2.69	2.56
Overall X		2.94	1.50	3.00	1.92	2.44	2.44	3.16	2.40	3.05	3.01	3.73	2.67	2.86	2.70
Overall Services															
Sanitation & Hygiene		1.00	3.00	5.00	4.00	2.20	3.00	3.53	3.00	2.80	4.00	3.67	3.00	3.27	3.19
Provision of light		4.00	1.00	5.00	4.00	3.80	4.00	3.89	4.00	3.20	4.00	3.33	2.00	3.82	3.54
Adequate accommodation		1.00	3.00	4.00	4.00	3.40	4.00	3.89	4.00	2.50	4.00	3.33	3.00	3.55	3.36
Clean drinking water		4.00	1.00	3.00	4.00	3.40	4.00	3.79	2.00	3.00	4.00	3.33	3.00	3.36	3.22
Cloak room & security		4.00	3.00	3.00	4.00	3.40	4.00	3.95	5.00	3.20	4.00	3.33	2.00	3.73	3.59
Adequate bedding		4.00	3.00	3.00	4.00	3.40	4.00	3.84	4.00	3.80	4.00	3.33	2.00	3.73	3.55
Adequate infrastructure		4.00	1.00	4.00	4.00	4.00	4.00	3.75	4.00	3.20	4.00	3.33	2.00	3.64	3.46
Feeling of safety		4.00	3.00	3.00	4.00	4.33	2.00	3.88	2.00	3.40	4.00	3.33	3.00	2.91	3.30
X5		3.25	2.25	3.75	4.00	3.49	3.63	3.82	3.50	3.14	4.00	3.37	2.50	3.50	3.40
Preference of Service															
Outside Katra X6		4.00	4.00	1.00	2.00	3.40	4.00	3.74	4.00	3.20	4.00	4.67	4.00	3.09	3.47

Table–4.14

Mean Score of Marketing Effectiveness Measured through Non-Local Female Non-Pilgrim Judgement in Hotel Services

Variables	Age / Income / Education	Age Group-I Above 25 Yrs.		Age Group-II 25-50 Yrs.			Age Group-III Above 50 Yrs.		X
		Inc-1 E-1	Inc-1 E-2	Inc-2 E-1	Inc-2 E-2	Inc-3 E-2	Inc-2 E-2	Inc-3 E-2	
(1)	(2)	(3)	(4)	(5)	(6)	(7)	(8)	(9)	(10)
Acc. Service at Katra									
Satisfactory		4.00	2.00	2.00	2.00	1.00	2.67	2.00	2.24
Easily available		4.00	1.60	2.00	2.50	4.00	2.67	1.00	2.54
Reasonable charges		3.50	1.60	2.00	1.00	4.00	2.67	1.00	2.25
X1		3.83	1.73	2.00	1.83	3.00	2.67	1.33	2.34
Food services at Katra									
Hygienic		3.00	2.00	3.00	2.00	1.00	3.50	3.00	2.50
Tasty & delicious		3.00	3.00	3.00	2.00	3.00	3.00	3.50	2.93
Cheap rates		3.00	2.80	3.50	1.50	1.00	3.50	2.50	2.54
Variety in food served		2.67	3.60	3.00	1.50	3.00	3.00	3.50	2.90
X2		2.92	2.85	3.13	1.75	2.00	3.25	3.13	2.72
X12		3.38	2.29	2.57	1.79	2.50	2.96	2.23	2.53
Acc. Service at Bhavan									
Satisfactory		4.00	2.00	2.00	3.00	4.00	3.00	3.00	3.00
Easily available		2.00	2.00	2.00	2.00	4.00	3.00	1.00	2.29

Contd......

(1)	(2)	(3)	(4)	(5)	(6)	(7)	(8)	(9)	(10)
Reasonable charges		3.50	2.00	2.00	1.00	3.00	3.00	1.00	2.21
X3		3.17	2.00	2.00	2.00	3.67	3.00	1.67	2.50
Food services at Katra									
Hygienic		3.00	1.60	3.50	2.00	1.00	3.33	2.50	2.42
Tasty & delicious		3.00	2.60	3.00	2.00	3.00	3.00	2.50	2.73
Cheap rates		2.00	2.80	2.50	1.50	1.00	3.33	3.50	2.38
Variety in food served		2.67	3.60	3.50	1.50	3.00	3.00	3.50	2.97
X4		2.67	2.65	3.13	1.75	2.00	3.17	3.00	2.62
X34		2.92	2.33	2.57	1.88	2.84	3.09	2.34	2.57
Overall X		3.15	2.31	2.57	1.84	2.67	3.03	2.29	2.55
Overall Services									
Sanitation & Hygiene		3.00	2.00	2.00	2.00	4.00	3.33	2.00	2.62
Provision of light		3.33	4.00	3.00	2.00	4.00	3.33	3.50	3.31
Adequate accommodation		3.33	4.00	3.50	2.50	4.00	4.00	3.50	3.55
Clean drinking water		3.33	4.00	2.50	3.00	4.00	3.00	4.00	3.40
Cloak room & security		3.33	3.60	2.50	3.00	4.00	3.00	3.50	3.28
Adequate bedding		3.67	3.60	3.00	3.50	4.00	4.33	2.00	3.44
Adequate infrastructure		3.33	4.50	2.50	1.00	4.00	4.00	4.00	3.33
Feeling of safety		2.33	4.00	3.50	1.00	2.00	3.33	3.50	2.81
X5		3.21	3.71	2.81	2.25	3.75	3.54	3.25	3.22
Preference of Services									
Outside Katra X6		3.67	2.40	3.00	3.50	4.00	3.67	3.00	3.32

Table–4.15

Mean Score of Marketing Effectiveness measured through Local Male Non-Pilgrim Judgement in Hotel Services

Variables	Age / Income / Education	Age Group-II 25 to 50 Yrs.			Age Group-III Above 50 yrs.		X
		Inc-1		Inc-2	Inc-3	Inc-3	
		E-2	E-1	E-2	E-2	E-2	X
(1)	(2)	(3)	(4)	(4)	(5)	(6)	(7)
Acc. Service at Katra							
Satisfactory		5.00	2.67	3.67	4.00	2.00	3.47
Easily available		4.00	3.33	2.67	1.00	2.00	2.60
Reasonable charges		4.00	2.67	3.00	1.00	1.00	2.33
X1		4.33	2.89	3.11	2.00	1.67	2.80
Food services at Katra							
Hygienic		2.00	3.33	3.00	1.00	4.00	2.67
Tasty & delicious		2.00	3.33	2.33	1.00	4.00	2.53
Cheap rates		2.00	2.67	3.00	1.00	4.00	2.53
Variety in food served		4.00	2.67	2.33	1.00	4.00	2.80
X2		2.50	3.00	2.67	1.00	4.00	2.63
X12		3.42	2.95	2.89	1.50	2.84	2.72
Acc. Service at Bhavan							
Satisfactory		5.00	3.00	4.00	1.00	1.00	2.80
Easily available		5.00	2.33	2.33	1.00	1.00	2.33

Contd......

(1)	(2)	(3)	(4)	(4)	(5)	(6)	(7)
Reasonable charges		3.00	2.00	4.00	1.00	2.00	2.40
X3		4.33	2.44	3.44	1.00	1.33	2.51
Food services at Katra							
Hygienic		2.00	3.00	2.67	1.00	2.00	2.13
Tasty & delicious		4.00	3.00	2.67	1.00	2.00	2.53
Cheap rates		4.00	2.67	3.33	1.00	2.00	2.60
Variety in food served		4.00	2.67	2.33	1.00	2.00	2.40
X4		3.50	2.84	2.75	1.00	2.00	2.42
X34		3.92	2.64	3.10	1.00	1.67	2.47
Overall X		3.67	2.80	3.00	1.25	2.26	2.60
Overall Services							
Sanitation & Hygiene		2.00	3.67	4.00	1.00	4.00	2.93
Provision of light		4.00	3.00	3.33	1.00	4.00	3.07
Adequate accommodation		2.00	4.00	3.67	1.00	4.00	2.93
Clean drinking water		4.00	4.00	1.67	1.00	2.00	2.53
Cloak room & security		3.00	4.00	2.00	1.00	2.00	2.40
Adequate bedding		3.00	4.00	4.00	1.00	4.00	3.20
Adequate infrastructure		4.00	4.00	3.00	1.00	1.00	2.60
Feeling of safety		2.00	3.33	3.67	1.00	1.00	2.20
X5		3.00	3.75	3.17	1.00	2.75	2.73
Preference of Services							
Outside Katra X6		5.00	2.67	4.00	3.00	4.00	3.73

Table–4.16

Overall Marketing Orientation and
Customer Assessment in Hotel Services

Grouping Pattern				Low Educaton				High Education				Over-all Mean			
Area (1)	Purpose (2)	Gender (3)	INCOME (4)	A (5)	B (6)	C (7)	X (8)	A (9)	B (10)	C (11)	X (12)	A (13)	B (14)	C (15)	X (16)
	PILGRIM	Male	Inc-1	2.42	2.25	3.25	2.64	1.98	2.27	2.21	2.15	2.20	2.26	2.73	2.40
			Inc-2	2.59	2.05	3.75	2.80	3.16	2.98	3.52	3.22	2.88	2.52	3.64	3.01
			Inc-3	–				2.59	2.92	4.00	3.17	2.59	2.92	4.00	3.17
			X1	2.51	2.15	3.50	2.72	2.58	2.72	3.24	2.85	2.55	2.44	3.37	2.79
		Female	Inc-1					3.42	3.42	3.75	3.53	3.42	3.42	3.75	3.53
			Inc-2	1.25	4	4	3.08	2.25	2.75	3.00	2.67	1.75	3.38	3.50	2.88
			Inc-3												
			X2	1.25	4	4	3.08	2.84	3.09	3.38	3.10	2.05	3.55	3.69	3.10
			X12	1.88	3.08	3.75	2.90	2.71	2.91	3.31	2.98	2.30	3.00	3.53	2.94
	NON-PILGRIM	Male	Inc-1					3.17	4.17	3.00	3.45	3.17	4.17	3.00	3.45
			Inc-2	2.95	2.78	4	3.24	3.06	2.87	2.84	2.92	3.01	2.83	3.42	3.09
			Inc-3					2.17	1.25	2.00	1.81	2.17	1.25	2.00	1.81
			X3	2.95	2.78	4.00	3.24	2.80	2.76	2.61	2.72	2.88	2.77	3.31	2.99
		Female	Inc-1												
			Inc-2												
			Inc-3												
			X4												

Contd......

(1)	(2)	(3)	(4)	(5)	(6)	(7)	(8)	(9)	(10)	(11)	(12)	(13)	(14)	(15)	(16)
Non-Local	PILGRIM	Local	X34	2.95	2.78	4.00	3.24	2.80	2.76	2.61	2.72	2.88	2.77	3.31	2.99
			X	2.42	2.93	3.88	3.07	2.76	2.84	2.96	2.85	2.59	2.89	3.42	2.97
		Male	Inc-1	3.04	2.28	3.70	3.01	2.86	3.33	3.60	3.26	2.95	2.81	3.65	3.14
			Inc-2	2.33	2.38	3.29	2.67	2.85	2.76	3.54	3.05	2.59	2.57	3.42	2.86
			Inc-3	2.89	2.57	3.58	3.01	2.96	2.29	3.37	2.87	2.93	2.43	3.48	2.95
			X1	2.75	2.41	3.52	2.90	2.89	2.79	3.50	3.06	2.82	2.60	3.51	2.98
		Female	Inc-1	2.14	2.54	3.65	2.78	2.13	1.63	3.48	2.41	2.14	2.09	3.57	2.60
			Inc-2	1.88	2.66	3.50	2.68	2.65	2.14	3.28	2.69	2.27	2.40	3.39	2.69
			Inc-3	2.67	2.25	3.00	2.64	2.35	2.30	3.34	2.66	2.51	2.28	3.17	2.65
			X2	2.23	2.48	3.38	2.70	2.38	2.02	3.37	2.59	2.31	2.25	3.38	2.65
			X12	2.49	2.45	3.45	2.80	2.64	2.41	3.44	2.83	2.57	2.43	3.45	2.82
	NON-PILGRIM	Male	Inc-1	2.76	2.17	4.00	2.98	2.84	2.82	3.20	2.95	2.80	2.50	3.60	2.97
			Inc-2	2.59	2.42	4.00	3.00	2.42	2.66	3.15	2.74	2.51	2.54	3.58	2.88
			Inc-3	2.46	2.63	3.13	2.74	3.35	2.34	3.32	3.00	2.91	2.49	3.23	2.88
			X3	2.60	2.41	3.71	2.91	2.87	2.61	3.22	2.90	2.74	2.51	3.47	2.91
		Female	Inc-1	3.42	2.95	3.42	3.26	2.07	2.30	3.80	2.72	2.75	2.63	3.61	3.00
			Inc-2	2.63	2.67	2.88	2.73	2.44	2.62	3.29	2.78	2.54	2.65	3.09	2.76
			Inc-3	-	-	-	-	1.82	2.54	3.63	2.66	1.82	2.54	3.63	2.66
			X4	3.03	2.81	3.15	3.00	2.11	2.49	3.57	2.72	2.57	2.65	3.36	2.86
			X34	2.82	2.61	3.43	2.96	2.49	2.55	3.40	2.81	2.66	2.58	3.42	2.89
		Non-Locals	X	2.66	2.53	3.44	2.88	2.57	2.48	3.42	2.82	2.62	2.51	3.43	2.85
		Overall	X	2.54	2.73	3.66	2.98	2.67	2.66	3.19	2.84	2.61	2.70	3.43	2.91

Table–4.17

Variable-wise Multiple Regression Coefficient Values of Pilgrim and Non-Pilgrim Visitors

	Pilgrims		Non-Pilgrims	
Variables	Locals	Non-locals	Locals	Non-Locals
A	0.583	0.154	0.666	0.030
B	-0.423	-0.206	-0.151	0.124
C	0.616	0.147	0.681	0.009
D	0.179	0.185	-0.071	0.244
Constant	0.429	2.460	0.012	2.322

Note   A= Accommodation at Katra
B=Accomodation at Bhavan
C=Food at Katra
D=Food at Bhavan

Table–4.18

Test of Significance Values

	Pilgrims		Non-Pilgrims	
Values	Locals	Non-locals	Locals	Non-Locals
R	0.85	0.43	0.93	0.42
R^2	0.72	0.19	0.87	0.17
F(cal.)	15.06	12.93	8.31	4.38
df (v^1v^2)	4,23	4,222	4,5	4,83
F(Tab) (at 5% level)	2.79	2.37	5.19	2.44

Table–4.19

Variable-wise Over-all Satisfaction and Percentage of Respondents
Falling under three Orientation Levels of Satisfaction

Variables	PILGRIMS				OVERALL SATISFACTION				NON-PILGRIMS			
	B.Avg (2)	%of resp. (3)	Avg (4)	%ofResp. (5)	A.Avg. (6)	% of Resp. (7)	B.Avg. (8)	% of Resp. (9)	Avg (10)	% of Resp (11)	A.Avg. (12)	% of Resp (13)
(1)												
Acc. Services at Katra												
Satisfactory	2.08	8.14	2.85	41.18	2.83	50.68	1.6	5.49	2.74	47.25	2.69	47.26
Easily available	3.06	8.11	2.78	41.89	2.95	50	1.75	4.35	2.5	47.83	2.8	47.82
Reasonable charges	2.5	8.18	2.24	42.27	2.55	49.55	1.2	5.62	2.21	46.07	2.65	48.31
X1		8.14		41.78		50.08		5.15		47.05		47.8
Food Services at Katra												
Hygienic	2.1	8.87	2.68	42.34	2.95	48.79	2.5	6.59	3.23	50.55	2.84	42.88
Cheap rates	2.32	8.87	2.38	43.15	2.71	47.98	2.83	6.25	2.93	48.96	2.55	44.79
X2		8.87		42.75		48.39		6.42		49.76		43.83
Acc. Services at Bhavan												
Satisfactory	1.54	7.22	2.84	45.56	2.93	47.22	1.75	5.48	2.89	53.42	3.4	41.1
Easily available	1.69	7.3	2.32	46.07	2.41	46.63	1.75	5.48	2.07	53.42	2.7	41.1

Contd.....

(1)	(2)	(3)	(4)	(5)	(6)	(7)	(8)	(9)	(10)	(11)	(12)	(13)
X3		7.26		45.82		46.93		5.48		53.42		41.1
Food Services at Katra												
Hygienic	2.05	9.84	2.97	42.21	2.91	47.95	1.83	6.45	3.04	47.31	2.74	46.24
Tasty & delicious	2.17	9.76	2.65	42.68	2.7	47.56	2	7.37	2.55	47.37	2.86	45.26
Variety in food served	1.71	9.43	2.57	43.03	2.79	47.54	2.85	7.78	2.6	45.56	2.9	46.66
X4		9.68		42.64		47.68		7.2		46.75		46.05
Overall Services												
Adequate accommodation	3.08	8.87	3.37	43.15	3.68	47.98	2.85	6.93	3.16	48.51	3.48	44.56
Clean drinking water	3.29	9.64	3.27	43.37	3.39	46.99	2.83	6.06	2.95	49.49	3.45	44.45
Cloak room & security	2.88	9.52	3.22	42.86	3.36	47.62	2.83	7.29	3.6	47.92	3.34	44.79
Adequate bedding	3.09	5.77	3.35	50.96	3.68	43.27	2.85	6.93	3.63	48.51	3.4	44.56
Pref. of services	2.77	8.4	3.38	42.44	3.16	49.16	3.57	6.93	3.22	48.51	3.22	44.55
Outside Katra												
X5	2.42	8.44	2.86	44.56	3	47	2.33	6.83	2.89	48.59	3	44.58
		8.48		43.51		48.02		6.22		49.11		44.67
No % age	23	9.2	107	42.8	120	48	7	7.14	47	47.96	44	44.9

References

Brooksbank, Roger N. (1991) "Successful Marketing Practice: A Literature Review and Checklist for Marketing Practitioners," *European Journal of Marketing*, Vol. 25 (5), 20-29.

Bryden, John M. (1973). Tourism and Development—A case Study of Common wealth Carribbean, Cambridge University Press, 195-220.

Burkart, A. J. & S. Medlik (1981). *Tourism: Past Present and Future* II ed., Heinemann, London, 199-219.

Czepial, John A. & Rosenberg, Larry J. (1987) "Customer Satisfaction: Concepts & Measurements" in Bellur, V.V. & H.W. Berkwar's (ed.), *Readings in Marketing Management*, Himalayan Publishing, Bombay.

Endris, A. Thabet & A. Meidan (1990) "On the Reliability of Psychographic Research: Encouraging Signs of Measurement Accuracy & Methodology in Consumer Research", *European Journal of Marketing*, Vol. 24, No.3 , 23.27.

Gunn, Clare A. (1994). " Tourism Planning : Basic Concepts and Cases, III ed., Taylor & Franics, 30-35.

Kaul, R.N (1985). Dynamics of Tourism—A Trilogy-Transportation. Sterling Publishers; New Delhi. 8-19, 47-52.

Middleton, Victor T.C. (1994) Marketing in Travel and Tourism, IInd ed., Butterworth, Heinemann: Oxford, 4-20, 54-66.

Moutinho, Luiz(1987) "Consumer Behaviour in Tourism, " *European Journal of Marketing*, Vol. 21 (10), 5-44.

Negi, Jagmohan (1982) Tourism & Hotellering—A world Wide Industry, Gitanjali Publishers, New Delhi., 108-131, 318-347.

Pearce, D.G. (1981) Tourism Development—Topics in Applied Geography, Longman, U.K., 5-10, 23-30.

Poon, Auliana (1993) Tourism Technology and Competitive strategies, C.A.B., International; U.K., 53-61,236-335.

Rebello, Andrey (1991) "Societal Response to Consumer Movement," Government, C.E.R.C. Publication, Ahmedabad.

Robinson, H. (1976) A Geography of Tourism, McDonald & Evans, London, 3-18.

Sivers, Angelika (1987) "The Significance of Pilgrimage Tourism in Sri Lanka (Ceylon)", *National Geographical Journal of India*, Vol. 33 (4), 430-445.

Smith, L.J.S. (1989) Tourism Analysis – A Handbook, Longman Scientific and Technical, U.K, 7-13,17-27.

Swan, John E & Combs Linda Jones (1976) "Product Performance and Consumer Satisfaction: A New Concept", *Journal of Marketing*, Vol.20 (2),25-30

Tewari, S.P. (1994) Tourism Dimensions, Atma Ram & Sons, New Delhi., 13-59.

Usha Bala (1990) Tourism in India—Policy and Perspectives, Aarushi Prakashan; New Delhi, 40-49, 113-225.

Witt, S.F. (1992) The Management of International Tourism, Routledge Publishers, U.K. 25-39.

MARKETING STRATEGY FOR PILGRIMAGE TOURISM WITH SPECIAL REFERENCE TO TRANSPORTATION SERVICES

Background

Tourist attractions of whatever kind would be of little value if their locations are inaccessible (Robinson 1976). Mobility is an essential element for encompassing a journey. The pursuit of travel and tourism has over the years developed into a grand and mass phenomenon involving millions of people visiting other countries and many more moving within their own (Kaul 1985). The choice of destination lies in the hands of a traveller but inadequate transport facilities are a clear handicap (Robinson 1976) even in case of the most revered pilgrimage destination. Improvement in quality of roads and transportation gave an unparalleled boost to the tourism industry as a whole with an abrupt increase in the number of places visited and the days spent by the tourist. Moreover, the economical and safe travel by railways and other transport services like motor car, taxis, etc. revolutionized the concept of travel with larger number of tourists moving individually or in groups (Kaul 1985). The transportation services include airlines, railways, buses, taxis, even porters etc. which form the principal touristic infrastructure at a pilgrimage destination (Negi 1982). Demand for a mode of transport for a tourist market is a derived demand, and its requirement is met by transporters providing a means to reach the destination and also a means of movement at and around that place (Burkart & Medlik 1981). The modern transport system changes old holiday or touring habits by adding new dimensions (Tewari 1994) to it with the technological advancement, marketing innovations, etc. (Poon 1993), which lay down adequate foundation for economical and comfortably designed adequate transportation services (Negi 1982). In other words, the tourism industry is primarily concerned with the movement where its ease and cost are the critical factors to improve and maintain the frequency of tourists and the expansion of tourist trade (Peters 1969). It is actually the job of carriers to transport a satisfied customer to and fro his travel and tour (Kaul 1985).

Exhibit–5.1

Time Schedule of AIRLINES and RAILWAYS connecting Jammu city

INDIAN AIRLINES	JET AIR WAYS	RAILWAYS				
(1)	(2)	(3) S.No	(4) Train	(5) UP/DN	(6) Arrival	(7) Departure
(I) FLIGHT No: IC 821	FLIGHT : IW 605/606					
(Daily) AB 320	(Connecting Delhi)	1	Shalimar Express	4545/4646	6:30 AM	8:55 PM
(Connecting Delhi, Mumbai)	ARRIVAL = 01:10	2	Sealdah Express	3151/3152	9:20 AM	6:55 PM
	DEPARTURE = 01:45	3	Jammu Mail	4033/4034	11:00 AM	3:45 PM
ARRIVAL = 12:50		4	Jhelum Mail	1077/1078	11:20 AM	9:40 PM
DEPARTURE = 13:30		5	Swaraj Express	2471/2472	3:25 PM	11:25 AM
					(Mon,Tues,Fri,Sat)	(Tues, Wed, Fri, Sat)
		6	Sarvodaya Express	2473/2474	3:25 PM	11:25 AM
					(Sun)	Thursday
(2) FLIGHT NO:IC 822	FLIGHT : IW 603/604	7	Rajkot Express	2475/2476	3:25 PM	11:25 AM
					(Thurs)	(Mon)
(Daily) AB 320	(Connecting Delhi)	8	Happa Express	2477/2478	3:25 PM	11:25 AM
					(Wed)	(Sun)
ARRIVAL = 15:25	ARRIVAL = 02:05	9	Mangalore Express	6687/6688	3:00 PM	10:35 PM
					(Thurs)	(Thurs)

Contd....

(1)	(2)	(3)	(4)	(5)	(6)	(7)
DEPARTURE = 16:05	DEPARTURE = 02:40	10	Lohit Express	5651/5652	12:55 PM	10:10 PM
(Connectng Delhi, Mumbai)					(Wed)	(Wed)
		11	Himsagar Express	6017/6018	3:00 PM	10:35 PM
					(Mon)	(Mon)
		12	Himgiri Express	3073/3074	12:55 PM	10:10 PM
					(Mon, Thurs, Sun)	(Mon, Sun)
		13	Gorakhpur Express	5087/5088	12:38 PM	10:10 PM
					(Fri, Sat)	(Fri, Sat)
		14	Baroni Express	5097A/5098A	12:38 PM	10:10 PM
					(Tuesday)	(Tues)
		15	Madras Express	6031/6032	3:00 PM	10:35 PM
					(Tues, Fri, Sat)	(Tues, Fri, Sat)
		16	Jodhpur Express	4805/4806	7:55 PM	7:15 AM
		17	Pooja Express	2403/2404	9:00 AM	6:05 PM
		18	Malwa Express	9367/9368	6:25 PM	8:30 AM
		19	Rajdhani Express	2425/2426	5:45 AM	8:30 PM
		20	Amritsar Express	4611/4612	4:00 AM	10:35 PM

Source: (i) Railways Time Table
(ii) Time Schedule of Indian Airlines and Jet Airways.

Nature and Scope of the Study

The transportation service is an integral part of any tourist destination, whether it is cultural, adventure, educational or a pilgrimage destination. Being situated mostly at very difficult and remote locations, the pilgrimage destinations require specialized transportation models and such services require special treatment from the marketers point of view, so that the visitors to such destination feel satisfied.

This chapter has exclusively been devoted to critically examine the various transportation services required by different pilgrim and non-pilgrim groups visiting Shri Mata Vaishno Devi Shrine on the basis of primary information gathered from visitors within the parameters of customer/pilgrim satisfaction-oriented marketing spread over-important aspects of transportation services necessary for such a pilgrimage tourism. The profile of the visitors and their mode of travelling as per the haltages en route to the shrine indicate the nature of the transport services available. After the entry of the pilgrims in the state, the first halt point towards the shrine is Jammu city which is connected by three means of transportation viz.: Roadways, Railways and Airways. Table-5.1 provides that between the place of residence and Jammu City 66% of the total 500 visitors contacted travelled by Train, 0.8 per cent by airways, approximately 21 per cent by roadways and 2 per cent both by road and railways. Only approximately 8 per cent of the visitors boarded the buses from Jammu Railway station towards Katra—the base camp of the shrine. The majority of them preferred to reach Jammu Bus Stand by local conveyances to take buses/taxis for Katra. About 30 per cent did not respond with regard to their experience in Jammu city. From Jammu, Katra is connected through road only and the modes of transportation available are buses and taxis; the majority of visitors travelled by bus. From Katra towards Ban Ganga, again it is roadways where taxis, autos, free bus service by the Shrine Board and private vehicles owned by hoteliers are available. More than 60 per cent walked on foot till Ban Ganga. More than 85% per cent walked on foot up to *Bhavan*, further from *Bhavan* to Bhaironghati the majoritity of them walked on foot, but some preference is shown for pony services (Exhibit-5.2). It is apparent that from the point of origin of the visitors to the destination i.e. the Shrine visitors have different haltages wherefrom different modes of transport are available.

The scope of the present study covers the transportation services available from Jammu city to *Bhavan*. For reaching Jammu city pilgrims prefer the railways. There are as many as twenty trains running between Jammu and all-important cities of the country (Exhibit-5.1) and out of these seven are daily services. The city receives two-to-three flights daily from Delhi and Bombay. From Jammu city more than 50 taxis out of a total the 4000 taxis registered with the Regional Transport Office and 150 buses are available for Katra under the operation of different agencies viz.—SRTC, JKTDC, Pvt. bus service and J&K Taxi Union (Table-5.2) at a fixed rate of Rs 15/- and Rs 18/- per head for ordinary buses, Rs. 35/-, Rs. 45/-and Rs. 50/- per head for different standards of deluxe buses, Rs 520/- and Rs. 1040/- per taxi per drop service and to and fro service respectively. In addition, approximately five buses of Inter State Bus Service also ply daily on the same route. The present pilgrim traffic of about 50 lakh

Exhibit-5.2

Rates of Palki, Pony and Pithu Services as per weight of visitors en route to the track.

S.No	Service	Weight of visitors	Rate per visitor
1	PALKI		
	(a) Katra-*Bhavan*-Katra	up to 75 Kgs	Rs 900/- + Rs 200 (for Bhairo Mandir)
	(Major visitors)	up to 100 Kgs.	Rs. 1050/-+Rs 272/-
	(b) Katra-*Bhavan*-Katra		Rs. 450/-
	(Minor has to be accompanied by a major visitor)		
2	PONY		
	(a) Katra-Adhkuwari-Katra	up to 75 Kgs	Rs.60/-
	(b) Adhkuwari-*Bhavan*-Adhkuwari	up to 100 kgs.	Rs. 80/-
	with below 7 yrs child	up to 75 kgs	Rs.80/-
	with below 7 yrs child	up to 100 kgs.	Rs. 85/-
	(c) Katra-*Bhavan*	up to 75 Kgs	Rs. 120/-
	with below 7 yrs. Child	up to 75 Kgs	Rs. 155/-
		up to 100 kgs.	Rs. 155/-
	with child	above 100 kgs.	Rs. 170/-
	(d) *Bhavan*- Bhairon Mandir-Katra	up to 75 Kgs	Rs. 145/-
	with below 7 yrs. Child	up to 75 Kgs	Rs. 180/-
		up to 100 kgs.	Rs. 180/-
	with child	above 100 kgs.	Rs. 200/-
	PITHU		
	(a) Katra-*Bhavan*-Katra		Rs. 160/-
	(b) For Bahiron Mandir		30/-
	* 8% of amount on prescribed rates has to be paid by yatri as commission.		

Source: Mata Vaishno Devi Yatri Guide, J&K Reporter (ed.) June 2000 P-6-7.

per year itself is an indication of the market potential for transportation services out of which 75 per cent visit purely for pilgrimage purposes (Exhibit-1.2). Demographic background and the purpose of visit of visitors have an impact on the choice, and the purpose of a visit of a visitor has an impact on the choice of the mode of transportation and other related requirements which serving such a fast growing pilgrim traffic, transporters have to concentrate on their requirements during the journey.

For this purpose information about pilgrim satisfaction about all these aforesaid modes of transportation covering reasonability of fare, maintenance of roads, proper and significant sign boards, etc. was gathered through a five point Likert scale [5————1] where 5 stands for excellent, 4 for good, 3 for fair, 2 for poor and 1 for very poor services.

Measurement of Customer Satisfaction—An Index of Marketing Effectiveness

For measuring the quality of transportation services in terms of customer satisfaction, the visitors were classified into different groups for determining the segment-wise level of satisfaction and strategic transport service package.

Satisfaction Among Non-local Pilgrims

Non-local pilgrims who require the transport service right from their point of origin constitute about 92.25 per cent of the total customers i.e. a target market of approximately thirty-five lakhs non-local pilgrims every year is available to the transporters. Their transport requirements right from the generation of idea of a pilgrimage trip in their mind are different as compared to the local pilgrims due to their distance from the destination and their style and purpose of travel. Therefore, their satisfaction regarding the transportation service has been worked out separately to study the relationship between the demographic characteristics of different pilgrims and their satisfaction about these services.

Satisfaction Among Non-local Male Pilgrims

The above over-all average level of 3.19 (Table-5.3) observed by non-local male pilgrims regarding the transportation services available right from Jammu city to *Bhavan* shows a satisfactory arrangement of such services. Different segments of these customers show different levels of satisfaction. It is the highly educated teenagers with an above average income level, who are highly satisfied (3.77). They show a higher score of 3.88 with respect to these services available from Jammu city to Katra followed by other transport-related services provided en route to the whole of the journey from Jammu to *Bhavan* at 3.83 level. The highly educated teenage pilgrims with an average-income level show a below average-level of 2.68 for such services taken together. This group further shows a below average-level of 2.34 score with respect to transportation services available from Katra to *Bhavan* indicating thereby the ineffective and inadequate services in this part of the journey. The table indicates that all the non-local male pilgrim groups show an above average-score of these services except for the ordinary bus service between Jammu and Katra (2.67), Pony and Pithu services from Katra to *Bhavan* (2.78) and responsibility of fare (2.80). This indicates that these aspects of the transportation services bring down the over-all satisfaction level.

Satisfaction Among Non-local Female Pilgrims

The non-local female pilgrims show only a near average score of 2.98 with respect to these services taken together. Half of the female groups show a below average and the rest an above average-level of satisfaction. The less educated old age females with an average income level show the highest above average score at 3.33 level (Table-5.4) along with the above average scores from all these services viz. (i) 3.50 for transport services from Katra to *Bhavan* (ii) 3.23 for transport services from Jammu to Katra and (iii) 3.27 for other transport related services throughout the pilgrimage. The group shows only an average score of 3 for reasonability of fare and a below average level of 2.71 for fixed fare. The low level of below average satisfaction at 2.47 has been shown by the highly educated teenage females with an above average income level. This segment has shown below average scores at 2.5 for transport services each from Jammu to Katra and Katra to *Bhavan* and 2.4 for other transport services. On the whole, the Table under reference gives a below average satisfaction of 2.49 with respect to safe transport services, 2.5 level for fixed fare, 2.53 level for satisfaction from taxi/auto services, 2.54 for ordinary bus service, 2.53 for reasonality of fare and 2.71 for satisfaction from pony and pithu service. Thus the females are not that much satisfied with respect to the transport services as compared to their male counterparts.

Satisfaction Among Non-Local Male Non-Pilgrims

The non-pilgrims non-local male visitors also show an above average level of 3.32 score showing similarity with their male non-local pilgrims group. The highest score of 4.04 has been shown by the highly educated teenagers with an above average income level. This group has shown the highest score of 4.13 for satisfaction and 4 each for transport service from Katra to *Bhavan* and other transport related services. The lowest of 2.73 score has been shown by low educated middle aged males with below average income level. The segment has shown the lowest score of 2.5 each with respect to transport services from Jammu to Katra & Katra to *Bhavan*. All the segments under the group taken together have shown an above average score for these services except for taxi and auto services at 2.94, reasonable fare at 2.96 and quality of roads from Jammu to Katra at 2.97 (Table-5.5).

Satisfaction Among Non-Local Female Non-Pilgrims

An above average of 3.24 level of satisfaction has been estimated in case of non-local female non-pilgrim visitors regarding the transportation services available between Jammu and *Bhavan*. The only segment of highly educated middle aged females with an average income has observed a below average of 2.72 for all the services taken together with a below average for transport services from Jammu to Katra (2.75), other transport related services (2.4) and 3 point for the transport services from Katra to *Bhavan*. All the female segments under the group have felt below average satisfaction with respect to safe transport (2.76), fixed fare (2.96) and reasonable fare

(2.58) indicating thereby the areas which need immediate and effective remedial marketing efforts for better transportation and related services (Table-5.6).

Satisfaction Among Local Male Pilgrims

The local male pilgrims also observe an above average level of satisfaction at 3.13 with respect to all the transportation services taken together. All the local male pilgrims show an above average score throughout except for the services like (Table-5.7) an ordinary bus service (2.61), pony/pithu service (2.7) and (2.31) for reasonable fare. The low educated teenaged males with an average income level has shown the lowest average of 2.58 with respect to all the services. A much lower score of 2 has been identified for other transport services and 2.5 points need for transport service from Katra to *Bhavan*, indicating the need for effective marketing efforts in such areas.

Satisfaction Among Local Female Pilgrims

All the segments of local female pilgrims have observed the satisfaction at an above average of 3.74 regarding all the transportation services taken together. The service between Jammu & Katra has secured a below average of 2.5 points from highly educated middle aged females having an average income (Table-5.7) revealing that all these female groups are enjoying above average satisfaction throughout and the highest of 4.13 has been shown by highly educated old aged females with an above average income level followed by highly educated middle aged females with average income at 3.87

Satisfaction Among Local Male Non-Pilgrims

The local non-pilgrim males indicate a below average level of satisfaction at 2.81 (Table-5.8). There are only five groups of such visitors out of which three groups viz. highly educated middle aged with below average income (3.68) and low educated middle aged with average income level (3.33) and highly educated middle aged with an average income level (3.71) show an above average score explaining their satisfaction with regard to such services taken together. The Table further reveals that all the segments have shown a below average level of satisfaction for these services except for a near average 3.33 for pony and pithu services, 3.13 each for taxi/auto services and adequacy of transport and 3.03 for reasonable fare and provision of significant sign boards.

Satisfaction Among Local Non-Pilgrim Females

There is only one group viz. highly educated youngsters with average income under this group who show again a near average of 3.05 satisfaction with respect to such services (Table-5.8)

The relationship between the group cum variable-wise customer satisfaction of the transport services with overall satisfaction has been identified with the help of four linear equations (Exhbit-5.3) of multiple regression which explain the nature of association between overall and variable-wise satisfaction among all the four groups. The results indicate that the pilgrims, whether they are local or non-local, show a positive association especially with variable 'C' (Other transport services like safe transport, fixed rates, reasonable fare, etc.) which has raised their level of satisfaction. This variable shows the highest significance in all the groups except for the local non-pilgrims (equation-3). The least important appears to be variable 'A' and 'C' in case of local non-pilgrims and variable 'B' in case of non-local non-pilgrims. The relative coefficient of multiple determination R^2 is shown in table 5.11. A reasonable level of 68% variation in satisfaction scores is explained by the given variables in linear equations. The multiple correlation 'R' between independent and dependent variables identifies positive, higher degrees of association at .83 and .53 only for local non-pilgrims and local pilgrims respectively. Since the calculated values (3.28 local pilgrims,19.99 non-local pilgrims, 6.41 local non-pilgrims, 5.67 non-local non-pilgrims) of 'F at 5 per cent level of significance is higher than the tabulated value (2.99, 2.60, 3.86, 2.68) in all the cases at d.f. (V1 V2 i.e. 3,25; 3,341; 3,9; 3,109) respectively. This states that with a confidence level of 95 per cent, the four variables under study do not have equal impact on the satisfaction of customers from the transport services.

Exhibit–5.3

S.No	GROUPS	FOUR LINEAR EQUATIONS
1	Local Pilgrims	1.221+.306(AX1)+100(BX2)+.404(CX3)
2	Non-Local Pilgrims	1.931+.044(AX1)+.093(BX2)+.460(CX3)
3	Local Non-Pilgrims	5.180-.364(AX1)+1.393(BX2)-1.519(CX3)
4	Non-Local Pilgrims	2.641+.231(AX1)-1.64(BX2)+.394(CX3)

Note :
A= Transport Service from Jammu to Katra
B= Transport Service from Katra to *Bhavan*
C= OtherTransport Services

Strategic Action

The extent of marketing orientation with reference to the over-all satisfaction (Table 5.9 & 5.12) indicates three types of strategies for creating and maintaining a marketing culture in the transportation services related to pilgrimage tourism.

The first type of strategic action emerging from the findings is such a marketing plan which not only retains the present level of marketing orientation regarding those aspects where both pilgrims and non-pilgrims enjoy an 'above average' score of orientation but also to takes it to the highest possible level on the satisfaction scale.

47.44% of pilgrims have shown an above average score of satisfaction with respect to the transport services from Jammu to Katra which make them more satisfactory followed by their satisfaction from luxury bus service, taxi and auto service, and ordinary bus service from Jammu to Katra.

48.33% of non-pilgrims have also indicated an above average score of satisfaction from such services. Here the taxi and auto services from Jammu to Katra have satisfied them more, followed by nearly a similar satisfaction from the quality of road from Jammu to Katra, luxury bus service and ordinary bus service.

46.11 % of pilgrims marked an above average score of satisfaction for the transport services from Katra to *Bhavan*. Here also the quality of road from Katra to *Bhavan* has made the pilgrims more contented followed by the only transportation mode of pony & pithu services.

48.88% of non-pilgrims scored an above average score of satisfaction for the transport services from Katra to *Bhavan*. These non-pilgrims scored more satisfaction from pony & pithu services as compared to the quality of road from Katra to *Bhavan*.

49.77% of pilgrims marked an above average score of satisfaction for the other transport related services where the highest satisfaction is scored from fixed fare charged for these transport services followed by safety while travelling, significant sign boards en route to the pilgrimage, adequacy in transport services and reasonability of fare for such transport (Table-5.12).

49.18% of non-pilgrims show the highest satisfaction of above average score for other transport related services out of which more than half of non-pilgrims are more satisfied from the fixed fare for such services. Reasonability of fare for transport and its adequacy made them equally satisfied followed by safety in these transport services and significance of sign boards en route to the pilgrimage.

Thus nearly half of the visitors concluded with an above average score of satisfaction from these transportation services en route to the pilgrimage.

The second type of strategy required improvement in the present level of marketing culture about all these services where pilgrims and non-pilgrims obtained an average level of satisfaction.

41.48% pilgrims showed an average level of satisfaction from such services where pony & pithu services from Katra to *Bhavan* make more pilgrims satisfied and significant provision of sign boards least effect on this satisfaction.

Similarly 42.95% non-pilgrims show the average score of satisfaction from these services where again pony and pithu services from Katra to *Bhavan* make more satisfied and least effective is the fixed fare for such services.

The third type of strategy gives stress upon immediate attention of policy makers, administrators and operators of such transportation services towards those aspects of marketing structure, which scored, below average level of satisfaction.

8% to 11% of the pilgrim and non-pilgrim visitors show a below average level of satisfaction from these transport services from Jammu to Katra and Katra to *Bhavan*. These visitors felt satisfied regarding safety in travel and fixed fare of such services.

Thus it may be concluded that these 'below average' scorers of satisfaction reduce the overall satisfaction to a great extent. Thus a sound strategy is required to improve such services so that they fall under the category of satisfiers.

Table–5.1

Modes of Transportation used by No. of Pilgrims between different halt points of the journey as per survey conducted

Halt Points S.No	Modes of Transportation	Origin to & fro Jammu Railway Station		Jammu Rly Station to & fro Bus stand		Bus stand to & fro Katra		Between Katra & Banganga		Between Banganga & Bhavan		Between Bhavan & Bhaironghati	
		No	%	No	%	No	%	No	%	No	%	No	%
1	TRAIN	332	66.4	-	-			-	-				
2	BUS	100	20	100	20	-	-						
3	TAXI	4	0.8	24	4.8	390	78	25	5				
4	AUTO	-	-	65	13	104	20.8	118	23.6				
5	AIR	4	0.8	-	-	-	-						
6	TRAIN & BUS	10	20	-	-	-	-						
7	MATADOR	-	-	122	24.4	-	-						
8	HOTELIERS	-	-	-	-	-	-	11	2.2				
	VEHICLE (TAXI)	-	-	-	-	-	-						
9	SHRINE BOARD FREE BUS	-	-	-	-	-	-	4	0.8				
10	FOOT	-	-	-	-	-	-	327	65.4	434	86.8	284	56.8
11	PONIES	-	-	-	-	-	-	3	0.6	58	11.6	119	23.8
12	FOOT &PONY			-	-	-	-			6	1.2	4	0.8
13	RLY STN BOUND BUS	-	-	38	7.6	-	-	8	1.6				
14	NO-RESPONSE	50	10	151	30.2	6	1.2	4	0.8	2	0.4	93	18.6
		500	100	500	100	500	100	500	100	500	100	500	100

Table–5.2

Fleet strucuture of different Transport Agencies plying from Jammu to Katra as Carriers for pilgrims

Transport Agency	No.of Vehicles	Seating Capacity	Other Features	Fares(in Rs.) Per head	Fares(in Rs.) Full Vehicle	Trips Per Day	Mainten-ance	Busines General	Busines Seasonal	Competitor
(1)	(2)	(3)	(3)	(4)	(5)	(6)	(7)	(8)	(9)	(10)
1.SRTC										At Katra
Super Deluxe Bus	15	18	Non-A/C	50/45	1000	2				with JKTDC
			2X1 (Push Back Seat)							for 18 seated
Deluxe Bus	15	31	Non-A/C	35	750-1000	2	Average	Good	Profitable during season	
		25	2X2 (Push Back Seat)							
		23								
		22								
Semi Deluxe	15	52	3X2 (Push Back Seat)	25	1300	2				
	15	35	Non A/c	25	900	2				
Ordinary Bus	10	52	3X2	18	950	2				
Pvt. Super Deluxe	1	18	Non A/c	50/45	900	2				
Pvt. Deluxe	19	35	Non A/c	35	650	2				
Total	90		2X2 (Push Back Seat)							
2.JKTDC										At Katra
Eicher Mitsubishi					4000					with Pvt. Travel agencies
Summer	5	25	Non A/C	45/35	3000	2		Throughout profitable		
Winter	12	18	Inclusive of							
		17	Driven & fuel	750/450	1800	2				
Mahinder Visor	2	7								

Contd.....

(1)	(2)	(3)	(3)	(4)	(5)	(6)	(7)	(8)	(9)	(10)
Imported Japanese										
Taxis (Not in Operation)	2	-	A/C	-	2000		Very Fast			Without of
Total	21									
3. JK TAXI UNION										
Taxis	50	-	Professional Drivers	520	1040	1 trip after		Not in profit except		union Pvt. Taxis
Total (150+800)						15 days per		with routine visting		regisitration
JKTDC Rly Stn						taxi		pilgrims		
+ 3000 Pvt.regd.										with R.T.O
Tata Sumo Total 160 Regd with Union	10		Professional Drivers	520	1040					3000 in number
Contessa Total 10 regd.with Union				520	1040					
Vans							Good			
Total 50 Regd with Union			Professional Drivers	520	1040					
4. Inter state Bus Service										
Delhi-Jammu-Katra										
Rajasthan-Jammu-Katra	5 per day	52								
Himachal-Jammu-Katra										
Haryana-Jammu-Katra										
Punjab-Jammu-Katra										
5. Bus Service at Bus Stand	40	35	Non-A/C	15	-	2				

Source :- J&KSRTC, JKTDC & J&K Taxi Union

Table–5.3

Mean Score of Marketing Effectiveness Measured through Non-Local Male Pilgrim Judgement in Transportation Services

Variables	Age Group-I Up to 25 Yrs.						Age Group-II 25 to 50 Yrs.						Age Group-III Above 50 Yrs.					
Income	Inc-1		Inc-2		Inc-3		Inc-1		Inc-2		Inc-3		Inc-1	Inc-2		Inc-3		X
Education	E-1	E-2	E-1	E-2	E-1	E-2	E-1	E-2	E-1	E-2	E-1	E-2	E-1	E-1	E-2	E-1	E-2	
(1)	(3)	(4)	(5)	(6)	(7)	(8)	(9)	(10)	(11)	(12)	(13)	(14)	(15)	(16)	(17)	(18)	(19)	(20)
Trpt Service from																		
Jammu to Katra																		
1. Lux. bus service	3.42	2.75	2.50	4.00	4.00	4.00	4.00	3.67	3.20	3.61	3.36	3.06	3.00	3.50	3.11	3.60	2.93	3.39
2. Ord. bus service	2.80	2.50	2.50	3.00	3.80	3.50	1.50	2.50	2.65	2.80	1.91	2.53	2.00	3.50	2.63	3.00	2.30	2.67
3. Taxi/Auto service	2.57	3.00	3.25	1.00	4.00	5.00	4.00	3.25	3.04	3.40	3.09	3.14	2.00	3.00	3.30	3.00	3.45	3.15
4. Quality of road from Jammu to Katra	3.23	3.50	2.25	3.75	3.00	3.00	3.50	3.50	3.38	3.46	2.91	3.45	3.50	3.67	3.50	3.60	3.31	3.32
X1	3.01	2.94	2.63	2.94	3.70	3.88	3.25	3.23	3.07	3.32	2.82	3.05	2.63	3.42	3.14	3.30	3.00	3.13

Contd......

(1)	(2)	(3)	(4)	(5)	(6)	(7)	(8)	(9)	(10)	(11)	(12)	(13)	(14)	(15)	(16)	(17)	(18)	(19)	(20)
Trpt Service from Katra to Bhavan																			
1. Pony/Pithu service		2.80	2.50	3.75	1.00	3.50	3.50	3.00	2.40	2.96	3.06	2.78	2.72	2.00	3.00	2.78	2.50	2.97	2.78
2. Quality of road from Katra to Bhavan		3.40	4.00	2.75	3.67	3.50	3.67	4.00	3.50	3.23	3.58	2.73	3.33	3.50	3.17	3.30	3.50	3.06	3.41
X2		3.10	3.25	3.25	2.34	3.50	3.59	3.50	2.95	3.10	3.32	2.76	3.03	2.75	3.09	3.04	3.00	3.02	3.09
X12		3.07	3.10	2.94	2.26	3.60	3.73	3.38	3.09	3.10	3.32	2.79	3.04	2.67	3.25	3.09	3.15	3.01	3.09
Other Transport Services																			
1. Safe transport		3.00	4.00	3.25	3.00	2.40	3.00	4.00	4.00	3.24	3.14	2.36	2.62	2.50	2.00	3.44	2.86	2.81	3.04
2. Fixed fare		3.43	4.00	3.50	4.00	3.20	3.67	4.50	3.50	3.90	3.64	3.89	3.20	3.00	2.00	3.11	2.88	3.27	3.45
3. Reasonable fare		2.77	2.00	3.00	3.00	2.00	4.50	3.50	3.33	2.67	2.46	2.18	2.95	3.50	2.50	2.35	2.13	2.83	2.80
4. Significant sign boards		3.31	2.00	3.00	3.75	3.00	3.67	3.50	3.50	3.41	3.56	3.36	3.41	3.50	3.67	3.60	3.70	3.28	3.37
5. Adequate transport		3.70	4.25	3.75	3.75	4.75	4.33	4.00	3.83	3.79	4.38	3.55	3.73	4.00	4.00	3.90	4.00	3.83	3.97
X3		3.24	3.25	3.30	3.50	3.07	3.83	3.90	3.63	3.40	3.44	3.07	3.18	3.30	2.83	3.28	3.12	3.20	3.33
X123		3.13	3.15	3.06	2.93	3.42	3.77	3.55	3.27	3.20	3.60	2.88	3.09	2.89	3.11	3.15	3.14	3.07	3.20

Table–5.4

Mean Score of Marketing Effectiveness through Non-Local Female Pilgrims Judgement in Transportation Services

Variables	Age Income Education	Age Group-I Up to 25 Yrs.				Age Group-II 25-50 Yrs.						Age Group-III Above 50 Yrs.						X
		Inc-1		Inc-2	Inc-3	Inc-1		Inc-2		Inc-3		Inc-1		Inc-2		Inc-3		
		E-1	E-2	E-1	E-2	E-1	E-2	E-1	E-2	E-1	E-2	E-1	E-2	E-1	E-2	E-1	E-2	
(1)	(2)	(3)	(4)	(5)	(6)	(7)	(8)	(9)	(10)	(11)	(12)	(13)	(14)	(15)	(16)	(17)	(18)	(19)
Trpt Service from Jammu to Katra																		
1. Lux. bus service		4.00	3.20	2.00	4.00	2.64	3.33	5.00	3.33	4.00	3.00	3.00	3.00	3.14	3.33	4.00	3.50	3.40
2. Ord. bus service		3.00	2.40	3.00	1.00	2.09	2.78	1.00	2.80	2.00	2.00	3.00	3.00	3.25	2.40	4.00	2.92	2.54
3. Taxi/Auto service		3.00	2.33	2.00	1.00	2.55	2.75	1.00	2.17	4.00	3.00	3.40	3.00	3.29	2.50	1.00	3.42	2.53
4. Quality of road from Jammu to Katra		3.33	3.80	4.00	4.00	3.55	3.24	4.00	3.27	2.00	3.00	2.71	4.00	3.25	3.40	1.00	3.21	3.24
X1		3.33	2.93	2.75	2.50	2.71	3.03	2.75	2.89	3.00	2.75	3.03	3.25	3.23	2.91	2.50	3.26	2.93

Contd.....

(1)	(2)	(3)	(4)	(5)	(6)	(7)	(8)	(9)	(10)	(11)	(12)	(13)	(14)	(15)	(16)	(17)	(18)	(19)
Trpt Service from Katra to *Bhavan*																		
1. Pony/Pithu service		3.00	2.00	3.00	1.00	2.11	2.88	5.00	2.88	2.00	3.50	3.40	1.00	3.50	2.50	3.00	2.57	2.71
2. Quality of road from Katra to *Bhavan*		3.67	3.20	4.00	4.00	3.36	3.53	1.00	3.56	4.00	2.50	3.14	4.00	3.50	3.40	3.00	3.50	3.34
X2		3.34	2.60	3.50	2.50	2.74	3.21	3.00	3.22	3.00	3.00	3.27	2.50	3.50	2.95	3.00	3.04	3.02
X12		3.34	2.77	3.13	2.50	2.72	3.12	2.88	3.06	3.00	2.88	3.15	2.88	3.37	2.93	2.75	3.15	2.98
Other Transport Services																		
1. Safe transport		1.00	4.00	1.00	2.00	3.00	2.70	1.00	3.00	4.00	4.00	1.33	1.00	3.14	3.00	3.00	2.67	2.49
2. Fixed fare		5.00	1.00	1.00	2.00	3.57	3.20	1.00	3.00	4.00	3.50	2.00	1.00	2.71	2.50	1.00	3.50	2.50
3. Reasonable fare		1.67	2.20	3.00	1.00	1.82	2.44	5.00	2.18	3.00	3.00	3.71	1.00	3.00	2.20	3.00	2.21	2.53
4. Significant sign boards		3.33	4.20	3.00	3.00	2.89	3.56	4.00	3.09	3.00	4.00	3.71	4.00	3.50	3.80	3.00	3.57	3.48
5. Adequate transport		4.00	3.80	4.00	4.00	3.82	3.50	5.00	4.27	3.00	3.50	3.57	4.00	4.00	4.20	4.00	4.00	3.92
X3		3.00	3.04	2.40	2.40	3.02	3.08	3.20	3.11	3.40	3.60	2.86	2.20	3.27	3.14	2.80	3.19	2.98
X123		3.16	2.86	2.75	2.47	2.82	3.11	2.98	3.07	3.13	3.12	3.05	2.65	3.33	3.00	2.77	3.16	2.96

Table–5.5

Mean Score of Marketing Effectiveness Measured through Non-Local Male Non-Pilgrim Judgement in Transportation Services

Variables	Age Group-I (Up to 25 Yrs.)			Age Group-II (25 to 50 Yrs.)						Age Group-III (Above 50 Yrs.)						
Income	Inc-1	Inc-2	Inc-3	Inc-1		Inc-2		Inc-3		Inc-1		Inc-2		Inc-3		X
Education	E-2	E-2	E-2	E-1	E-2	E-1	E-2	E-1	E-2	E-1	E-2	E-1	E-2	E-1	E-2	
(1)	(3)	(4)	(5)	(6)	(7)	(8)	(9)	(10)	(11)	(12)	(13)	(14)	(15)	(16)	(17)	(18)
Trpt Service from Jammu to Katra																
1. Lux. bus service	4.00	2.33	4.50	3.00	3.00	3.50	3.61	4.00	4.00	4.00	4.00	4.00	3.33	4.00	3.43	3.65
2. Ord. bus service	4.00	2.33	4.50	3.00	1.80	3.00	3.26	3.00	3.43	3.00	4.00	2.00	3.00	3.00	3.00	3.09
3. Taxi/Auto service	1.00	3.00	4.50	1.00	2.40	3.00	2.76	3.00	3.57	3.00	4.00	4.00	3.00	3.00	2.94	2.94
4. Quality of road from Jammu to Katra	3.00	3.00	3.00	3.00	3.00	2.50	3.00	3.00	3.00	3.00	3.00	3.00	3.00	3.00	3.00	2.97
X1	3.00	2.67	4.13	2.50	2.55	3.00	3.16	3.25	3.50	3.25	3.75	3.25	3.08	3.25	3.09	3.16

Contd.....

(1)	(2)	(3)	(4)	(5)	(6)	(7)	(8)	(9)	(10)	(11)	(12)	(13)	(14)	(15)	(16)	(17)	(18)
Trpt Service from Katra to Bhavan																	
1. Pony/Pithu service		4.00	2.67	4.00	1.00	3.60	3.00	3.16	3.00	3.00	4.00	4.00	4.00	3.33	4.00	3.57	3.36
2. Quality of road from Katra to Bhavan		1.00	3.00	4.00	4.00	3.40	4.00	3.55	3.00	3.25	4.00	4.00	4.00	3.33	3.00	3.43	3.40
X2		2.50	2.84	4.00	2.50	3.50	3.50	3.36	3.00	3.13	4.00	4.00	4.00	3.33	3.50	3.50	3.38
X12		2.75	2.76	4.07	2.50	3.03	3.25	3.26	3.13	3.32	3.63	3.88	3.63	3.21	3.38	3.30	3.27
Other Transport Services																	
1. Safe transport		2.67	3.00	3.50	4.00	4.33	2.00	3.79	2.00	3.29	4.00	4.00	3.00	3.33	3.00	3.13	3.27
2. Fixed fare		2.67	2.33	3.50	2.00	2.33	4.00	3.68	3.00	3.00	4.00	4.00	3.00	3.33	4.00	3.19	3.20
3. Reasonable fare		4.33	3.33	4.00	2.00	3.80	2.00	2.76	2.00	1.89	4.00	4.00	1.00	3.33	3.00	3.00	2.96
4. Significant sign boards		4.00	3.67	4.00	4.00	3.40	4.00	3.81	4.00	3.78	4.00	1.00	4.00	3.33	3.00	3.31	3.55
5. Adequate transport		5.00	3.00	5.00	4.00	4.60	3.50	4.14	4.00	4.44	4.00	4.00	4.00	4.00	4.00	4.19	4.12
X3		3.73	3.07	4.00	3.20	3.69	3.10	3.64	3.00	3.28	3.75	3.40	3.00	3.46	3.40	3.36	3.42
X123		3.08	2.86	4.04	2.73	3.25	3.20	3.39	3.09	3.30	3.75	3.72	3.42	3.29	3.38	3.32	3.32

Table–5.6

Mean Score of Marketing Effectiveness Measured through
Non-Local Female Non-Pilgrim Judgement in Transport Service

Variables	Age	Age Group-I Up to 25 Yrs.		Age Group-II 25-50 Yrs.			Age group-III Above 50 yrs.		
	Income	Inc-1	Inc-1	Inc-2	Inc-2	Inc-3	Inc-2	Inc-3	X
	Education	E-1	E-2	E-1	E-2	E-2	E-2	E-2	
(1)	(2)	(3)	(4)	(5)	(6)	(7)	(8)	(9)	(10)
Trpt Service from Jammu to Katra									
1. Lux. bus service		4.00	3.20	4.00	3.00	4.00	3.86	3.00	3.58
2. Ord. bus service		3.33	3.20	3.50	2.50	4.00	2.86	3.00	3.20
3. Taxi/Auto service		3.00	3.60	4.00	2.50	2.00	2.71	4.00	3.12
4. Quality of road from Jammu to Katra		3.00	3.00	3.00	3.00	3.26	3.00	3.00	3.04
X1		3.33	3.25	3.63	2.75	3.32	3.11	3.25	3.24

Contd.....

(1)	(2)	(3)	(4)	(5)	(6)	(7)	(8)	(9)	(10)
Trpt Service from Katra to *Bhavan*									
1. Pony/Pithu service		3.33	3.20	4.00	3.00	2.00	2.71	4.00	3.18
2. Quality of road from Katra to *Bhavan*		3.33	3.20	3.50	3.00	4.00	4.00	2.50	3.36
X2		3.33	3.20	3.75	3.00	3.00	3.36	3.25	3.27
X12		3.33	3.23	3.69	2.88	3.16	3.24	3.25	3.26
Other Transport Services									
1. Safe transport		2.33	4.00	3.50	1.00	2.00	3.00	3.50	2.76
2. Fixed fare		2.67	4.00	3.50	1.00	2.00	3.57	4.00	2.96
3. Reasonable fare		3.33	1.60	2.50	2.50	4.00	2.14	2.00	2.58
4. Significant sign boards		3.33	4.00	3.50	3.00	4.00	3.43	3.50	3.54
5. Adequate transport		4.33	4.40	3.00	4.50	4.00	4.71	4.50	4.21
X3		3.20	3.60	3.20	2.40	3.20	3.37	3.50	3.21
X123		3.29	3.35	3.53	2.72	3.17	3.28	3.33	3.24

Table-5.7

Mean Score of Marketing Effectiveness Measured through Non-Local Male and Female Non-Pilgrim Judgement in Transportation Services

Variables	MALE PILGRIMS										FEMALE PILGRIMS						
	Age Group-I Up to 25 Yrs.			Age Group-II 25-50 Yrs.				Age Group-III Above 50 Yrs.			Age Group-II 25 to 50 Yrs.			Age Group-III Above 50 Yrs.			
Income	Inc-1	Inc-1	Inc-2	Inc-1	Inc-1	Inc-2	Inc-3	Inc-2	Inc-3	X	Inc-1	Inc-2	Inc-3	Inc-1	Inc-2	Inc-2	X
Education	E-1	E-2	E-1	E-2	E-1	E-2	E-1	E-2	E-2		E-1	E-2	E-2	E-2	E-1	E-2	
(1)	(3)	(4)	(5)	(6)	(7)	(8)	(9)	(10)	(11)	(12)	(13)	(14)	(15)	(16)	(17)	(18)	(19)
Trpt Service from Jammu to Katra																	
1. Lux. bus service	2.00	3.00	4.00	2.67	4.00	3.50	3.00	3.25	4.00	3.27	3.00	2.00	3.50	4.00	4.00	4.00	3.42
2. Ord. bus service	2.00	2.00	2.00	2.33	3.00	3.25	3.00	2.40	3.50	2.61	3.00	2.00	3.00	4.00	4.00	4.00	3.33
3. Taxi/Auto service	2.00	3.00	3.00	2.67	4.00	3.50	3.00	3.40	3.50	3.12	3.00	2.00	3.50	4.00	4.00	4.00	3.42
4. Quality of road from Jammu to Katra	4.00	4.00	4.00	3.33	4.00	4.25	1.00	3.20	2.50	3.36	3.00	4.00	4.00	4.00	4.00	4.00	3.83
X1	2.50	3.00	3.25	2.75	3.75	3.63	2.50	3.06	3.38	3.09	3.00	2.50	3.50	4.00	4.00	4.00	3.50

Contd.....

(1)	(2)	(3)	(4)	(5)	(6)	(7)	(8)	(9)	(10)	(11)	(12)	(13)	(14)	(15)	(16)	(17)	(18)	(19)
Trpt Service from Katra to *Bhavan*																		
1. Pony/Pithu service		2.00	2.00	1.00	3.67	3.00	4.00	3.00	2.60	3.00	2.70	3.00	3.50	4.00	4.00	4.00	4.00	3.75
2. Quality of road from Katra to *Bhavan*		3.00	4.00	4.00	3.67	2.00	4.75	3.00	3.60	4.00	3.56	4.00	4.00	4.00	4.00	4.00	4.00	4.00
X2		2.50	3.00	2.50	3.67	2.50	4.38	3.00	3.10	3.50	3.13	3.50	3.75	4.00	4.00	4.00	4.00	3.88
X12		2.50	3.00	2.88	3.21	3.13	4.01	2.75	3.08	3.44	3.11	3.25	3.13	3.75	4.00	4.00	4.00	3.69
Other Transport Services																		
1. Safe transport		3.00	3.00	1.00	3.67	4.00	3.50	3.00	3.40	3.50	3.12	4.00	3.00	4.00	4.00	4.00	5.00	4.00
2. Fixed fare		4.00	3.00	1.00	2.00	4.00	3.50	4.00	3.40	4.00	3.21	3.00	3.00	3.50	4.00	3.00	4.00	3.42
3. Reasonable fare		2.00	4.00	1.00	3.00	1.00	2.50	1.00	3.80	2.50	2.31	3.00	2.00	4.00	4.00	3.00	4.00	3.33
4. Significant sign boards		3.00	3.00	3.00	2.67	4.00	4.00	4.00	4.20	4.50	3.60	4.00	4.00	4.00	4.00	4.00	4.00	4.00
5. Adequate transport		3.00	4.00	4.00	3.67	3.00	4.25	3.00	3.80	4.00	3.64	4.00	4.00	4.50	5.00	4.00	5.00	4.42
X3		3.00	3.40	2.00	3.00	3.20	3.55	3.00	3.72	3.70	3.17	3.60	3.20	4.00	4.20	3.60	4.40	3.83
X123		2.67	3.13	2.58	3.14	3.15	3.85	2.83	3.29	3.53	3.13	3.37	3.15	3.83	4.07	3.87	4.13	3.74

Table–5.8

Mean Score of Marketing Effectiveness Measured through
Local Male & Female Non-Pilgrim Judgement in Transport Service.

Variables	Age	Male				Age Group-III Above 50 Yrs.		Female Age Group-I Up to 25 Yrs.
		Age Group-II 25 to 50 Yrs.					X	
	Income	Inc-1		Inc-2	Inc-3	Inc-3		Inc-1
	Education	E-2	E-1	E-2	E-2	E-2		E-2
(1)	(2)	(3)	(4)	(5)	(6)	(7)	(8)	(9)
Trpt Service from Jammu to Katra								
1. Lux. bus service		3.00	3.00	4.00	2.00	1.00	2.60	1.00
2. Ord. bus service		5.00	2.67	3.00	2.00	1.00	2.73	3.00
3. Taxi/Auto service		5.00	2.67	4.00	3.00	1.00	3.13	1.00
4. Quality of road from Jammu to Katra		2.00	2.33	3.50	1.00	4.00	2.57	4.00
X1		3.75	2.67	3.63	2.00	1.75	2.76	2.25

Contd.....

(1)	(2)	(3)	(4)	(5)	(6)	(7)	(8)	(9)
Trpt Service from Katra to Bhavan								
1. Pony/Pithu service		5.00	3.67	4.00	3.00	1.00	3.33	3.00
2. Quality of road from Katra to Bhavan		2.00	4.00	4.00	1.00	1.00	2.40	4.00
X2		3.50	3.84	4.00	2.00	1.00	2.87	3.50
X12		3.63	3.26	3.82	2.00	1.38	2.82	2.88
Other Transport Services								
1. Safe transport		2.00	3.33	3.50	1.00	1.00	2.17	3.00
2. Fixed fare		3.00	4.00	4.00	1.00	1.00	2.60	4.00
3. Reasonable fare		5.00	3.67	2.50	2.00	2.00	3.03	2.00
4. Significant sign boards		4.00	2.67	3.50	1.00	4.00	3.03	4.00
5. Adequate transport		5.00	3.67	4.00	2.00	1.00	3.13	4.00
X3		3.80	3.47	3.50	1.40	1.80	2.79	3.40
X123		3.68	3.33	3.71	1.80	1.52	2.81	3.05

Table–5.9

Over-all Marketing Orientation & Customer Assessment in Transport Services

Grouping Pattern				Low Education				High Education				Over all Mean			
rea	Purpose	Gender	Income	A	B	C	X	A	B	C	X	A	B	C	X
(1)	(2)	(3)	(4)	(5)	(6)	(7)	(8)	(9)	(10)	(11)	(12)	(13)	(14)	(15)	(16)
Local	PILGRIM	Male	Inc-1	2.50	2.50	3.00	2.67	2.88	3.34	3.20	3.14	2.69	2.92	3.10	2.90
			Inc-2	3.50	2.25	2.40	2.72	3.35	3.74	3.64	3.58	3.43	3.00	3.02	3.15
			Inc-3	2.50	3.00	3.00	2.83	3.38	3.50	3.70	3.53	2.94	3.25	3.35	3.18
			X	2.83	2.58	2.80	2.74	3.20	3.53	3.51	3.41	3.02	3.06	3.16	3.08
		Female	Inc-1					3.50	3.75	3.90	3.72	3.50	3.75	3.90	3.72
			Inc-2	4.00	4.00	3.60	3.87	3.25	3.88	3.80	3.64	3.63	3.94	3.70	3.76
			Inc-3					3.50	4.00	4.00	3.83	3.50	4.00	4.00	3.83
			X	4.00	4.00	3.60	3.87	3.42	3.88	3.90	3.73	3.71	3.94	3.75	3.80
			X	3.42	3.29	3.20	3.30	3.31	3.71	3.71	3.58	3.37	3.50	3.46	3.44
Non-Local		Pilgrims	Inc-1					3.75	3.50	3.80	3.68	3.75	3.50	3.80	3.68
			Inc-2	2.67	3.84	3.47	3.33	3.63	4.00	3.50	3.71	3.15	3.92	3.49	3.52
			Inc-3					1.50	1.25	1.30	1.35	1.50	1.25	1.30	1.35
			X	2.67	3.84	3.47	3.33	2.96	2.92	2.87	2.92	2.82	3.38	3.17	3.12
		Female	Inc-1					1.75	3.50	3.40	2.88	1.75	3.50	3.40	2.88
			Inc-2												
			Inc-3												
			X	1.75				1.75	3.50	3.40	2.88	1.75	3.50	3.40	2.88

Contd.....

(1)	(2)	(3)	(4)	(5)	(6)	(7)	(8)	(9)	(10)	(11)	(12)	(13)	(14)	(15)	(16)
Non-Local	Pilgrim		X	2.67	3.84	3.47	3.33	2.36	3.21	3.14	2.90	2.52	3.53	3.31	3.12
		Locals	X	3.05	3.57	3.34	3.32	2.84	3.46	3.43	3.24	2.95	3.52	3.39	3.29
		Male	Inc-1	2.96	3.13	3.48	3.19	3.09	3.10	3.44	3.21	3.03	3.12	3.46	3.20
			Inc-2	3.05	3.15	3.35	3.18	3.05	2.73	3.41	3.06	3.05	2.94	3.38	3.12
			Inc-3	3.27	3.09	3.09	3.15	3.31	3.21	3.40	3.31	3.29	3.15	3.25	3.23
			X	3.09	3.12	3.31	3.17	3.15	3.01	3.42	3.19	3.12	3.07	3.37	3.19
		Female	Inc-1	3.02	3.12	2.89	3.01	3.07	2.77	2.64	2.83	3.05	2.95	2.77	2.92
			Inc-2	2.74	3.17	2.69	2.87	2.90	3.09	3.13	3.04	2.82	3.13	2.91	2.95
			Inc-3	2.75	3.00	3.00	2.92	2.67	2.68	3.06	2.80	2.71	2.84	3.03	2.86
			X	2.84	3.10	2.86	2.93	2.88	2.85	2.94	2.89	2.86	2.98	2.90	2.91
	Non-Pilgrim		X	2.97	3.11	3.09	3.06	3.02	2.93	3.18	3.04	3.00	3.02	3.14	3.05
		Male	Inc-1	2.75	3.00	3.60	3.12	3.02	3.33	3.54	3.30	2.89	3.17	3.57	3.21
			Inc-2	3.13	3.75	3.05	3.31	2.97	3.18	3.32	3.16	3.05	3.47	3.19	3.24
			Inc-3	3.25	3.25	3.20	3.23	3.57	3.54	3.55	3.55	3.41	3.40	3.38	3.40
			X	3.04	3.33	3.28	3.22	3.19	3.35	3.47	3.34	3.12	3.34	3.38	3.28
		Female	Inc-1	3.33	3.33	3.20	3.29	3.25	3.20	3.60	3.35	3.29	3.27	3.40	3.32
			Inc-2	3.63	3.75	3.20	3.53	2.93	3.18	2.69	2.93	3.28	3.47	2.95	3.23
			inc-3					3.29	3.13	3.35	3.26	3.29	3.13	3.35	3.26
			X	3.48	3.54	3.20	3.41	3.16	3.17	3.21	3.18	3.32	3.36	3.21	3.30
			X	3.26	3.44	3.24	3.31	3.18	3.26	3.34	3.26	3.22	3.35	3.29	3.29
		Non Locals	X	3.12	3.28	3.17	3.19	3.10	3.10	3.26	3.15	3.11	3.19	3.22	3.17
		Overall	X	3.09	3.43	3.26	3.26	2.97	3.28	3.35	3.20	3.03	3.36	3.31	3.23

Table–5.10

Variable-wise Multiple Regression Coefficient
Values of Pilgrim and Non-Pilgrim Visitors

Variables	PILGRIMS		NON-PILGRIMS	
	Local	Non-Local	Local	Non-Local
A	0.306	0.044	-0.364	0.231
B	0.100	0.093	1.393	-0.164
C	0.404	0.460	-1.519	0.394
Constant	1.221	1.931	5.180	2.641

Note :

A=Transport service from Jammu to Katra

B=Transport service from Katra to *Bhavan*

C=Other transport services

Table–5. 11

Test of Singificance

Values	PILGRIMS		NON-PILGRIMS	
	Local	Non-Local	Local	Non-Local
R	0.531	0.387	0.825	0.367
R2	0.282	0.15	0.681	0.135
F′ (Cal.)	3.279	19.998	6.407	5.668
df(v¹v²)	(3,25)	3,341	(3,9)	3,109
F(Tab) (at 5% level)	2.9912	2.6049	3.8626	2.6802

Table-5.12

Variable-wise Over-all Satisfaction and Percentage of Respondents Falling under three Orientation Levels of Satisfaction

Variables	OVER ALL SATISFACTION											
	Pilgrims						Non-Pilgrims					
	B.Avg	%of Resp	Avg	%of Resp	A.Avg	% of Resp	B.Avg	% of Resp	Avg	%of Resp	A.Avg	% of Resp
Trpt Service from Jammu to Katra												
1. Lux. bus service	3.29	11.84	3.23	40.50	3.37	47.66	3.30	8.85	3.63	42.48	3.60	48.67
2. Ord. bus service	2.55	11.55	2.65	42.25	2.66	46.20	2.70	8.33	3.12	43.33	3.21	48.33
3. Taxi/Auto service	3.10	10.98	3.02	42.05	3.25	46.97	3.00	8.57	2.75	41.90	3.46	49.53
4. Quality of road from Jammu to Katra	3.56	11.62	3.22	39.46	3.46	48.92	3.40	8.00	3.50	43.20	3.66	48.80
X1		11.50		41.07		47.44		8.44		42.73		48.83
Trpt Service from Katra to Bhavan												
1. Pony/Pithu service	2.50	11.84	2.91	44.41	3.01	43.75	3.14	6.48	3.17	44.44	3.43	49.08
2. Quality of road from Katra to Bhavan	3.26	11.76	3.32	39.78	3.54	48.46	2.60	8.85	3.44	42.43	3.49	48.67
X2		11.80		42.10		46.11		7.67		43.46		48.88
X12												
Other Transport Services	2.27	4.35	2.96	44.27	3.12	51.38	3.33	8.49	3.14	43.40	3.38	48.11
1. Safe transport	2.50	5.58	3.37	43.03	3.48	51.39	2.44	8.18	3.36	40.00	3.42	51.82
2. Fixed fare	2.37	11.72	2.61	40.33	2.72	47.95	2.70	8.06	2.64	42.74	2.93	49.19
3. Reasonable fare	3.56	11.62	3.33	39.19	3.57	49.19	3.40	8.06	3.38	44.35	3.80	47.59
4. Significant sign boards	4.09	11.56	3.88	39.52	3.90	48.92	4.00	8.06	4.17	42.74	4.33	49.19
5. Adequate transport	3.00	8.97	3.14	41.27	3.28	49.77	3.09	8.17	3.30	42.65	3.52	49.18
X3		10.76		41.48				8.09		42.25		
X123	45.00	12.03	145.00	38.77	184.00	49.20	10.00	7.94	55.00	43.65	61.00	48.41

References

Burkart, A. J. & S. Medlik (1981) *Tourism: Past Present and Future* IIed., Heinemann, London, 47-107, 210-215.

Kaul, R.N. (1985) Dynamics of Tourism—A Trilogy-Transportation. Sterling Publishers; New Delhi.1-52, 91-115.

Negi, Jagmohan (1990) Tourism and Travel Concepts and Principles, Gitanjali Publishers, New Delhi. 100-153.

Peters, M. (1969) International Tourism—The Economics & Development of Internal Tourism Trade, Hutchinson; London, 114-119, 140-161.

Poon, Auliana (1993) Tourism Technology and Competitive Strategies, C.A.B., International; U.K., 53-61, 236-335.

Robinson, H. (1976) A Geography of Tourism, McDonald & Evans, London, 3-75.

Tewari, S.P. (1994) Tourism Dimensions, Atma Ram & Sons, New Delhi., 181-205, 216-249.

MARKETING STRATEGY FOR PILGRIMAGE TOURISM WITH SPECIAL REFERENCE TO RETAIL SERVICES

Background

Besides the provision of basic facilities like accommodation, access and attraction, tourism requirements prominently include retail services (Pearce 1981, Negi 1982 & Witt 1992). This service is readily needed everywhere and as such its easy accessibility, location and proper exposure (Kaul 1985) affect the success of a destination area. Traditionally speaking, a tourist was categorised as a 'guest' and the locals as 'hosts', but the increase in density of tourism has developed the concept of commercial outlets i.e. shops thereby changing the earlier relation to that of a 'seller-customer' type. In such a less friendly relation if the tourist feels cheated, it will lead to dissatisfaction and resentment (Bryden 1973) because before visiting a place visitors have many dreams of new horizons, exotic places, fascinating ways of life, art and culture etc. A properly planned tourism market provides the means to convert these essential experiences into happy memories of different forms like memory ticklers and objects, which may otherwise be called 'Souvenirs' (Kaul 1985 & Jha 1992). Such a shopping has become now an essential sport and a recreational pursuit which is based upon tourist consumption and frivolous spending. In India approximately 10% domestic tourist budget and 30% foreign tourist budget is every year earmarked for shopping, entertainment, etc. (Subramanya 1995), but the expenditure on shopping varies from place to place depending upon the financial status and social standing of the shoppers. Further, it has been estimated that women are 25% more prone to shopping than men especially during old age when there is more tendency to shop frequently and spend more due to more leisure time (Kaul 1985). This service is responsible for transferring huge amounts of money from a tourist generating area to the tourist receiving area (Rai & Kumar 1988, Tewari 1994) because a tourist directly spends on shopping (Shaw & Williams 1989), thereby creating and supporting a variety of part time, full time and seasonal trading jobs (Hartley & Hooper 1992) as shopping at a tourist destination is like any other economic activity involving an exchange process between a buyer and a seller of goods. At any destination area, promotion and proper functioning of shopping yield economic benefits and satisfies customers. It also helps the development of handicraft, art and cultural activities at the pilgrimage destination area.

Nature & Scope of the Study

Pilgrimage destinations receive bulk tourists in India and at every such destination tourists want to purchase souvenirs, pieces of art and craft, pictures or idols of diety i.e. they want to retain their experience for ever in some physical way. This is made possible by commercial outlets dealing with such articles and other articles of general use which every visitor may require during a trip.

This chapter has been exclusively devoted to critically examine the various shopping services available at Katra and *Bhavan* on the basis of primary information gathered from visitors within the parameters of customer satisfaction-oriented marketing spread over important aspects of shopping necessary for such pilgrimage destination.

Every year this shrine receives approximately 50 lakh visitors amounting to about 10 to 14 thousand visitors daily and the number gets doubled during the peak season, viz.—navratras and summer vacations in schools and colleges. Everyone who visits the Shrine requires some commodities or souvenirs for retaining their memories and also to gift them to their dear ones. To meet this shopping requirement both of general and particular nature, Katra, the base camp, has a large number of shops and stores, beyond Katra and en route to the shrine there are different kinds of shops catering to such needs. These shops are run mostly on commercial consideration out of which some are owned by the Shri Mata Vaishno Devi Shrine Board and some by local people. The retail service available may be classified mainly into (Table 6.1.) souvenir shops, dry fruit shops, handicraft stores and 460 general provision stores. Both the handicraft stores are Government-owned and other shops are private. Mostly all the shops are fixed price shops. The highest profit margin of cost +20% is enjoyed by the handicraft stores; the dry fruit shops and souvenir shops are run on cost +10 to 15 per cent profit margin. Most of the commodities in general stores are sold on cost +40 to 50 paise margin. Most of the commodities in general stores are sold on cost +40 to +50 paise margin. From the visitor's point of view dry fruit store owners feel abundant demand for walnut and at an average 10 to 30 kgs of walnut is sold in a store in a day. Other items in dry fruit stores generally include almond, dry apple, amlok, anardana, rajmash ajwain, kishmish, cashewnut, ampapad, coated saunf, etc. Pashmina shawls, wood carvings, papier-mâché and leather fur, embroidery work, silk & pashmina, carpets, namda, crival bags, saffron and honey, etc., are high in demand. There are 17 crafts in our state but only 5 to 6 craft items are available in stores at Katra. These handicraft stores receive at an average 50 customers per day but items like saffron, honey and leather fur, etc. are in short supply since 1994-95. Government-owned handicraft stores are running at a loss. These shops on an average receive daily 20 to 50 customers mainly from Delhi, Mumbai, Calculta, M.P., U.P. & Punjab etc. There is no provision for bargaining in these shops.

Measurement of Customer Satisfaction—An Index of Marketing Effectiveness

For measuring the effectiveness of the retail services available in terms of customer satisfaction, the visitors were classified into different demographic groups for determining the segment-wise level of satisfaction and strategic developing retail services package for the future (Exhibit–1.3).

Satisfaction Among Non- Local Male Pilgrims

An over-all above average level of 3.08 satisfaction (Table-6.2) observed by non-local male pilgrims with respect to retail/shopping services available right form Katra to *Bhavan* shows a near average level of effectiveness regarding such services. Different segments of the non-local male pilgrims reflect different levels of satisfaction. The highly educated teenagers with an above-average income level are satisfied at 3.41 level. This segment showed much higher satisfaction at 3.67 score with respect to such services available at *Bhavan* followed by the services at Katra (3.33). This segment is followed by highly educated teenagers with the average-income level at 3.38 score of satisfaction. This segment complains about cheating by shopkeepers during shopping; otherwise they rank every other service at an above average level. Taking all these segments together it is only the quality of souvenirs available which make them highly satisfied at 3.89 score followed by over-all satisfactory shopping service (3.82), enjoyable shopping at Katra (3.12) and enjoyable shopping at *Bhavan* (3.03).

Satisfaction Among Non-Local Female Pilgrims

Among the non-local female pilgrims only four segments viz. less educated middle aged females with an average income (3.55), highly educated middle aged females with an above average income (3.05), less educated middle aged females with an above average income (3.00) and less educated teenaged females with an average income level (3.00), show an average or above average scores of satisfaction with regard to the retail services en route to the Shrine. This group as a whole shows an over-all below average of 2.8 score of satisfaction. The lowest score of satisfaction at 2 points has been marked by highly educated teenage females with an average income level (Table-6.3).

Satisfaction Among Local Male Pilgrims

The over-all near average satisfaction at 2.99 level achieved by the local male pilgrims indicate that most of the local male pilgrim segments under study have shown an average and above average satisfaction with respect to these retail services. The highest score of 3.44 has been enjoyed by highly educated middle aged males with an above average income level. This segment has observed the highest of 4.33 for other retail services. A below average of 2.33 point has been estimated by low educated teenaged males with an average income. This segment shows a very low level of 1 point from fixed prices during shopping en route to the Shrine. All the local male pilgrim segments show the highest of 3.76 score for the quality of souvenirs available followed by over-all satisfaction from these retail services (3.65). The lowest score of 1.76 has been observed for fair shopping available at Katra followed by cooperative behaviour of the shopkeepers at Katra (2.27) Table-6.4.

Satisfaction Among Local Female Pilgrims

An over-all above average of 3.12 level of satisfaction has been reflected by all the local female pilgrims (Table-6.5). The highest of 3.67 has been observed by highly educated middle aged female pilgrims with an above average income followed by highly educated old age female pilgrims with an average income level (3.66). This segment has shown the highest of 4 points for other retail services. All these local female pilgrim segments taken together have also observed an above average of 3.36 for other retail services available. Among all the retail services en route, this group as a whole has enjoyed an above average of 3.83 for good quality of souvenirs purchased followed by enjoyable shopping at *Bhavan* (3.75). The lowest score of 2.33 has been observed for fair shopping at Katra and 2.58 at *Bhavan* respectively.

Satisfaction Among Non-Local, Non-Pilgrim Males

The whole group of non-local non pilgrim male visitors has observed a below average of 2.69 for all the retail services during the pilgrimage (Table-6.6). The highest score of 3. 5 has been observed by highly educated young teenage with an above average income level. This segment has observed 3.83 score for other retail services followed by 3.29 score for highly educated middle aged males with a below average income level. They also reflect an above average of 3.8 level for other retail services. All the non-local non-pilgrim male visitors have expressed the highest of 3.65 for over-all satisfactory shopping followed by 3.46 for the quality of souvenirs purchased during the trip. On the other hand fair shopping at *Bhavan* (1.53) and at Katra (1.55) has acquired a lower level of satisfaction.

Satisfaction Among Non-Local Female Non-Pilgrims

A below average of 2.75 score has been experienced by all non-local female, non-pilgrim visitors. Among all, there is only one segment which has shown an above average of 3.22 level, i.e., highly educated middle aged females with an above average income level followed by an average score by two segments viz. (i) low educated teenage females with a below average income level and (ii) low educated middle aged females with an average income level. This group as a whole expressed an above average of 3.43 level for other retail services. They show a highest of 4.12 for over-all satisfactory shopping followed by 3.6 for the quality of souvenirs purchased. They all expressed the lowest level of 1.54 for fair shopping at *Bhavan* and 1.25 at Katra (Table-6.7).

Satisfaction Among Local Non-Pilgrim Males

A marginally above average of 3.02 level of satisfaction score has been expressed by local non-pilgrim male visitors (Table-6.8). The highest of 4.11 has been explained by highly educated middle aged male visitors with a below average income level. This segment showed a highest of 4.33 level with respect to other retail services. This segment is followed by highly educated middle aged male non-pilgrims with an above average income level. All these visitors have observed an above average score of 4 points for good quality of souvenirs purchased followed by over-all satisfactory shopping at 3.81. The below average score of 1.43 and 1.5 points has been observed by all these visitors for fair shopping at *Bhavan* and Katra respectively.

Satisfaction Among Local Non-Pilgrim Females

There is only one segment, i.e., highly educated teenage females with a below average income level in the group under study. They show an over-all below average score of 2.67 from these retail services during the visit (Table-6.8).

The relationship between the group-cum-variable-wise customer satisfaction of retail services with the over-all satisfaction has been identified with the help of four linear equations (Exhibit-6.1) of multiple regression which explain the nature of association between over-all and variable-wise satisfaction among all the four groups. The over-all value of customer satisfaction refers to the mean values calculated from directly obtained response from each respondent. The results indicate that the pilgrims whether they are local or non-local show both positive and negative association. The highest significance has been shown by variable 'B' (Cooperation of retailers) of retail services at Katra and variable 'B' of other retail services i.e. quality of souvenirs purchased. The least important variable appears to be variable 'A' of retail services at Katra i.e. enjoyable shopping for which all the groups have shown a negative association with the over-all satisfaction. The relative coefficients of multiple determination R^2 as shown in Table-6.11 explain a reasonable level of 74% and 64% variation in satisfaction scores for local non-pilgrims and local pilgrims respectively. The multiple correlation 'R' between dependent and independent variables also identify a positive and higher degree of association at .93 and .80 only for local non-pilgrims and local pilgrims respectively. Since the calculated values of 'F' at 5 per cent level of significance is higher in the case of three groups under study, viz. 3.807 (local pilgrims), 4.937 (non-local pilgrims) and 3.081 (non-local non-pilgrims) than the table values of 2.4227, 1.8799 and 1.9588 at $v_1 v_2$ (d.f) of 9,19; 9,335 and 9,103 respectively, which indicates that with a confidence level of 95 per cent the variables under study do not have equal impact on the satisfaction of customer from retail services. They show a varying effect on the over-all customer satisfaction and marketing effectiveness. The only group of local non-pilgrims which show a 74 per cent variation in satisfaction scores has the calculated value of 'F' at 95 per cent confidence level (3.055) less than its table value (3.8378) at (8.4) d.f. This states that with a confidence level of 95 per cent, the three variables under study show an equal impact on the satisfaction of this group from the retail services during the trip. Marketing orientation and customer satisfaction which arrived at 2.92 (Table-6.9) has been proved convergently valid as the proportion of pilgrims and non-pilgrims falling under the average region of over-all satisfaction at 3.23 and 3.26 (Table-6.12) has been estimated as 43.55% and 43.38% respectively as against 9.68% and 46.77% of below average and above average in case of pilgrims and 7.83% and 48.69% of non-pilgrims respectively.

Strategic Action

The extent of marketing orientation with reference to over-all satisfaction (Table-6.9 & 6.12) indicate three types of strategies for creating and maintaining marketing culture in retail services related to pilgrimage tourism.

The first type of strategic action emerging from the findings is such a marketing plan which not only retains the present level of marketing orientation regarding those aspects where both pilgrims and non-pilgrims enjoy an 'above average' score of orientation but also to take it to the highest possible level on the satisfaction scale.

46.22% of pilgrims have shown an above average score of satisfaction with respect to retail services at Katra, cooperation of shopkeepers during shopping by pilgrims has made more of them satisfactory at 46.5% followed by enjoyable shopping and fairness in such retail services. 48.27% of non-pilgrims have reflected an above average satisfaction with respect to the retail services at Katra. More of the non-pilgrims enjoy these services at Katra followed by fair shopping and cooperation by shopkeepers.

Regarding these retail services at *Bhavan* 46.92% of pilgrims enjoy an above average satisfaction. This group explains more of fairness in such retail services. 48.23% of non-pilgrims explain an above average level of satisfaction regarding retail services at *Bhavan*. They enjoyed the shopping at *Bhavan* and explain fairness in shopping.

Other retail services at *Bhavan* and Katra make 47.51% pilgrims and 48.67% non-pilgrims satisfied at an above average level. 49.46% pilgrims and 49.18% non-pilgrims explain over-all above average satisfaction from such shopping followed by fixed prices during the shopping at such destination. 47.71% of non-pilgrims and 46.45% of pilgrims are satisfactory at an above average level with respect to the quality of souvenirs purchased during shopping (Table-6.12). Thus nearly half of the pilgrim and non-pilgrim visitors have scored an above average satisfaction from these retail services en route to the pilgrimage.

The second type of strategy requires constant improvement in the present level of marketing culture about all those services where both pilgrim and non-pilgrim groups obtain an average level of satsifaction score.

43.52% of pilgrims and 43.84% of non-pilgrims scored an average level of satisfaction from such retail services at the destination out of which 45.39% of pilgrims are satisfied at an average level regarding the quality of sourvnirs purchased followed by enjoyable shopping at *Bhavan* by 44.98% of pilgrims. 44.44% non-pilgrims show an average level of satisfaction from the cooperative nature of shopkeepers at *Bhavan* and the quality of sourvenirs purchased during shopping at a pilgrimage trip.

The third type of strategy draws immediate attention of policy makers, administrators and operators of such retail services towards those aspects of marketing efforts, which scored, below average level of satisfaction regarding these retail services. 11.18% pilgrims show a below average satisfaction from fair shopping at Katra followed by over-all satisfaction in shopping by 11.14% pilgrims 8.26% non-pilgrims show a below average satisfaction from the cooperative nature of shopkeepers at *Bhavan* and the quality of sourvnirs purchased during the visit. These visitors feel less satisfied regarding satisfaction from retail services en route to the Shrine.

It may be concluded that these below average scores of satisfaction reduce the over-all satisfaction to a great extent. Thus a sound strategy for such services is required for improvement and converting dissatisfied customers into satisfied ones.

Exhibit–6.1

S.No	GROUPS	FOUR LINEAR EQUATIONS
1	Local Pilgrims	4.742-.329(AX1)+.214(BX2)+.019(CX3)+.181(AX4)-.438(BX5)-.227(CX6)+.112(AX7)+.034(BX8)
2	Non-Local Pilgrims	4.027-0.68(AX1)+0.30(BX2)-0.92(CX3)+.107(AX4)-1.095(BX5)+.117(CX6)-.190(AX7)+.012(BX8)
3	Local Non-Pilgrims	-37.381-3.333(AX1)+4.155(BX2)+0.655(CX3)-2.190(BX5)+3.250(CX6)+2.310(AX7)+7.583(BX8)
4	Non-Local Non-Pilgrims	3.004-.228(AX1)+.213(BX2) +0.56(CX3)-.031(AX4)+0.45(BX5)-0.39(CX6)-.098(AX7)+.044(BX8)

Note:

Katra

A

B

C=Retail Services at Katra

Bhavan

A

B

C=Retail Services at Bhavan

Common

A

B= Other Retail Services

Table–6.1

Structure of Retail Services at Katra—The base camp of Shri Mata Vaishno Devi Shrine Retail Services

	Souvenirs Shop	Dry Fruit Shops	Karayana/ General Shops	Handicraft Stores
No. of Shops	15	50	460	2
Ownership	Private	Private	Private	Private
Pricing Strategy	Fixed Price	As per supply & Season	Fixed Price	Fixed Price
Profit %	Cost+15%	Cost + 15%	Cost+50 Paise	Price fixed by govt.
Nature of Merchandise	Souvenirs	Walnuts Almond Dry apple Amlok Anardana Rajmash Ajwan Kishmish Cashewnut Ampapad Coated saunf	General Items of daily use	Shawls Papier Mâché Embroidery Silk Pashmina Carpets Namda Crival bags Leather bags Saffron Honey
Bargaining	Up to Rs. 5 per item	Upto Rs.5 per item	No Bargain	No Bargain
Competitors	None	None	None	Poshish
Average sales per customer	20-to-30 Customer	10-to-30 Kgs.	50 customers	50-to-60 Customer
More demand of	Idols of Diety in different forms	Walnuts	Rice Rajamash	Shawls Papier Mâche Costly wood carvings Leather fur
Earning	Profits	Profits	Profits	Loss
Visitors mainly from	Delhi Mumbai Kolkata UP MP	Delhi Mumbai Kolkata UP MP Punjab Haryana	All over India	Delhi Kolkata Mumbai
Shrine Board support	No	No	No	No
Inadqaute Supply	–	–	–	Costly wood carvings Furniture Leather fur Saffron Honey
Problems faced	Services of Pawan Hans	Holding of Dry fruits by suppliers	No storage sheds at bust stand No porters available at bus stand	Shortage of craft items Out of 17 crafts of the state only 5-to-6 crafts are in supply

Source : Retailers Association, Katra

Table–6.2

Mean Score of Marketing Effectiveness Measured through Non-Local Male Pilgrim Judgement in Retail Services

Variables	Age Group-I Upto 25 Yrs.						Age Group-II 25 to 50 Yrs.						Age Group-III Above 50 Yrs.					X
Income	Inc-1		Inc-2		Inc-3		Inc-1		Inc-2		Inc-3		Inc-1	Inc-2		Inc-3		
Education	E-1	E-2	E-1	E-2	E-1	E-2	E-1	E-2	E-1	E-2	E-1	E-2	E-1	E-1	E-2	E-1	E-2	X
Service at Katra																		
1. Enjoyable shopping	2.91	3.33	3.00	3.50	3.83	3.67	2.00	2.50	3.33	3.24	2.91	3.50	3.00	3.33	2.94	3.14	2.91	3.12
2. Cooperative shopkeepers	3.27	3.33	2.50	3.50	3.50	3.33	2.00	2.75	2.85	2.97	2.45	2.41	2.00	3.00	2.22	2.57	2.74	2.79
3. Fair shopping	1.73	2.34	2.75	2.67	2.17	3.00	4.00	2.00	3.00	2.48	2.27	2.47	4.00	2.00	2.22	3.15	2.56	2.64
X1	2.64	3.00	2.75	3.22	3.17	3.33	2.67	2.42	3.06	2.90	2.54	2.79	3.00	2.78	2.46	2.95	2.74	2.85
Services at Bhavan																		
1. Enjoyable shopping	3.38	3.00	2.50	3.33	3.25	4.50	3.00	2.33	3.45	3.31	3.09	3.42	2.00	2.00	2.85	3.14	2.90	3.03
2. Cooperative shopkeepers	3.38	3.67	2.75	3.50	2.50	3.50	3.00	2.00	3.24	2.93	3.27	2.76	2.00	3.00	3.00	2.86	2.71	2.95
3. Fair shopping	1.25	1.67	2.75	2.67	2.25	3.00	2.50	2.84	2.76	2.66	2.64	2.50	3.00	2.00	2.93	3.15	2.55	2.54
X2	2.67	2.78	2.67	3.17	2.67	3.67	2.83	2.39	3.15	2.97	3.00	2.89	2.33	2.33	2.93	3.05	2.72	2.84
Other Retail Services																		
1. Fixed prices	3.50	2.33	2.75	3.00	2.75	2.00	3.00	2.17	3.38	3.40	3.64	3.55	3.00	3.00	2.80	2.86	2.84	2.94
2. Quality of souvenirs	4.75	4.00	4.00	4.00	4.00	4.00	4.50	3.33	4.03	3.79	3.91	3.89	2.00	5.00	3.77	3.14	4.07	3.89
3. Satisfactory shopping	3.92	3.50	3.50	4.25	4.75	3.67	4.50	3.67	3.94	3.95	3.45	3.32	3.50	3.83	3.70	4.20	3.36	3.82
X3	4.06	3.28	3.42	3.75	3.83	3.22	4.00	3.06	3.78	3.71	3.67	3.59	2.83	3.94	3.42	3.40	3.42	3.55
X123	3.12	3.02	2.95	3.38	3.22	3.41	3.17	2.62	3.33	3.19	3.07	3.09	2.72	3.02	2.94	3.13	2.96	3.08

Table–6.3

Mean Scores of Marketing Effectiveness Measured through Non-Local Female Pilgrims Judgement in Retail Services

Variables	Age Group-I Up to 25 Yrs.				Age Group-II 25 to 50 Yrs.						Age Group-III Above 50 Yrs.						X
Income	Inc-1		Inc-2	Inc-3	Inc-1		Inc-2		Inc-3		Inc-1		Inc-2		Inc-3		
Education	E-1	E-2	E-1	E-2	E-1	E-2	E-1	E-2	E-1	E-2	E-1	E-2	E-1	E-2	E-1	E-2	
Service at Katra																	
1. Enjoyable shopping	3.33	3.60	4.00	1.00	2.45	3.29	5.00	3.09	4.00	3.50	3.00	3.00	1.88	3.20	4.00	2.71	3.19
2. Cooperative shopkeepers	3.00	3.40	2.00	2.00	2.18	2.53	4.00	2.73	2.00	2.50	2.71	3.00	1.75	2.80	3.00	2.57	2.64
3. Fair shopping	1.33	1.60	2.00	1.00	1.92	1.47	1.00	1.45	1.00	1.50	1.29	2.00	1.50	1.60	1.00	2.00	1.48
X1	2.55	2.87	2.67	1.33	2.18	2.43	3.33	2.42	2.33	2.50	2.33	2.67	1.71	2.53	2.67	2.43	2.44
Services at Bhavan																	
1. Enjoyable shopping	2.00	2.00	3.00	2.00	2.40	3.27	4.00	2.90	4.00	3.50	3.33	3.00	3.29	2.67	4.00	3.25	3.04
2. Cooperative shopkeepers	2.00	2.00	4.00	2.00	2.60	2.64	4.00	2.82	2.00	3.00	3.33	3.00	2.71	1.67	3.00	2.17	2.68
3. Fair shopping	1.00	1.00	2.00	1.00	1.90	2.00	2.00	2.00	2.00	2.00	2.00	2.00	1.80	1.00	1.00	2.20	1.68
X2	1.67	1.67	3.00	1.67	2.30	2.64	3.33	2.57	2.67	2.83	2.89	2.67	2.60	1.78	2.67	2.54	2.47
Other Retail Services																	
1. Fixed prices	2.00	1.33	3.00	1.00	3.40	2.90	3.00	2.40	3.00	4.00	3.67	3.00	3.00	2.67	3.00	3.17	2.78
2. Quality of souvenirs	5.00	3.67	4.00	4.00	3.70	3.36	4.00	3.80	5.00	4.50	3.67	3.00	4.00	3.67	3.00	3.92	3.89
3. Satisfactory shopping	4.00	3.40	3.00	4.00	3.64	3.61	5.00	4.09	4.00	3.00	3.71	3.00	3.78	3.80	4.00	4.14	3.76
X3	3.67	2.80	3.33	3.00	3.58	3.29	4.00	3.43	4.00	3.83	3.68	3.00	3.59	3.38	3.33	3.74	3.48
X123	2.63	2.45	3.00	2.00	2.69	2.79	3.55	2.81	3.00	3.05	2.97	2.78	2.63	2.56	2.89	2.90	2.79

Table-6.4

Mean Score of Marketing Effectiveness Measured through Local Male Pilgrim Judgement in Retail Services

Variable	Age Group-I Up to 25 Yrs.			Age Group-II 25 to 50 Yrs.					Age Group-III Above 50 Yrs.		X
Income	Inc-1		Inc-2	Inc-1	Inc-2		Inc-3		Inc-2	Inc-3	
Education	E-1	E-2	E-1	E-2	E-1	E-2	E-1	E-2	E-2	E-2	
Service at Katra											
1. Enjoyable shopping	2.00	3.00	3.00	3.00	2.00	4.00	2.00	4.00	2.80	3.50	2.93
2. Cooperative shopkeepers	1.00	2.00	2.00	1.67	2.00	3.33	2.00	4.00	2.20	2.50	2.27
3. Fair shopping	2.00	2.00	2.00	1.67	3.00	1.25	2.00	1.00	1.20	1.50	1.76
X1	1.67	2.33	2.33	2.11	2.33	2.86	2.00	3.00	2.07	2.50	2.32
Services at Bhavan											
1. Enjoyable shopping	4.00	3.00	2.00	3.33	4.00	4.00	3.00	4.00	3.40	4.00	3.47
2. Cooperative shopkeepers	4.00	5.00	2.00	2.00	4.00	3.33	4.00	4.00	3.20	4.00	3.55
3. Fair shopping	3.00	5.00	2.00	2.00	2.00	2.00	3.00	1.00	2.20	3.00	2.52
X2	3.67	4.33	2.00	2.44	3.33	3.11	3.33	3.00	2.93	3.67	3.18
Other Retail Services											
1. Fixed prices	4.00	3.00	1.00	1.33	4.00	3.25	3.00	4.00	2.80	3.50	2.99
2. Quality of souvenirs	5.00	3.00	4.00	4.00	5.00	3.00	3.00	4.00	2.60	4.00	3.76
3. Satisfactory shopping	3.00	3.00	3.00	4.00	4.00	3.50	3.00	5.00	4.00	4.00	3.65
X3	4.00	3.00	2.67	3.11	4.33	3.25	3.00	4.33	3.13	3.83	3.47
X123	3.11	3.22	2.33	2.55	3.33	3.07	2.78	3.44	2.71	3.33	2.99

Table-6.5

Mean Score of Marketing Effectiveness Measured through Local Female Pilgrim Judgement in Retail Services

Variable	Age Group-II 25 to 50 Yrs.			Age Group-III Above 50 Yrs.			
Income	Inc-1	Inc-2	Inc-3	Inc-1	Inc-2	Inc-2	
Education	E-2	E-1	E-2	E-2	E-1	E-2	X
Service at Katra							
1. Enjoyable shopping	3.00	3.00	4.00	4.00	1.00	5.00	3.33
2. Cooperative shopkeepers	3.00	3.00	4.00	4.00	1.00	4.00	3.17
3. Fair shopping	3.00	2.00	3.00	3.00	2.00	1.00	2.33
X1	3.00	2.67	3.67	3.67	1.33	3.33	2.94
Services at *Bhavan*							
1. Enjoyable shopping	3.00	3.50	4.00	4.00	4.00	4.00	3.75
2. Cooperative shopkeepers	3.00	3.00	4.00	1.00	1.00	5.00	2.83
3. Fair shopping	3.00	1.50	3.00	4.00	3.00	1.00	2.58
X2	3.00	2.67	3.67	3.00	2.67	3.33	3.05
Other Retail Services							
1. Fixed prices	3.00	1.50	2.00	1.00	4.00	4.00	2.58
2. Quality of souvenirs	3.00	4.00	4.00	4.00	4.00	4.00	3.83
3. Satisfactory shopping	1.00	3.00	5.00	4.00	4.00	5.00	3.67
X3	2.33	2.83	3.67	3.00	4.00	4.33	3.36
X123	2.78	2.72	3.67	3.22	2.67	3.66	3.12

Table-6.6

Mean Score of Marketing Effectiveness Measured through Non-Local Male Non- Pilgrim Judgement in Retail Services

Variable	Age Group-I Up to 25 Yrs.				Age Group-II 25 to 50 Yrs.						Age Group-III Above 50 Yrs.						X
	Inc-1		Inc-2	Inc-3	Inc-1		Inc-2		Inc-3		Inc-1		Inc-2		Inc-3		
Education	E-1	E-2	E-2	E-2	E-1	E-2	E-1	E-2	E-1	E-2	E-1	E-2	E-1	E-2	E-1	E-2	
Service at Katra																	
1. Enjoyable shopping	2.00	4.00	2.33	4.50	1.00	3.40	2.00	3.10	2.00	3.25	2.00	4.00	4.00	2.67	2.00	2.64	2.81
2. Cooperative shopkeepers	2.50	2.67	1.67	4.00	2.00	3.80	2.00	2.75	2.00	2.78	2.00	4.00	4.00	2.67	2.00	2.36	2.70
3. Fair shopping	2.25	1.67	1.67	2.00	1.00	1.40	1.00	1.40	1.00	1.22	1.00	2.00	2.00	1.67	2.00	1.53	1.55
X1	2.25	2.78	1.89	3.50	1.33	2.87	1.67	2.42	1.67	2.42	1.67	3.33	3.33	2.34	2.00	2.18	2.35
Services at Bhavan																	
1. Enjoyable shopping	3.40	2.00	3.00	4.50	1.00	3.20	2.00	3.00	3.00	4.00	2.00	4.00	4.00	2.67	2.00	2.71	2.91
2. Cooperative shopkeepers	3.20	1.67	2.33	4.00	2.00	4.00	1.00	2.55	3.00	3.25	2.00	4.00	4.00	2.67	2.00	2.08	2.73
3. Fair shopping	2.00	1.00	1.67	1.00	1.00	2.40	2.00	1.47	2.00	2.00	1.00	1.00	1.00	1.67	2.00	1.26	1.53
X2	2.87	1.56	2.33	3.17	1.33	3.20	1.67	2.34	2.67	3.08	1.67	3.00	3.00	2.34	2.00	2.02	2.39
Other Retail Services																	
1. Fixed prices	3.20	2.00	4.00	2.50	2.00	4.00	2.00	3.05	4.00	3.00	3.00	3.00	3.00	3.00	2.00	2.43	2.89
2. Quality of souvenirs	4.00	4.67	3.00	4.50	4.00	4.00	3.00	3.55	3.00	3.75	4.00	2.00	2.00	4.00	2.00	3.93	3.46
3. Satisfactory shopping	3.20	4.00	4.00	4.50	2.00	3.40	3.50	3.95	3.00	3.22	4.00	4.00	4.00	4.00	4.00	3.64	3.65
X3	3.47	3.56	3.67	3.83	2.67	3.80	2.83	3.52	3.33	3.32	3.67	3.00	3.00	3.67	2.67	3.33	3.33
X123	2.86	2.60	2.63	3.50	1.78	3.29	2.06	2.76	2.56	2.94	2.34	3.11	3.11	2.78	2.22	2.51	2.69

Table-6.7

Mean Score of Marketing Effectiveness Measured through
Non-Local Female Non-Pilgrim Judgement in Retail Service

Variables	Age Group-I Up to 25 yrs.		Age Group-II 25 to 50 Yrs.					Age Group-III Above 50 Yrs.		X
Income	Inc-1	Inc-2	Inc-1		Inc-2		Inc-3	Inc-1	Inc-2	
Education	E-1	E-1	E-1	E-2	E-1	E-2	E-2	E-2	E-2	
Service at Katra										
1. Enjoyable shopping	3.67	3.00	4.00	2.40	4.00	2.50	4.00	3.00	2.00	3.17
2. Cooperative shopkeepers	2.67	1.00	3.00	1.60	3.00	2.00	4.00	2.60	2.00	2.43
3. Fair shopping	1.33	1.00	2.00	1.20	1.50	1.00	1.00	1.20	1.00	1.25
X1	2.56	1.67	3.00	1.73	2.83	1.83	3.00	2.27	1.67	2.28
Services at *Bhavan*										
1. Enjoyable shopping	3.30	3.00	3.00	3.60	4.00	2.50	4.00	3.20	3.50	3.34
2. Cooperative shopkeepers	3.00	2.00	2.00	1.33	3.50	2.00	4.00	2.80	4.00	2.74
3. Fair shopping	2.00	1.00	2.00	1.20	1.50	1.00	2.00	2.20	1.00	1.54
X2	2.77	2.00	2.33	2.04	3.00	1.83	3.33	2.73	2.83	2.54
Other Retail Services										
1. Fixed prices	3.00	3.00	3.00	1.20	3.00	2.00	3.00	3.00	2.00	2.58
2. Quality of souvenirs	3.67	3.00	3.00	4.00	3.50	4.00	3.00	4.20	4.00	3.60
3. Satisfactory shopping	4.33	5.00	4.00	4.00	3.00	4.50	4.00	3.71	4.50	4.12
X3	3.67	3.67	3.33	3.07	3.17	3.50	3.33	3.64	3.50	3.43
X123	3.00	2.45	2.89	2.28	3.00	2.39	3.22	2.88	2.67	2.75

Table-6.8

Mean Score of Marketing Effectiveness Measured through Local Male & Female Non-Pilgrim Judgement in Retail Services

Variable	MALE						FEMALE	
Age	Age Group-II 25 to 50 Yrs				Age Group-III Above 50 Yrs		Age Group-I Upto 25 Yrs	
Income	Inc-1		Inc-2		Inc-3	Inc-3		Inc-1
Education	E-1	E-2	E-1	E-2	E-2	E-2	X	E-2
Service at Katra								
1. Enjoyable shopping	3.00	5.00	3.33	3.00	4.00	1.00	3.22	3.00
2. Cooperative shopkeepers	4.00	5.00	3.33	3.00	4.00	2.00	3.56	3.00
3. Fair shopping	2.00	2.00	1.47	2.00	1.00	1.00	1.58	1.00
X1	3.00	4.00	2.71	2.67	3.00	1.33	2.79	2.33
Services at Bhavan								
1. Enjoyable shopping	3.00	5.00	2.67	3.50	4.00	2.00	3.36	4.00
2. Cooperative shopkeepers	4.00	5.00	2.00	3.00	4.00	2.00	3.33	3.00
3. Fair shopping	1.00	2.00	2.00	2.00	1.00	1.00	1.50	1.00
X2	2.67	4.00	2.22	2.83	3.00	1.67	2.73	2.67
Other Retail Services								
1. Fixed prices	4.00	3.00	3.00	2.50	4.00	3.00	3.25	2.00
2. Quality of souvenirs	3.00	5.00	4.00	4.00	4.00	4.00	4.00	4.00
3. Satisfactory shopping	4.00	5.00	3.67	4.00	5.00	2.00	3.95	3.00
X3	3.67	4.33	3.56	3.50	4.33	3.00	3.73	3.00
X123	3.11	4.11	2.83	3.00	3.44	2.00	3.08	2.67

Table–6.9

Over-all Marketing Orientation and Customer Assessment in Retail Services

(1)	(2)	Gender (3)	Income (4)	Low Educated				High Educated				Over-all X			
				A (5)	B (6)	C (7)	X (8)	A (9)	B (10)	C (11)	X (12)	A (13)	B (14)	C (15)	X (16)
Local	Pilgrims	Male	Inc-1	1.67	3.67	4.00	3.11	2.22	3.39	3.06	2.89	1.95	3.53	3.53	3.00
			Inc-2	2.30	2.67	3.50	2.82	2.47	3.19	3.19	2.95	2.40	2.93	3.35	2.89
			Inc-3	2.00	3.33	3.00	2.78	2.75	3.34	4.08	3.39	2.38	3.34	3.54	3.09
			X1	2.00	3.22	3.50	2.91	2.48	3.31	3.44	3.08	2.24	3.27	3.47	2.99
		Female	Inc-1	-				3.00	3.00	3.13	3.04	1.50	1.50	1.57	1.52
			Inc-2	1.33	2.67	4.25	2.75	3.00	3.00	3.82	3.27	2.17	2.84	4.04	3.02
			Inc-3	-				3.67	3.67	3.63	3.66	1.84	1.84	1.82	1.83
			X2	1.33	2.67	3.88	2.63	3.22	3.22	3.53	3.32	2.28	2.95	3.89	3.04
			X12	1.67	2.95	3.67	2.76	2.85	3.27	3.49	3.20	2.26	3.11	3.69	3.02
	Non-Pilgrims	Male	Inc-1	3.00	2.67	3.56	3.08	4.00	4.00	4.33	4.11	3.50	3.34	4.00	3.61
			Inc-2	2.71	2.22		1.64	2.67	2.83	3.50	3.00	2.69	2.53	3.53	2.92
			Inc-3	-		3.62	1.21	2.17	2.34	3.67	2.73	1.09	1.17	1.84	1.37
			X3	2.86	2.45		1.77	2.95	3.06	3.83	3.28	2.91	2.76	3.73	3.13
		Female	Inc-1	-				2.33	2.67	3.00	2.67	1.17	1.34	1.50	1.34
			Inc-2	-											
			Inc-3	-											
			X4	-				2.33	2.67	3.00	2.67	1.17	1.34	1.50	1.34

Contd......

(1)	(2)	(3)	(4)	(5)	(6)	(7)	(8)	(9)	(10)	(11)	(12)	(13)	(14)	(15)	(16)
		Local	X34	2.86	2.45	3.62	2.98	2.64	2.87	3.42	2.98	2.75	2.66	3.52	2.98
			X	2.27	2.70	3.75	2.91	2.75	3.07	3.46	3.09	2.51	2.89	3.61	3.00
Non-Local	Pilgrims	Male	Inc-1	2.77	2.61	3.63	3.00	2.71	2.59	3.17	2.82	2.74	2.60	3.40	2.91
			Inc-2	2.86	2.72	3.71	3.10	2.86	3.02	3.63	3.17	2.86	2.87	3.67	3.13
			Inc-3	2.89	2.91	3.63	3.14	2.95	3.09	3.41	3.15	2.92	3.00	3.52	3.15
			X1	2.84	2.75	3.66	3.08	2.84	2.90	3.40	3.05	2.84	2.83	3.53	3.07
		Female	Inc-1	2.35	2.29	3.64	2.76	2.66	2.33	3.14	2.71	2.51	2.31	3.39	2.74
			Inc-2	2.57	2.98	3.64	3.06.	2.48	2.18	3.41	2.69	2.53	2.58	3.53	2.88
			Inc-3	2.50	2.67	3.67	2.95	2.09	2.35	3.52	2.65	2.30	2.51	3.60	2.80
			X2	2.47	2.65	3.65	2.92	2.41	2.29	3.36	2.69	2.44	2.47	3.51	2.81
			X12	2.66	2.70	3.66	3.01	2.63	2.60	3.38	2.87	2.65	2.65	3.52	2.94
	Non-Pilgrims	Male	Inc-1	1.75	1.96	3.27	2.33	2.99	2.55	3.45	3.00	2.37	2.26	3.36	2.66
			Inc-2	2.50	2.92	2.92	2.78	2.22	2.34	3.62	2.73	2.36	2.63	3.27	2.75
			Inc-3	1.84	3.00	3.00	2.61	2.70	2.76	3.49	2.98	2.27	2.88	3.25	2.80
			X3	2.03	2.63	3.06	2.57	2.64	2.55	3.52	2.90	2.24	2.59	3.29	2.71
		Female	Inc-1	2.78	2.56	3.50	2.95	1.73	2.04	3.07	2.28	2.26	2.30	3.29	2.62
			Inc-2	2.25	2.50	3.42	2.72	1.97	2.20	3.49	2.55	2.11	2.35	3.46	2.64
			Inc-3	-			2.34		3.08	3.42	2.95	1.17	1.54	1.71	1.47
			X4	2.52	2.53	3.46	2.84	2.01	2.44	3.33	2.59	2.27	2.49	3.40	2.72
			X34	2.28	2.58	3.26	2.71	2.33	2.50	3.43	2.75	2.31	2.54	3.35	2.73
		Non-Local	X	2.47	2.64	3.46	2.86	2.48	2.55	3.41	2.81	2.48	2.60	3.44	2.84
		Over-all	X	2.37	2.67	3.61	2.88	2.62	2.81	3.44	2.96	2.50	2.75	3.53	2.93

Table–6.10

Variable-wise Multiple Regression Coefficient
Values of Pilgrim and Non-Pilgrim Visitors

		PILGRIMS		NON-PILGRIMS	
	Variables	Local	Non-Local	Local	Non-Local
Katra	A	-0.329	-0.068	-3.333	-0.228
	B	0.214	0.030	4.155	0.213
	C	0.019	0.092	0.655	0.560
Bhavan					
	A	0.181	0.107		-0.031
	B	-0.438	-1.095	-2.190	0.045
	C	-0.227	0.117	3.250	-0.039
Common					
	A	0.112	-0.190	2.310	-0.098
	B	0.034	0.120	7.583	0.044
Constant		4.742	4.027	-37.381	3.004

Table–6.11

Test of Significance

Values	PILGRIMS		NON-PILGRIMS	
	Local	Non-Local	Local	Non-Local
R	0.802	0.342	0.931	0.461
R2	0.643	0.117	0.741	0.212
F(Cal)	3.807	4.937	3.055	3.081
df (V^1V^2)	(9,19)	-9,335	(8,4)	-9,103
F (Tab.) at 5 % level	2.4227	1.8799	3.8378	1.9588

Table–6.12
Variable-wise over-all satisfaction and percentage of Respondents falling under three orientation levels

Variables	PILGRIMS		OVER-ALL SATISFACTION						NON-PILGRIMS			
	B.Avg.	% of Resp.	Avg	%of Resp	A.Avg.	% of Resp	B.Avg	Avg.	% of Resp	%of Resp	Avg	% of Resp
Service at Katra												
1. Enjoyable shopping	2.94	10.33	3.03	43.77	3.19	45.90	2.56	7.96	3.10	43.36	2.98	48.67
2. Cooperative shopkeepers	2.67	10.94	2.54	42.55	2.82	46.50	2.11	7.69	2.73	44.44	2.73	47.86
3. Fair Shopping	3.47	11.18	3.55	42.55	3.29	46.27	4.11	7.76	3.63	43.97	3.45	48.28
X1		10.82		42.96		46.22		7.80		43.92		48.27
Service at Bhavan												
1. Enjoyable shopping	2.30	8.30	3.14	44.98	3.37	46.71	2.56	7.69	3.24	43.59	3.23	48.72
2. Cooperative shopkeepers	2.44	8.74	2.80	44.76	3.05	46.50	2.11	8.26	2.92	44.04	2.81	47.71
3. Fair Shopping	3.38	9.09	3.35	43.36	3.22	47.55	4.11	7.89	3.56	43.86	3.44	48.25
X2		8.71		44.37		46.92		7.95		43.83		48.23
Other Retail Services												
1. Fixed Prices	2.00	8.45	3.13	44.93	3.12	46.62	2.75	7.02	2.70	43.86	2.8	49.12
2. Quality of Souvenirs	3.70	8.16	3.82	45.39	3.89	46.45	3.22	8.26	3.81	44.04	3.83	47.71
3. Satisfactory shopping	3.83	11.14	3.74	39.40	3.74	49.46	3.70	8.20	3.62	43.44	3.97	49.18
X3	2.97	9.25	3.23	43.24	3.30	47.51	3.03	7.83	3.26	43.78	3.25	48.67
X123		9.59		43.52		46.88		7.86		43.84		48.39
No/ % age	30	9.68	135	43.55	145	46.77	9	7.83	50	43.48	56	48.69

References

Bryden, John M. (1973) *Tourism & Development—A Case Study of Commonwealth Caribbean*, Cambridge University Press, 57-73, 213-221.

Hartley, Keith & Nicholas Hooper (1992) "Tourism Policy: Market Failure & Public Choice", in Peter Johnson & Barry Thomas (ed.), Perspective on Tourism Policy, Durham, 15-27.

Jha, S.M. (1995) Tourism Marketing, Himalayan Publishing House, New Delhi, 32-70, 119-127.

Kaul, R.N. (1985). Dynamics of Tourism—A Trilogy-Transportation, Sterling Publishers; New Delhi.1-52, 91-115.

Negi, Jagmohan (1990) Tourism and Travel Concepts and Principles, Gitanjali Publishers, New Delhi. 100-153.

Pearce, D.G. (1981) Tourism Development—Topics in Applied Geography, Longman, U.K.,5-13, 25-30.

Rai, Lajipathi H. & J. S. Kumar (1988) "Poverty & Prosperity through Tourism in Third World", Southern Economist.

Shaw, Gerath & Allan M. Williams (1989) Tourism & Economic Development, Western European Experience, Belheaven Press; London, 5-11,230-239.

Subramanya, K.N. (1995). " Rejuvenating India's Tourism Industry", Southern Economist 1-3.

Tewari, S.P. (1994) Tourism Dimensions, Atma Ram & Sons, New Delhi, 181-205,216-249.

Witt, S.F. (1992) The Management of International Tourism, Routledge Publishers, U.K., 25-39,80-103.

SUPERVISORY EFFECTIVENESS OF SHRI MATA VAISHNO DEVI SHRINE BOARD ASSESSED THROUGH CUSTOMER/PILGRIM JUDGEMENT

Background

Shri Mata Vaishno Devi Shrine Board came into existence in August 1986 with the prime objectives to provide better amenities to the pilgrims during their entire pilgrimage through better and improved infrastructure, its maintenance and monitoring. The Board comprises a chairman and nine other members. The Governor of Jammu and Kashmir State is the *ex-officio* chairman of the board. Other nine members include I.A.S officers, some industrialists and prominent personalities (Exhibit-7.1). The Shrine Board organises its activities through a large number of independent but interconnected departments for the delivery of better services to the pilgrims. These departments are the account section, security wing, administration, engineering & non-engineering stores, personnel section, purchase section, development section, civil section and forest wing (Exhibit-7.2). All these departments work in coordination with each other to provide different facilities and services to the visitors en route to the Shrine especially at *Bhavan, Sanjichat, Adhkumari, Banganga*. These services include revenue collection maintenance of funds, provision of accommodation, bhojanalyas, dispensaries, cloakrooms, security, sanitation and hygiene, prasad, souvenir and general shops, water supply and electricity (Exhibit-7.3).

Besides these sections, the Board manages a Yatra Registration counter located at the main bazar, 'Katra'. The main function of this counter is the issuing of yatra slips. Statistically, this counter is very significant as it records the influx of yatris for which registers are maintained. In a day it permits only 18,000 yatris to move ahead with an army quota of 750 yatris which is raised to 1050 on weekends. This counter is open from 7 AM to 11 PM; afterwards no slips are issued. Keeping into consideration the rush at the yatra slip counter, a second yatra slip counter has been opened at Katra. Here slips are granted to the yatris coming in big groups e.g. a 'whole bus' of yatris. A single slip is issued to a group and the report is sent to the main centre.

Exhibit–7.1

Present Board Members of
Shri Vaishno Devi Shrine Board

Source: Shrine Board Development Report 2000

Many developmental works like the construction of an alternate track between Adhkumari and *Bhavan*, operationalisation of Manokamna Bhavan at Darbar Vaishno Deviji, an additional block of Niharika Yatri Niwas, a New Yatra registration counter at Katra, the commissioning of a helipad at Katra, the computerization of a railway reservation counter, the construction of a sewage treatment plant at *Bhavan* and a sarai building at Katra, etc., have been undertaken by the Board recently. These works are carried on to make the yatra smooth and enjoyable for the visitors.

The Shri Mata Vaishno Devi Shrine Board provides proper facilities to the yatris and channelises the resources for the development of the Shrine and the smooth functioning of the yatra. Besides making arrangements for the proper conduct of Puja at the shrine, it undertakes the construction work of buildings for accommodation, sanitary work, medical relief, safety and the insurance of the pilgrims, improvement in the communication network.

Since the last one decade the developmental works for satisfaction of the visitors to the Shrine includes a 16.2 km track from Katra to *Bhavan* including Bhaironghati , which has been laid with titles, widened, smoothened with parapets on the valley side and retaining walls to prevent landslides and slips. Along the track rain-cum-shelter sheds, view points, cafeterias and drinking water-stand posts have been constructed. Also powerful sodium vapour lamps have been installed for making the yatra easy. Considerable progress has been made to cover the highly vulnerable stretches between Sanjichat and *Bhavan*. A number of vatikas en route to Banganga

Exhibit–7.2
Organisational Structure of Shrine Board

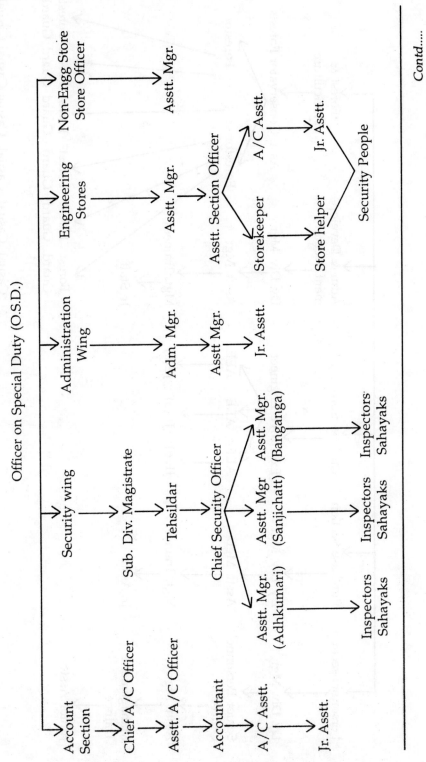

Contd.....

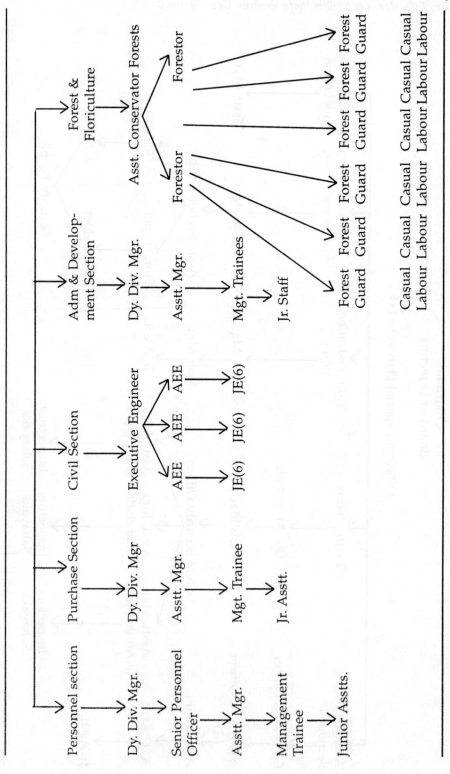

Source : Shrine Board Development Report 2000

Exhibit–7.3

Different Sections of Administration in Shrine Board

Bhavan

Adm. Section

1. Accommodation
2. Stores
3. Bhojanalaya
4. Sanitation
5. Dispensary
6. Issue of Blankets
7. Electric Wing
8. Prasad shop
9. Souvenir shop

Accounts Section

1. Revenue Collection
2. Collection, Maintenance Security of Strong Room
3. Salary Administration
4. Monitoring cash & non-cash funds

Security Wing

1. Regulating & Facilitating yatra smoothly
2. Security at Bathing Ghats
3. Security while waiting in queues & while Darshan
4. Checking of yatra slips
5. Frisking of visitors
6. Coordinating activities of different forces viz. Police, BSF, CRPF etc.

Contd.....

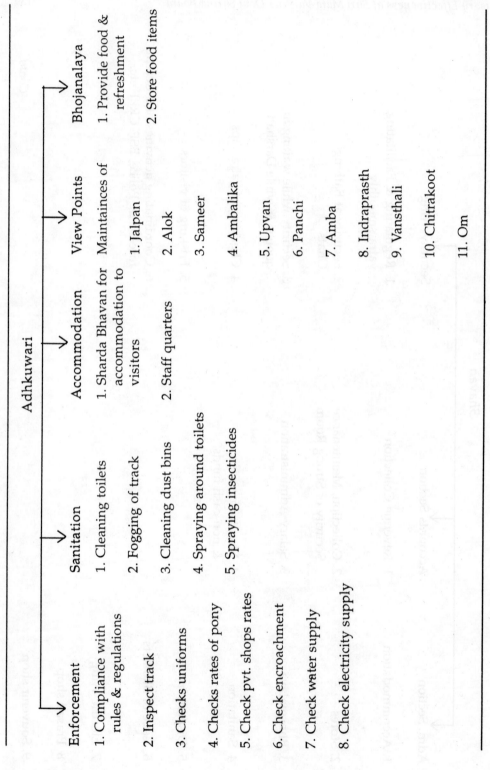

Adhkuwari

Enforcement	Sanitation	Accommodation	View Points	Bhojanalaya
1. Compliance with rules & regulations	1. Cleaning toilets	1. Sharda Bhavan for accommodation to visitors	Maintainces of	1. Provide food & refreshment
2. Inspect track	2. Fogging of track	2. Staff quarters	1. Jalpan	2. Store food items
3. Checks uniforms	3. Cleaning dust bins		2. Alok	
4. Checks rates of pony	4. Spraying around toilets		3. Sameer	
5. Check pvt. shops rates	5. Spraying insecticides		4. Ambalika	
6. Check encroachment			5. Upvan	
7. Check water supply			6. Panchi	
8. Check electricity supply			7. Amba	
			8. Indraprasth	
			9. Vansthali	
			10. Chitrakoot	
			11. Om	

Contd.....

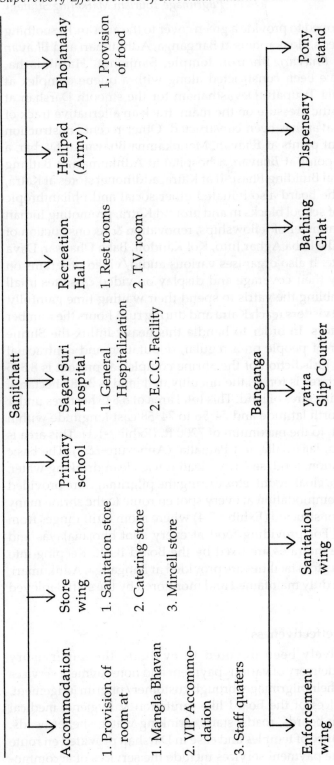

Sanjichatt

Accommodation
1. Provision of room at
   1. Mangla Bhavan
   2. VIP Accommodation
   3. Staff quaters

Store wing
1. Sanitation store
2. Catering store
3. Mircell store

Primary school

Sagar Suri Hospital
1. General Hospitalization
2. E.C.G. Facility

Recreation Hall
1. Rest rooms
2. T.V. room

Helipad (Army)

Bhojanalay
1. Provision of food

Banganga

Enforcement wing
1. Checking uniform
2. Checking pony rates
3. Checking begging
4. Checking ID cards
5. Checking encroachment
6. Checking water supply

Sanitation wing
1. Bathroom cleaning
2. Cleaning track

yatra Slip Counter
1. Issue general slips
2. Issue priority slips

Bathing Ghat

Dispensary

Pony stand

Source : SMVDSB Development Report 2000

and to *Bhavan* have been developed to provide a green cover to the area and a soothing feeling to the pilgrims. Pony sheds, cloak rooms at Banganga, Adhkumari and *Bhavan* and shopping complexes at *Bhavan*, Bhairon temple, Sanjichat, Hathimatha, Adhkumari and Banganga have been constructed along with a queue complex at *Bhavan* on the lines of Tirumula Tirupati Devasthanam for the smooth Darshan at the Cave. In order to reduce traffic pressure on the main track an alternative track of 5.5 km from Adhkumari to *Bhavan* has been constructed. Other recent construction works include sewage treatment plants at *Bhavan*, Manokamna Bhavan at Darbar, a staff colony near Panchi view point at *Bhavan*, a hospital at Adhkumari, a Bathing ghat at Banganga, Niharika, Sarai Building Phase-II at Katra, additional stores at Katra, Pony stands near Katra, etc. The board also initiated other social and philanthropic activities like the construction of school blocks in and around Katra, promoting Indian culture studies by providing a number of fellowships, renovation & reconstruction of religious and historical places like Baba Aghar Jitto, Kol Kandoli, Baba Dhansar, Deva Mai Temple, Bhim Ghar fort, etc. It also organises various audio/video programs on religious festivals supported by their coverage and display on video cassettes in all the buildings at *Bhavan* for enabling the yatris to spend their waiting time gainfully. In a day an average 10000-15000 visitors reach Katra and during rush hours the number may reach to 20000-25000 visitors. In order to handle this heavy influx the Shrine Board employs a large number of people on a regular, deputation and contractual basis. The total area within the jurisdiction of the Shrine complex at present is 8,845 hectares out of which 3,783 hectares is forest, the uncultivated land is 3,783 hectares, buildings are constructed on 21 hectares of land. This total area of 8,845 hectares under the Board lies $32^0 59'$ to $33^0 3'$ north latitude and $74^0 56$ to $74^0 58$ east longitude within the minimum altitude of 2700 ft. to the maximum of 7200 ft. (Exhibit-1.1). This area is steep and watered by Anzinalla, Jajjarnalla and Painalla. (Annexure-2&3). The basic needs like those of accommodation, food, security, clean track, clean drinking water, provision of blankets, sanitation, cloak room, etc., during the pilgrimage are provided by the Board. For providing accommodation at every spot en route to the shrine many bhavans (building) have been constructed (Exhibit-7.4) where room tariff ranges from Rs 300/- to Rs. 600/- per day. For providing food at every spot bhojanalayas and cafeteria are constructed where the rates are fixed by the Board itself. Keeping into consideration the needs of the visitors facilities are provided at Banganga, Adhkumari, Sanjichat and *Bhavan* which are duly maintained and monitored by the staff deployed by the Board for this purpose.

Measurement of supervisory effectiveness

This chapter has exclusively been devoted to evaluate the supervisory effectiveness of the Board in the delivery of various payment and non-payment services to the pilgrims/visitors during their pilgrimage through customer/pilgrim judgement. The various non-payment services of the Board like sanitation & hygiene, medical facility, telecommunication, sign boards, roads, stairs, drinking water, shelter heads, cloak rooms, blankets, maintenance of temples and ease in Darshan provided en route are taken into consideration. The payment services include the services of accommo-

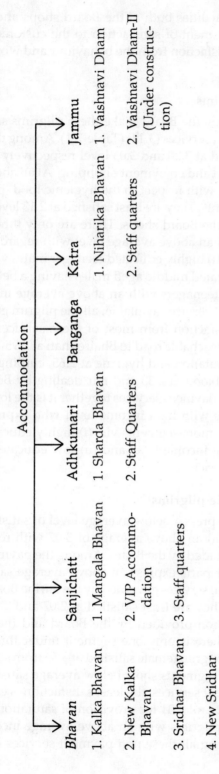

Exhibit-7.4

Accommodation at different spots of the pilgrimage

Accommodation

Bhavan

Sanjichatt
1. Kalka Bhavan
2. New Kalka Bhavan
3. Sridhar Bhavan
4. New Sridhar Bhavan
5. Lakshmi Bhavan
6. Saraswati Bhavan
7. Durga Bhavan
8. Gauri Bhavan
9. Vaishnavi Bhavan

Adhkumari
1. Sharda Bhavan
2. Staff Quarters

Banganga
1. Niharika Bhavan
2. Staff quarters

Katra
2. VIP Accommodation
3. Staff quarters

Sanjichatt
1. Mangala Bhavan

Jammu
1. Vaishnavi Dham
2. Vaishnavi Dham-II (Under construction)

Source : Shrine Board Development Report 2000

dation, food, catering and retailing facilities both at the Board shops and the shops given on contractual basis. The assessment of satisfaction to the customers in these services is complemented by their satisfaction from the behaviour and working of the supervisory staff of the Board.

Satisfaction among local male pilgrims

The payment services provided by the Board make these pilgrims satisfied less (2.79) as compared to the non-payment services (3.14) (Table-7.1). Among the payment services this group feels more satisfied at 3.20 and 3.03 level respectively for fairness of retail service, governed by the Board and enjoyment-shopping. At an above average level of 3.01 they observe satisfaction with respect to the hygienic food provided by the Board outlets, dhabas and restaurants. They are least satisfied at 2.13 level regarding the fixed price of commodities from the Board shops. There are only three segments under this group who feel satisfied at an above average level with regard to all these payment services taken together viz. (i) highly educated teenager males with a below average income(3.39), (ii) highly educated middle aged males having a below average income (3.13) and (iii) low educated teenagers with an above average income (3.02) respectively. Among the non-payment services available, all the pilgrim groups taken together observe above average satisfaction from most of these services except for maintenance of Garbjoon at 2.95, approachable road to Bhairoghati at 2.95, helpfulness of Board staff at 2.74, provision of sanitation and hygiene at 2.65, curbing of begging practice at 2.58, easy darshan at Garbjoon at 2.33 and fair dealing by Board staff at 1.82 respectively. Taking all these non-payment services together it is the low-educated middle aged non-local male pilgrims with high income level who express a below average of 2.81 level followed by two more segments viz. (i) highly educated old age male pilgrims with an above average income level and (ii) low educated teenagers with an average income level at 2.91 each.

Satisfaction among non-local female pilgrims

The female non-local pilgrims express a below average level of satisfaction from the payment services at 2.61 level and an above average of 3.07 with respect to the non-payment services (Table-7.2) provided by the Board. Among the payment services these females like their male counter parts express an above average satisfaction of 3.38 level regarding fairness in the retail services governed by the Shrine Board followed by enjoyable shopping at 3.1 level. They are least satisfied at 2.07 and 2.1 level from the easy availability of accommodation provided by the Board and the reasonable charges for such accommodation. There is only one segment under this group viz. low educated middle aged non-local pilgrim female satisfied at 3.55 from such payment services by the Board while all other segments show below average satisfaction from such services. Among the non-payment services, the least satisfaction is expressed for fair dealing by the Board staff at 2.02 and 2.31 for provision of sanitation & hygiene. The highly young non-local female pilgrims with an above average income express least satisfaction at 2.75 level regarding all these non-payment services of the Board taken together. However, their low educated teenager counterparts with a below average income level express the highest satisfaction at 3.43 score.

Satisfaction among local male pilgrims

Like their non-local counter parts, the local male pilgrims show a below average satisfaction at 2.7 with respect to non-payment services provided by the board (Table-7.3). Among these services it is the fairness in shopping, enjoyable shopping and cooperation of shop place above average level of 3.18, 3.47 & 3.55 respectively. All other payment services satisfy them at a below average level and the least satisfaction is derived from fixed prices in these relevant services during shopping. There are only three segments among this group viz. (i) low educated middle aged males with an above average income 3.35, (ii) low educated income (3.09) and (iii) high educated old aged males with an above average income (3.00) who are satisfied at a near average and above average level. However, all other segments express below average satisfaction. This group derives an above average of 3.18 satisfaction from the non-payment services.

Among all these services this group is satisfied by the over-all working of the Board at 4.04 of above average level followed by satisfaction from the infrastructure provided by the Board at 3.73 and maintenance of temples at 3.73. It is the fairness in dealing by Shrine Board staff which turns the pilgrims less satisfied at 1.42 level followed by provision of sanitation and hygiene at 2.17. It is the low educated middle aged males with a below average income level who derive the highest above average satisfaction of 3.76 level from such non-payment services taken altogether followed by high educated old aged male, with an above average income at 3.4 level.

Satisfaction among local female pilgrims

All the local female pilgrim segments under study are satisfied at an above average level with respect to the payment and non-payment services at 3.18 and 3.44 respectively. Among the payment services they are highly satisfied with the provision of tasty and delicious food provided by Shrine Board outlets at 3.83 level; similarly among the non-payment services they show the highest satisfaction of 4.00 each from the provision of better infrastructure, approachable temples and proper positioning of sign boards along the whole track. The highest of above average satisfaction from payment services at 4.09 and 3.9 for non-payment services has been derived by high educated old aged females with an average income level. However, the non-payment services taken together make all this local female group satisfied at an above average level. (Table–7.3)

Satisfaction among non-local male non-pilgrims

Like their non-local male pilgrims, the non-local male non-pilgrims reflect a below average of 2.91 for the payment services of the Board and an above average of 3.34 for the non-payment services (Table-7.4). Among the payment services it is the fixed price of retail services at 2.27 and reasonable food prices at 2.64 from which visitors derive least satisfaction.

Among the non-payment services, fair dealing by the Board staff (1.82) and easy darshan at Garbjoon (2.56) which bring down the level of satisfaction, all other non-payment services show an above average satisfaction level. The Table further reflects that the least satisfied segments in his group with respect to payment services are (i) low educated middle aged males with a below average income (2.09), (ii) low educated counter parts with an average income (2.14) and (iii) low educated teenagers with a below average income (2.43). Further there are only two segments viz. (i) low educated teenagers with a below average income (2.81) and low educated middle aged males with an average income (2.97) who show a below average satisfaction with respect to all the non-payment services taken together.

Satisfaction among non-local female non-pilgrims

A below average of 2.27 and a near average of 3.1 level with respect to payment and non-payment services by the Board respectively is reflected by the female non-pilgrims non-local visitors (Table-7.5). The least satisfying payment services are (i) fixed price of retail services (2.33), (ii) reasonable tariff for accommodation (2.37) (iii) cheapness in food prices (2.53) etc. Among the non-payment services the least satisfying are (i) fairness in dealing by the Board staff (1.54), (ii) easily approachable road to Bhairoghati (2.43) and easy darshan at Garbjoon (2.48) etc. The Table further explains that all the segments under this group show a below average score of satisfaction except for high educated middle aged females with an above average income (3.00) which show only an average satisfaction from the payment services. Half of the segments in the female non-pilgrim group are satisfied at an above average level of satisfaction and half of them show a below average satisfaction from these non-payment services of the Board. The highly satisfied is the low educated old aged females with a below average income segment (3.51) and the least satisfied is the high educated middle aged females with an average income (2.64).

Satisfaction among local non-pilgrim males

Throughout a below average satisfaction score has been expressed with regard to the payment (2.88) and non-payment services (2.77) of the Board by the local non-pilgrim male visitors (Table-7.6). There are only three payment services viz. (i) enjoyment in retail services (3.42) (ii) fairness in retailing (3.36) and (iii) cooperative retailers (3.29) which make these visitors satisfied at an above average level. Among the non-payment services it is the (i) over-all satisfactory working of the Board (3.86), (ii) provision of proper lighting (3.39) (iii) provision of proper sign boards (3.36), (iv) provision of adequate blankets (3.36) (v) provision of telecom facility (3.08) (vi) maintenance of temples (3.04), (vii) sanitation and hygiene (3.04) which keep the satisfaction score high. The least below average satisfaction score of 1.91 and 1.97 has been derived by high educated middle aged males with an above average income and high educated old age males with an average income respectively from the payment services of the Board. Further, the Table reflects that the aforesaid two segments again show the least satisfaction score of 1.34 and 1.86 from the non-payment services.

Exhibit-7.5

Profile of Accommodation provided by Shrine Board with Tariff and Free of Cost Facilities

S.No	Name	No. of Rooms	Tariff	Free of cost facilities			
				Cloak room	Blanket Counter	Bhojanalaya	Laundry
(1)	(2)	(3)	(4)	(5)	(6)	(7)	(8)
	At Bhavan						
1	Kalika Bhavan	42		-	-	-	-
	a) 4 beds room	-	Rs.450/-				
	b) 2 beds room	-	Rs.300/-				
	c) Extra person		Rs.45/-				
2	New Kalika Bhavan	10	"	-	-	-	-
3	Sridhar Bhavan	18	"	1	1	-	-
4	Lakshmi Bhavan	-	-			-	-
	a) VIP accommodation	-	-			-	-
	b) Rooms for staff	-	-			-	-
5	Saraswati Bhavan	3	"	1	1		
	a) Rooms for BSF personnel	-					
	b) Rooms for P.H.E. staff	-					
	c) 3 big halls (free of cost)	-					
6	Durga Bhavan	-		1	1	1	1
	a) Rooms for CID personnel	-					
7	Gauri Bhavan	10					
	a) 13 rentable huts	-					
8	Vaishnavi Bhavan	12					

Contd.....

(1)	(2)	(3)	(4)	(5)	(6)	(7)	(8)
	At Sanjichatt						
1	Mangala Bhavan	8			1		
	a) 1 Dormitory of 10 beds						
	b) VIP accommodation						
	c) Rooms for staff						
	At Katra						
1	Niharika Bhavan	44					
	a) 28 double beds room						
	I) Carpeted		Rs.375/-				
	ii) Non-carpeted		Rs. 300/-				
	b) 16 four beds room	–					
	ii) Carpeted		Rs.525/-				
	ii) Non-carpeted		Rs. 450/-				
	c) VVIP accommodation highly furnished	3					
2	Vishram ghar at Niharika complex	–					
	a) 10 beds dormitory		Rs. 300/-				
	b) 8 beds dormitory		Rs.240/-				
	c) Extra person		Rs 30/-				
	At Jammu						
1	Vaishnavi Dham	12	Rs 450/-	1		1	
	a) 12 A/C rooms	–					
	b) 11 dormitories		Rs 25 per bed				
	c) 4 VIP suits						

Source: Shrine Board Central Office, Katra

Exhibit–7.6
Retail Outlets of Shrine Board

S.No	Outlet	Retail Activity
1	Bhaint Shop at *Bhavan*	Selling Prasad, coconut, chuni etc. @ Rs. 21/- per prashad pack
2	Souvenir Shop at *Bhavan*	Selling Chuni, Chola, sarees offered or touched with Deity as Souvenirs Cassettes of Mata bhaints and bhajans
3	Cafeterias en route	Selling tea, coffee, snacks & milk at no-profit no-loss basis en route to the track
4	Souvenir shop at Vaishnavi Dham, Jammu	Selling Chuni, Chola, sarees offered or touched with Deity as Souvenirs Selling Prashad Sells cassettes of Mata bhaints and bhajans

Satisfaction among local non-pilgrim females

There is only one segment under this group viz. high educated young females with an average income under study. This segment throughout reflects an above average and near average score of satisfaction. viz. 3.00 for the payment services and an above average of (3.07) score for the non-payment services of the Board (Table-7.6).

The relationship among group-cum variable-wise customer satisfaction regarding the supervision of the Shrine Board during the Vaishno Devi Pilgrimage with the over-all satisfaction has been identified with the help of four linear equations (Exhibit-7.7) of multiple regression which explain the nature of association between over-all and variable-wise satisfaction among all the four groups. The results indicate that non-local visitors, whether they are pilgrims or non-pilgrims, show positive association with all the variables except for variable 'B' (non-payment services like sanitation, drinking water, cloak room, blankets, telecom, etc), which has lowered the over-all satisfaction level in case of non-local pilgrim group (equation-2). Here variable 'C' (maintenance of temples by the Shrine Board) has shown the highest significance followed by variable 'D' (supervision by the Shrine Board Staff) (equation-2). The local visitors have expressed both positive and negative association. They have expressed variable 'C' as least important (equation (1&3). The relative coefficients of

Exhibit–7.7

S.No	Groups	Four Linear Equations
1	Local Pilgrims	2.213+0.572(AX1)+0.402(BX2)-0.237(CX3)-0.2000(DX4)
2	Non-Local Pilgrims	2.367+0.009(AX1)-0.492(BX2)+0.530(CX3)+0.492(DX4)
3	Local Non-Pilgrims	4.332-0.572(AX1)+1.397(BX2)-1.462(CX3)+0.794(DX4)
4	Non-Local Non-Pilgrims	0.899+0.044(AX1)+0.134(BX2)+0.360(CX3)+0.495(DX4)

Note:

    A = Payment Services of Shrine Board

    B= Non-Payment Services of Shrine Board

    C= Maintenance of Temples by Shrine Board

    D= Supervision of Shrine Board Staff

multiple determination R^2 are shown in Table 7.9. A reasonable level of 60% variation in satisfaction scores is explained for local non-pilgrims whereas no other group explains a higher level of variation in satisfaction. These equations when plotted on a regression plane showed larger scatterness. The multiple 'R' between independent and dependent variables identifies a positive, higher degree of association at .78 and .56 only for local non-pilgrims and local pilgrims respectively. Since the calculated values of 'F' at 5 per cent level of significance is higher in the case of two groups under study viz. 7.97 for non-local pilgrims and 5.05 for non-local non-pilgrims than the table values of 2.37 and 2.45 at V_1V_2 (d.f.) of 4,340 and 4,108 respectively. This indicates that with a confidence level of 95 per cent the variables under study do not have equal impact on the satisfaction of customers regarding supervision by the Shrine Board and show varying effect on the over-all customer satisfaction. The other two groups have the lower calculated values at 95 per cent confidence level at 2.67 for local pilgrims and 3 for local non-pilgrims against a lesser Table value of 2.78 and 3.84 at 4,24 and 4,8 d. f.(v1 v2) respectively. This states that with a confidence level of 95 per cent, the variables under study show an equal impact on the satisfaction of these groups during their pilgrimage.

The marketing orientation and customer satisfaction which arrived at only a near average of 3.09 (Table-7.7) has been proved convergently valid as the proportion of pilgrims and non-pilgrims falling under average region of over-all satisfaction at 3.02 and 3.14 (Table 7.10) has been estimated as 40.11 and 44.44 respectively as against 11.76 and 48.13 of below average and above average in case of pilgrims and 7.14 and 48.42 of non-pilgrims respectively.

Strategic Action

The extent of marketing orientation with reference to over-all satisfaction (Table 7.7 & 7.10) within the framework of pilgrimage requirements suggests a well-planned and properly monitored strategic action for creating and maintaining marketing culture in the services of the Shri Mata Vaishno Devi Shrine Board.

One of the strategic actions emerging from the findings suggests marketing efforts not only to retain the present level of marketing orientation regarding those services where both pilgrim and non-pilgrim groups not only enjoy an 'above average' score of satisfaction but also to take it to the highest possible level on the 5 point (5———1) satisfaction scale.

47.48% of the pilgrims and 47.02 of non-pilgrims expressed an above average score of satisfaction regarding the payment services offered by the Board. It is the availability of choicest food and affordable/cheap prices of food items that make 50% of the pilgrims satisfied at an above average level followed by hygienic food and fixed price in the retailing outlets governed by the Board. Mostly the highly educated pilgrim and non-pilgrim male visitors with average and above average income level within all three age groups express an above average satisfaction regarding these aforesaid services (Table 7.1 to 7.6). Similarly most of the highly educated male pilgrim and non-pilgrim visitors having an average and above-average income within all the given age groups are highly satisfied regarding the prices fixed at retailing outlets governed by the Board (Table 7.1 to 7.4).

Regarding the non-payment services offered by the Board 48.56% pilgrims and 48.37% non-pilgrims enjoy an 'above average' satisfaction where 49.59 % of non-pilgrims show an 'above average' satisfaction regarding maintenance of stairs with railings provided en route to the track to the cave followed by 49.19% of pilgrims who are satisfied at the same level with respect to provision of proper sign boards en route to the track. Here again the highly educated visitors falling in the average and above average income group and mostly of middle and old age show the highest satisfaction above the average level from these non-payment services (Table 7.1 to 7.5).

The maintenance of temples en route make 48.58% pilgrims and 47.22% non-pilgrims satisfied at an above average level whereas 49.16% of the pilgrims and 48.67% of non-pilgrims approve of good maintenance of temples and easy approachable road to these temples respectively. Such maintenance of temples is approved by highly educated, average and high income earning middle and old age visitors. The satisfaction from the payment and non-payment services offered by the Board is complemented with the over-all supervision of the Board and its staff where 49.81% pilgrims and 49.06% of non-pilgrims are satisfied with respect to the Board services at an average level. Here 52.25% non-pilgrims and 51.38 % pilgrims feel safe and protected during the journey, particularly between Katra and *Bhavan* due to the proper arrangement by the Board. These arrangements en route are highly satisfactory for more knowledgeable, average and high income earner middle and old age pilgrims and non-pilgrims (Table 7.1 -to-7.6).

It is, therefore, reflected that the pilgrims and non-pilgrims visitors with more knowledge and above average and average income standards are satisfied with such services even if they pay higher prices for them. Moreover, irrespective of the prices they expect better quality of service at such destinations.

Constant improvement in the present level of marketing culture is required under the second type of strategy about all such services where only an average level of satisfaction is observed by the pilgrim and non-pilgrim groups. 45.93% non-pilgrims and 42.11% pilgrims observe an average satisfaction from the payment services offered by the Board. 43.6% non-pilgrims and 39.93% pilgrims are satisfied at an average level regarding the non-payment services. The maintenance of temples makes 44.09% non-pilgrims and 39.95% pilgrims satisfied at an average level followed by the supervision of the Board for which 42.77% non-pilgrims and 42.08% pilgrims express an average satisfaction. An average satisfaction with respect to reasonable charges for the accommodation provided by the Board is expressed by as many as 54.43% of non-pilgrims who have different educational backgrounds with low and average income level falling both middle and old age groups. (Table 7.1 to 7.6)

46.43% non-pilgrims show an average satisfaction for easy approachable road to Bhairoghati followed by telecom services which make 44.92% non-pilgrims falling in all-age groups but mostly low educated and earning not more than an average income (Table 7.1–7.6), at an average level. It is the over-all working of the Shrine Board which makes 45.46% of non-pilgrims satisfactory at an average level followed by helpfulness of the Board staff and the feeling of being in safe and protected hands which make 44.58% and 44.27% middle and old age pilgrims with less education and earning average and less than average income, satisfied respectively at an average level (Table 7.1–7.6). Here average satisfaction is reflected by an average and less than average income earner with a low educational background who cannot afford to pay much but expects an average satisfaction from whatever he pays for these services.

Among the payment and non-payment services 12.11% highly educated pilgrims falling in all the age groups and earning more than average income express a below average satisfaction score regarding the medical facilities provided by the Board. 11.94% and 11.91% of the middle and old age pilgrims with high educational back-ground, earning either average or more than average income show a below average satisfaction from cheap rates of food items and provision of tasty and delicious food respectively.

The over-all working of the Shrine Board and the easily approachable road to the temples en route made 12.24% and 11.76% middle and old age highly educated pilgrims with average and above average income, non-satisfied and put these services in a below average region (Table 7.1–7.6 & 7.10)

These segments of visitors expressing a below average satisfaction reduce the over-all satisfaction to a great extent and thus they need immediate attention for constant improvement and immediate action for providing them satisfactory services and supervision so that they become an asset by speaking good words about the functioning of the Board.

Table–7.1

Mean Scores of Marketing Effectiveness Measured through Non-Local Male Pilgrim Judgement w.r.t Supervisory Effectiveness of Shrine Board

Variables	Age Group-I Up to 25 Yrs.						Age Group-II 25 to 50 Yrs.						Age Group-III Above 50 Yrs.					
Income →	Inc-1		Inc-2		Inc-3		Inc-1		Inc-2		Inc-3		Inc-1	Inc-2		Inc-3		X
Education →	E-1	E-2	E-1	E-2	E-1	E-2	E-1	E-2	E-1	E-2	E-1	E-2	E-1	E-1	E-2	E-1	E-2	
(1)	(3)	(4)	(5)	(6)	(7)	(8)	(8)	(9)	(10)	(11)	(12)	(13)	(14)	(15)	(16)	(17)	(18)	(19)
Paid Services of Shrine Board																		
1. Adequate accommodation	2.67	3.33	2.50	2.00	3.00	1.00	2.50	3.50	2.71	3.00	2.91	3.00	4.00	4.00	2.83	3.60	2.50	2.89
2. Easily available accommodation	2.44	3.67	2.50	2.00	2.00	2.00	3.00	3.50	2.42	2.58	1.64	2.63	3.00	4.00	2.25	3.20	2.25	2.65
3. Reasonable Charge	2.67	3.33	2.00	2.00	3.00	2.00	2.00	3.50	2.36	2.70	2.45	2.60	3.00	2.00	2.80	3.60	1.91	2.58
4. Hygienic food	3.08	3.25	3.50	3.67	3.17	3.00	2.00	3.33	2.94	2.85	2.55	2.71	3.00	3.20	2.95	2.75	3.21	3.01
5. Tasty & delicious food	2.77	3.50	3.00	2.67	3.17	3.00	2.00	3.33	2.77	2.61	2.27	2.53	3.00	3.00	2.58	2.75	2.92	2.82
6. Cheap rates of food	2.69	3.25	3.00	2.00	3.50	3.67	3.00	3.80	2.55	3.03	2.00	1.79	4.00	2.40	2.00	2.63	2.22	2.80
7. Food of different variety	2.77	3.25	2.75	2.00	3.17	2.00	2.50	3.17	2.61	2.85	2.91	2.47	2.50	2.80	2.74	2.63	2.56	2.69
8. Enjoyable shopping	3.38	3.00	2.50	3.33	3.25	4.50	3.00	2.33	3.45	3.31	3.09	3.42	2.00	2.00	2.85	3.14	2.90	3.03
9. Cooperative shopkeepers	3.38	3.67	2.75	3.50	2.50	3.50	3.00	2.00	3.24	2.93	3.27	2.76	2.00	2.00	3.00	2.86	2.71	2.89
10. Fair shopping	3.75	4.33	2.75	3.33	3.75	3.00	2.50	3.17	3.24	3.34	3.36	3.50	3.00	2.00	3.08	2.86	3.45	3.20
11. Fixed price at shops	1.50	2.67	2.25	2.00	2.75	2.00	2.00	2.83	1.63	1.60	1.37	3.55	2.00	1.00	2.80	2.14	2.17	2.13
X1	2.83	3.39	2.68	2.59	3.02	2.70	2.50	3.13	2.72	2.80	2.53	2.81	2.86	2.58	2.72	2.92	2.62	2.79
Non-Payment Services																		
1. Telecommunication	2.82	3.75	2.75	4.00	3.50	3.33	4.00	3.67	3.38	3.68	3.00	3.09	3.50	4.00	3.25	3.38	3.19	3.43
2. Medical facility	3.08	2.75	3.50	4.00	3.50	2.50	3.00	2.83	3.07	3.05	3.09	3.09	3.50	3.40	3.26	3.90	2.88	3.20
3. Sanitation & Hygiene	2.54	2.75	2.50	3.67	3.00	2.67	1.00	2.83	2.61	2.74	1.82	2.68	3.50	2.50	2.60	3.20	2.42	2.65
4. Better roads	3.23	3.50	2.25	3.75	3.00	3.00	3.50	3.50	3.38	3.46	2.91	3.45	3.50	3.67	3.50	3.60	3.31	3.32

Contd.....

(1)	(2)	(3)	(4)	(5)	(6)	(7)	(8)	(8)	(9)	(10)	(11)	(12)	(13)	(14)	(15)	(16)	(17)	(18)	(19)
5. Provision of proper light		3.77	3.75	3.75	3.50	4.00	4.00	3.50	3.67	3.33	3.36	2.82	3.77	3.50	3.67	3.45	3.90	3.19	3.58
6. Provision of proper sign boards		3.31	2.00	3.00	3.75	3.00	3.67	3.50	3.50	3.41	3.56	3.36	3.41	3.50	3.67	3.60	3.70	3.28	3.37
7. Stairs with railing		3.77	3.75	2.00	2.75	2.50	3.00	1.50	2.40	3.64	2.90	3.09	3.23	3.50	3.50	3.50	3.30	2.92	3.01
8. Provision of shelter sheds		3.54	2.25	3.50	3.50	3.17	3.00	1.50	3.67	3.48	3.66	2.91	3.38	3.50	4.00	3.30	4.10	2.94	3.26
9. Clean drinking water		3.85	4.25	3.50	3.75	3.67	3.67	2.50	2.67	3.45	3.31	3.09	3.62	3.50	3.50	3.25	4.10	3.25	3.47
10. Efficient Cloak Room		3.54	4.00	2.50	3.75	3.67	4.33	5.00	3.80	3.58	3.38	3.55	3.68	3.50	3.67	3.20	4.10	3.22	3.67
11. Adequate blankets		3.85	4.50	3.50	3.50	4.00	5.00	4.50	3.80	3.35	3.64	3.36	3.41	3.50	3.33	3.45	3.90	3.47	3.77
X2		3.39	3.39	2.98	3.63	3.36	3.47	3.05	3.30	3.33	3.34	3.00	3.35	3.50	3.54	3.31	3.74	3.10	3.34
Maintenance of Temples																			
1. Well maintained temples		3.31	4.00	3.50	4.00	3.50	4.00	4.00	3.83	3.42	3.46	3.18	3.32	4.00	3.25	3.25	3.80	3.49	3.61
2. Easily approachable temples		3.46	4.00	2.75	3.67	3.50	3.67	4.00	3.50	3.23	3.58	2.73	3.33	3.50	3.17	3.30	3.50	3.06	3.41
3. Well maintained Garbjoon		2.92	3.67	2.00	3.33	2.17	3.00	2.50	3.40	2.91	3.16	2.27	3.14	3.50	2.83	3.00	3.56	2.73	2.95
4. Easy darshan Garbjoon		2.54	3.67	2.00	2.00	1.50	1.50	2.00	3.40	2.42	2.24	2.00	2.59	3.00	2.00	2.20	2.57	2.03	2.33
5. Easily approchable Bharioghati		3.00	3.67	2.50	3.33	2.33	4.00	2.50	3.50	3.15	2.53	2.00	2.55	3.00	3.50	2.80	3.11	2.64	2.95
X3		3.05	3.80	2.55	3.27	2.60	3.23	3.00	3.53	3.03	2.99	2.44	2.99	3.40	2.95	2.91	3.31	2.79	3.05
Supervision of Shrine Board																			
1. Good behaviour of the staff		3.42	3.25	3.75	4.00	3.67	4.00	2.50	3.50	3.41	3.36	2.91	2.86	4.00	3.33	3.42	2.88	3.36	3.39
2. Fair dealing of the staff		1.50	1.50	2.00	3.00	2.00	1.33	2.50	1.80	1.97	1.79	1.64	1.62	1.50	1.84	1.69	1.37	1.85	1.82
3. Helpful staff		2.86	2.00	3.25	3.00	2.80	3.00	3.50	2.25	3.05	3.04	2.37	2.53	3.00	2.00	2.89	2.63	2.42	2.74
4. Better infrastrucutre		3.57	4.00	3.75	4.00	3.80	3.67	4.00	3.75	3.78	3.43	3.27	3.37	3.00	2.00	3.67	3.13	3.08	3.49
5. Feeling of safety		3.00	4.00	3.25	3.00	2.40	3.00	4.00	3.50	3.24	3.14	3.89	2.62	2.50	2.00	3.44	2.88	2.81	3.10
6. Efficient Management of Shrine		3.00	4.00	3.50	3.00	2.20	3.67	4.00	2.25	4.14	3.46	3.55	3.30	3.00	2.00	4.00	3.00	3.30	3.26
7. Curb begging practice		2.84	2.25	1.75	3.00	2.33	2.00	2.50	2.80	2.84	2.87	2.73	3.05	3.00	2.17	2.63	2.75	2.31	2.58
8. Overall satisfactory working of board		4.18	3.50	4.25	4.00	4.25	4.00	3.50	4.50	3.77	3.91	3.64	3.50	4.00	3.75	4.06	4.00	3.62	3.91
X4		3.05	3.06	3.19	3.38	2.93	3.08	3.31	3.04	3.28	3.13	3.00	2.86	3.00	2.39	3.23	2.83	2.84	3.04
X234		3.16	3.39	2.91	3.43	2.96	3.26	3.12	3.29	3.21	3.15	2.81	3.07	3.30	2.96	3.29	3.10	2.91	3.14

Table-7.2

Mean Score of Marketing Effectiveness Measured through
Non-Local Female Pilgrim Judgement w.r.t. Supervisory Effectiveness of Shrine Board

Variables	Education	Age Group-I Up to 25 Yrs.				Age Group-II 25 to 50 Yrs.						Age Group-III Above 50 Yrs.						
		Inc-1		Inc-2	Inc-3	Inc-1		Inc-2		Inc-3		Inc-1		Inc-2		Inc-3		X
		E-1	E-2	E-1	E-2	E-1	E-2	E-1	E-2	E-1	E-2	E-1	E-2	E-1	E-2	E-1	E-2	
(1)	(2)	(3)	(4)	(5)	(6)	(7)	(8)	(9)	(10)	(11)	(12)	(13)	(14)	(15)	(16)	(17)	(18)	(19)
Paid Services of Shrine Board																		
1. Adequate accommodation		3.00	2.00	1.00	3.00	2.36	2.46	3.00	2.45	3.00	3.00	3.33	3.00	3.67	1.00	4.00	2.64	2.68
2. Easily available accommodation		1.00	2.00	1.00	3.00	2.27	2.00	3.00	2.00	2.00	1.50	3.00	3.00	3.00	1.00	1.00	2.29	2.07
3. Reasonable Charge		1.00	2.00	1.00	3.00	2.10	2.45	3.00	2.44	2.00	1.00	2.33	3.00	2.00	3.00	1.00	2.29	2.10
4. Hygienic food		3.33	3.20	3.00	2.00	2.82	2.89	4.00	2.82	3.00	3.50	3.43	1.00	3.38	1.40	1.00	2.57	2.71
5. Tasty & delicious food		3.33	3.00	3.00	4.00	2.64	2.67	4.00	3.33	3.00	3.00	2.43	1.00	2.75	2.60	1.00	2.43	2.76
6.Cheap rates of food		2.00	2.80	1.00	4.00	2.45	2.33	4.00	2.33	3.00	2.00	2.43	1.00	2.50	2.20	1.00	2.36	2.34
7. Food of different variety		2.67	3.20	2.00	4.00	2.27	2.44	4.00	2.55	3.00	2.50	2.00	1.00	3.25	2.80	1.00	2.43	2.60
8. Enjoyable shopping		3.00	2.00	3.00	2.00	2.40	3.27	4.00	2.90	4.00	3.50	3.33	3.00	3.29	2.67	4.00	3.25	3.10
9. Cooperative shopkeepers		3.00	2.00	4.00	2.00	2.60	2.64	4.00	2.82	2.00	3.00	3.33	3.00	2.71	1.67	3.00	2.17	2.75
10. Fair shopping		4.00	4.00	3.00	4.00	3.10	3.00	4.00	3.00	3.00	3.00	3.00	3.00	3.20	4.00	4.00	2.83	3.38
11. Fixed price at shops		3.00	3.67	2.00	1.00	1.60	2.10	2.00	2.60	2.00	1.00	1.33	2.00	3.00	2.33	2.00	3.17	2.18
X1		2.67	2.72	2.18	2.91	2.42	2.57	3.55	2.66	2.73	2.45	2.72	2.18	2.98	2.24	2.09	2.58	2.61
Non-Payment Services																		
1.Telecommunication		4.00	2.60	3.00	2.00	3.36	3.06	4.00	4.10	2.00	2.00	3.00	2.00	3.63	2.80	1.00	3.23	2.86
2. Medical facility		4.00	3.20	3.00	4.00	3.18	3.12	3.00	3.78	4.00	2.00	3.43	2.00	3.38	3.40	1.00	3.14	3.10
3. Sanitation & Hygiene		4.00	3.00	1.00	2.00	2.18	2.44	3.00	2.73	2.00	2.00	2.71	2.00	2.75	2.00	1.00	2.14	2.31
4. Better roads		3.33	3.80	4.00	4.00	3.55	3.24	4.00	3.27	2.00	3.00	2.71	4.00	3.25	3.40	1.00	3.21	3.24

Contd.....

(1)	(2)	(3)	(4)	(5)	(6)	(7)	(8)	(9)	(10)	(11)	(12)	(13)	(14)	(15)	(16)	(17)	(18)	(19)
5. Provision of proper lights		3.33	4.00	3.00	3.00	3.33	3.67	4.00	3.36	4.00	2.50	3.57	4.00	3.75	3.60	3.00	3.57	3.48
6. Provision of proper sign boards		3.33	4.20	3.00	3.00	2.89	3.56	4.00	3.10	3.00	4.00	3.71	4.00	3.50	3.80	3.00	3.57	3.48
7. Stairs with ralling		4.00	4.00	3.00	2.00	3.18	3.50	4.00	3.73	3.00	2.50	3.29	2.00	2.63	2.60	3.00	2.71	3.07
8. Provision of shelter sheds		4.00	3.40	3.00	2.00	3.36	3.28	4.00	3.27	2.00	3.50	3.29	4.00	3.63	3.40	3.00	2.79	3.25
9. Clean drinking water		4.00	3.60	4.00	4.00	3.27	3.39	4.00	3.27	3.00	2.50	3.57	4.00	3.88	4.00	3.00	3.14	3.54
10. Efficient Cloak Room		4.00	3.80	3.00	4.00	3.73	3.56	4.00	3.00	4.00	4.00	4.00	4.00	3.71	3.40	3.00	3.50	3.67
11. Adequate blankets		4.00	3.80	3.00	4.00	3.18	3.56	4.00	3.55	3.00	3.50	3.86	4.00	3.71	3.80	3.00	3.50	3.59
X2		3.82	3.58	3.00	3.09	3.20	3.31	3.82	3.38	2.91	2.86	3.38	3.27	3.44	3.29	2.27	3.14	3.24
Maintenance of Temples																		
1. Well maintained temples		4.00	3.20	4.00	3.00	3.55	3.65	3.00	3.64	3.00	3.50	3.43	4.00	3.75	2.80	3.00	3.50	3.44
2. Easily approachable temples		3.67	3.20	4.00	2.00	3.36	3.53	3.00	3.56	4.00	2.50	3.14	4.00	3.50	3.40	3.00	3.50	3.34
3. Well maintained Garbjoon		3.67	3.20	3.00	2.00	2.91	3.06	3.00	3.00	2.00	2.50	2.00	4.00	2.50	2.40	3.00	3.00	2.83
4. Easy darshan Garbjoon		2.67	2.80	1.00	2.00	2.18	2.65	3.00	3.18	2.00	3.00	2.00	4.00	2.00	1 20	3.00	2.57	2.45
5. Easily approchable Bharioghati		3.00	3.20	2.00	3.00	2.36	2.76	3.00	2.82	2.00	1.00	2.71	4.00	2.38	2.40	3.00	2.50	2.63
X3		3.40	3.12	2.80	2.40	2.87	3.13	3.00	3.24	2.60	2.50	2.66	4.00	2.83	2.44	3.00	3.01	2.94
Supervision of Shrine Board																		
1. Good behaviour of the staff		4.00	2.60	4.00	4.00	3.45	3.29	4.00	3.18	3.00	2.00	2.71	4.00	3.25	3.60	4.00	3.00	3.38
2. Fair dealing of the staff		2.00	2.00	2.00	1.00	2.00	2.23	2.00	1.92	3.00	3.50	2.43	2.00	1.50	1.60	2.00	1.17	2.02
3. Helpful staff		3.00	1.00	3.00	2.00	2.86	2.90	3.00	3.38	3.00	3.50	1.33	3.00	2.71	2.00	4.00	3.07	2.92
4. Better infrastrucutre		4.00	1.00	3.00	4.00	3.57	3.30	3.00	3.63	3.00	2.50	3.00	3.00	3.71	3.50	4.00	3.50	3.23
5. Feeling of safety		3.00	4.00	3.00	2.00	3.00	2.70	3.00	3.00	4.00	4.00	1.33	3.00	3.14	3.00	3.00	2.67	2.99
6. Efficient Management of Shrine		3.00	4.00	3.00	1.00	3.43	2.90	3.00	3.00	3.00	3.00	3.33	3.00	3.14	1.50	3.00	3.07	2.90
7. Curb begging practice		1.67	3.20	4.00	4.00	2.55	2.16	3.00	3.00	3.00	1.50	2.43	2.00	3.37	3.60	3.00	3.17	2.85
8. Over-all satisfactory working of Board		4.00	3.60	3.00	4.00	3.64	3.80	5.00	3.89	4.00	4.13	3.71	4.00	3.75	4.00	4.00	4.00	3.91
X4		3.08	2.68	3.13	2.75	3.06	2.91	3.25	3.13	3.25	3.02	2.53	3.00	3.07	2.85	3.38	2.96	3.00
X234		3.43	3.11	2.95	2.75	3.04	3.12	3.36	3.25	2.92	2.76	2.86	3.42	3.11	2.86	2.88	3.04	3.05

Table–7.3

Mean Scores of Marketing Effectiveness Measured through Local Male & Female Pilgrim Judgement w.r.t. Supervisory Effectiveness of Shrine Board

Variables	Age / Income / Education	MALE											FEMALE						
		Age Group-I Up to 25 Yrs.					Age Group-II 25 to 50 Yrs.				Age Group-III Above 50 Yrs.		Age Group-II 25 to 50 Yrs.			Age Group-III Above 50 Yrs.			
		Inc-1	Inc-1	Inc-2	Inc-2	Inc-1	Inc-2	Inc-2	Inc-3	Inc-2	Inc-3		Inc-1	Inc-1	Inc-2	Inc-1	Inc-2	Inc-2	
(1)	(2)	E-1 (3)	E-2 (4)	E-1 (5)	E-1 (6)	E-2 (7)	E-1 (8)	E-2 (9)	E-1 (10)	E-2 (11)	E-2 (12)	X (13)	E-1 (14)	E-2 (15)	E-2 (16)	E-2 (17)	E-1 (18)	E-2 (19)	X (20)
Paid Services of Shrine Board																			
1. Adequate accommodation		2.00	1.00	1.00	3.00	1.00	3.00	4.00	2.00	3.25	4.00	2.43	3.50	4.00	4.00	2.00	4.00	4.00	3.58
2. Easily available accommodation		1.00	3.00	1.00	3.00	2.00	2.00	3.00	1.00	2.00	3.00	2.10	3.00	3.00	1.00	2.00	3.00	5.00	2.83
3. Reasonable Charge		1.00	1.00	1.00	3.00	2.50	2.00	3.25	2.00	2.00	3.00	2.08	3.00	3.00	1.00	2.00	3.00	4.00	2.67
4. Hygienic food		3.00	3.00	3.00	4.00	2.33	2.00	3.50	3.00	3.00	3.00	2.98	4.00	3.00	2.50	4.00	4.00	5.00	3.75
5. Tasty & delicious food		2.00	3.00	2.00	3.00	2.33	2.00	3.50	2.00	2.00	3.00	2.48	3.00	4.00	3.00	4.00	4.00	5.00	3.83
6. Cheap rates of food		2.00	3.00	2.00	3.00	2.67	3.00	3.50	3.00	2.80	3.00	2.80	2.50	4.00	3.00	4.00	1.00	4.00	3.08
7. Food of different variety		4.00	4.00	1.00	3.00	2.00	4.00	3.00	4.00	2.60	2.00	2.96	3.50	3.00	3.50	1.00	4.00	5.00	3.33
8. Enjoyable shopping		4.00	3.00	2.00	4.00	3.33	4.00	4.00	3.00	3.40	4.00	3.47	4.00	3.00	3.50	4.00	4.00	4.00	3.75
9. Cooperative shopkeepers		4.00	5.00	2.00	4.00	2.00	4.00	3.33	4.00	3.20	4.00	3.55	4.00	3.00	3.00	1.00	1.00	5.00	2.83
10. Fair shopping		3.00	1.00	4.00	3.00	4.00	4.00	4.00	3.00	2.80	3.00	3.18	3.00	3.00	3.50	4.00	3.00	3.00	3.25
11. Fixed price at shops		1.00	2.00	1.00	1.00	2.67	1.00	1.75	2.00	2.20	1.50	1.71	3.00	2.00	3.50	2.00	1.00	1.00	2.08
X1		2.45	2.64	1.82	3.09	2.44	2.82	3.35	2.64	2.66	3.05	2.70	3.32	3.18	2.86	2.73	2.91	4.09	3.18
Non-Payment Services																			
1. Telecommunication		2.00	4.00	4.00	4.00	3.00	3.00	3.50	4.00	3.20	3.00	3.37	4.00	4.00	2.50	4.00	4.00	5.00	3.92
2. Medical facility		1.00	3.00	4.00	3.00	2.67	3.00	3.00	2.00	3.40	4.00	2.91	3.50	4.00	3.00	1.00	4.00	4.00	3.25
3. Sanitation & Hygiene		1.00	2.00	4.00	3.00	2.00	1.00	3.00	1.00	2.20	2.50	2.17	3.00	3.00	2.50	1.00	4.00	4.00	2.92
4. Better roads		4.00	4.00	4.00	3.00	3.33	4.00	4.25	1.00	3.80	2.50	3.39	4.00	3.00	4.00	4.00	4.00	4.00	3.83

Contd......

(1)	(2)	(3)	(4)	(5)	(6)	(7)	(8)	(9)	(10)	(11)	(12)	(13)	(14)	(15)	(16)	(17)	(18)	(19)	(20)
5. Provision of proper lights		4.00	1.00	3.00	4.00	3.33	3.00	4.50	2.00	3.40	3.50	3.17	4.00	3.00	4.00	4.00	4.00	4.00	3.83
6. Provision of proper sign boards		3.00	3.00	3.00	4.00	2.67	4.00	4.00	4.00	4.20	4.50	3.64	4.00	4.00	4.00	4.00	4.00	4.00	4.00
7. Stairs with railing		2.00	3.00	4.00	4.00	1.00	4.00	2.75	3.00	3.40	4.00	3.12	4.00	4.00	3.50	1.00	4.00	4.00	3.42
8. Provision of shelter sheds		4.00	2.00	4.00	4.00	2.33	4.00	3.25	3.00	4.00	3.50	3.41	4.00	4.00	3.00	1.00	4.00	4.00	3.33
9. Clean drinking water		2.00	1.00	4.00	4.00	2.33	3.00	3.00	4.00	3.40	3.50	3.02	3.50	3.00	3.00	4.00	4.00	4.00	3.58
10. Efficient Cloak Room		3.00	4.00	4.00	3.00	3.00	3.00	4.00	5.00	3.20	4.00	3.62	3.00	4.00	4.00	1.00	4.00	4.00	3.33
11. Adequate blankets		4.00	3.00	4.00	3.00	3.00	4.00	3.50	4.00	3.60	4.00	3.61	3.00	4.00	4.00	1.00	4.00	4.00	3.33
X2		2.73	2.73	3.82	3.55	2.61	3.27	3.52	3.00	3.44	3.55	3.22	3.64	3.64	3.41	2.36	4.00	4.09	3.52
Maintenance of Temples																			
1. Well maintained temples		4.00	3.00	4.00	4.00	4.00	4.00	4.00	4.00	2.80	3.50	3.73	3.50	5.00	3.00	4.00	4.00	4.00	3.92
2. Easily approachable temples		3.00	4.00	4.00	4.00	3.67	2.00	4.75	3.00	3.60	4.00	3.60	4.00	4.00	4.00	4.00	2.00	4.00	4.00
3. Well maintained Garbjoon		2.00	4.00	2.00	4.00	2.67	2.00	4.75	3.00	3.20	3.00	3.06	3.50	4.00	4.00	4.00	2.00	4.00	3.58
4. Easy darshan Garbjoon		3.00	2.00	2.00	3.00	2.33	2.00	2.50	1.00	3.00	2.00	2.28	3.00	2.00	2.00	4.00	2.00	3.00	2.67
5. Easily approchable Bhairoghati		2.00	4.00	4.00	3.00	3.33	3.00	2.00	1.00	2.60	3.50	2.84	3.00	4.00	3.50	1.00	2.00	3.00	2.75
X3		2.80	3.40	3.20	3.60	3.20	2.60	3.60	2.40	3.04	3.20	3.10	3.40	3.80	3.30	3.40	2.80	3.60	3.38
Supervision of Shrine Board																			
1. Good behaviour of the staff		3.00	3.00	4.00	5.00	2.00	2.00	4.25	2.00	3.00	3.00	3.13	4.00	4.00	3.00	4.00	4.00	4.00	3.83
2. Fair dealing of the staff		2.00	1.00	1.00	1.00	0.67	3.00	2.00	1.00	1.00	1.50	1.42	1.00	3.00	1.50	3.00	1.00	1.00	1.75
3. Helpful staff		4.00	2.00	3.00	5.00	3.00	3.00	4.00	3.00	3.40	4.00	3.44	4.00	3.00	3.00	4.00	2.00	5.00	3.50
4. Better infrastrucutre		2.00	4.00	3.00	5.00	3.00	4.00	4.25	4.00	4.00	4.00	3.73	4.00	4.00	3.00	4.00	4.00	5.00	4.00
5. Feeling of safety		3.00	3.00	3.00	5.00	3.67	4.00	3.50	3.00	3.40	3.50	3.51	4.00	4.00	3.00	4.00	3.00	5.00	3.83
6. Efficient Management of Shrine		3.00	4.00	2.00	4.00	2.50	4.00	3.00	4.00	3.80	4.50	3.48	4.00	4.00	2.00	4.00	3.00	4.00	3.50
7. Curb begging practice		3.00	3.00	3.00	3.00	2.00	3.00	2.50	4.00	2.60	3.00	2.91	3.00	2.00	2.50	4.00	3.00	4.00	3.08
8. Over-all satisfactory working of Board		4.00	5.00	4.00	5.00	3.33	3.00	4.50	4.00	3.60	4.00	4.04	4.50	3.00	4.00	4.00	4.00	4.00	3.92
X4		3.00	3.13	2.88	4.13	2.52	3.25	3.50	3.13	3.10	3.44	3.22	3.56	3.38	2.75	3.88	3.00	4.00	3.43
X234		2.84	3.09	3.30	3.76	2.78	3.04	3.54	2.84	3.12	3.40	3.18	3.53	3.61	3.15	3.21	3.27	3.90	3.44

Table-7.4

Mean Scores of Marketing Effectiveness Measured through Non-Local Male Non-Pilgrim Judgement w.r.t Supervisory Effectiveness of Shrine Board

Variables	Age Group-I Up to 25 Yrs.						Age Group-II 25 to 50 Yrs.						Age Group-III Above 50 Yrs.						
	Inc-1		Inc-2		Inc-3		Inc-1		Inc-2		Inc-3		Inc-1		Inc-2		Inc-3		X
Income / Education	E-1	E-2	E-1	E-2	E-1	E-2	E-1	E-2	E-1	E-2	E-1	E-2	E-1	E-2	E-1	E-2	E-1	E-2	
(1)	(3)	(4)	(5)	(6)	(7)	(8)	(9)	(10)	(11)	(12)	(13)	(14)	(15)	(16)	(17)	(18)	(19)	(20)	(21)
Paid Services of Shrine Board																			
1. Adequate accommodation	4.00	3.00	3.33	3.00	4.00	5.00	2.00	3.50	-3.50	3.60	3.00	4.00	4.00	2.00	4.00	4.00	2.00	3.10	3.39
2. Easily available accommodation	2.00	3.00	3.33	3.00	3.00	5.00	2.00	1.00	2.50	3.13	2.00	3.00	4.00	4.00	4.00	2.00	2.00	2.70	2.76
3. Reasonable Charge	2.00	3.00	3.33	3.00	3.00	5.00	1.00	2.50	2.00	3.07	2.00	3.67	2.00	3.00	2.00	2.67	3.00	2.80	2.72
4. Hygienic food	3.33	2.67	4.00	3.00	2.00	4.00	2.00	2.67	1.50	3.19	4.00	3.50	4.00	4.00	4.00	4.67	3.00	2.75	3.24
5. Tasty & delicious food	3.67	2.67	3.00	3.00	3.00	4.00	3.00	2.67	1.50	2.95	3.00	3.25	4.00	3.00	4.00	4.67	3.00	2.50	3.16
6. Cheap rates of food	2.00	1.00	3.50	3.00	3.00	4.00	2.00	1.33	2.00	2.90	3.00	3.50	2.00	4.00	1.00	4.00	3.00	2.29	2.64
7. Food of different variety	2.00	1.00	3.25	3.00	3.00	4.00	2.00	3.67	2.50	3.24	2.00	3.25	4.00	4.00	3.00	4.00	3.00	2.50	2.86
8. Enjoyable shopping	1.67	2.00	3.40	3.00	4.00	4.50	1.00	3.20	2.00	3.00	3.00	4.00	4.00	2.67	4.00	2.67	2.00	2.71	2.90
9. Cooperative shopkeepers	2.00	1.67	3.20	2.33	3.00	4.00	3.00	4.00	1.00	2.55	3.00	3.25	2.00	4.00	4.00	2.67	2.00	2.08	2.76
10. Fair shopping	4.00	3.67	3.00	3.33	3.00	4.00	4.00	2.60	2.00	3.63	3.00	3.00	4.00	3.00	4.00	3.33	2.00	3.85	3.30
11. Fixed price at shops	2.00	3.00	1.80	1.00	4.00	2.50	1.00	1.00	3.00	3.05	1.00	2.00	2.00	2.00	4.00	2.00	3.00	2.43	2.27
X1	2.61	2.43	3.19	2.79	3.18	4.18	2.09	2.56	2.14	3.12	2.64	3.31	2.73	3.36	3.45	3.33	2.55	2.70	2.91
Non-Payment Services																			
1. Telecommunication	4.00	4.00	4.40	3.67	4.00	3.00	4.00	3.80	4.00	3.63	4.00	2.20	4.00	3.00	4.00	4.00	4.00	4.00	3.77
2. Medical facility	4.00	1.00	3.00	3.00	4.00	5.00	4.00	3.20	4.00	3.50	4.00	4.00	4.00	4.00	4.00	3.33	4.00	3.43	3.64
3. Sanitation & Hygiene	4.00	1.00	3.40	3.00	4.00	5.00	4.00	2.20	3.00	3.48	3.00	3.56	4.00	4.00	2.00	3.67	3.00	3.13	3.30
4. Better roads	4.00	4.00	4.00	3.00	4.00	4.50	4.00	3.40	3.50	3.67	4.00	3.56	4.00	4.00	4.00	3.67	3.00	3.63	3.77

Contd.....

(1)	(2)	(3)	(4)	(5)	(6)	(7)	(8)	(9)	(10)	(11)	(12)	(13)	(14)	(15)	(16)	(17)	(18)	(19)	(20)	(21)
5. Provision of proper lights		4.00	4.00	2.60	3.00	4.00	4.50	4.00	3.80	4.00	3.90	4.00	3.78	4.00	4.00	4.00	3.33	2.00	3.88	3.71
6. Provision of proper sign boards		4.00	4.00	3.40	3.67	4.00	4.00	4.00	3.40	4.00	3.81	4.00	3.78	4.00	3.00	4.00	3.33	3.00	3.31	3.71
7. Stairs with railing		3.33	2.00	2.60	2.33	4.00	3.50	2.00	3.40	4.00	3.38	4.00	3.89	4.00	4.00	4.00	3.33	3.00	2.88	3.31
8. Provision of shelter sheds		4.00	4.00	3.80	3.67	4.00	4.50	4.00	3.40	4.00	3.80	4.00	3.25	4.00	4.00	3.00	3.33	3.00	3.69	3.75
9. Clean drinking water		4.00	3.33	2.80	4.00	4.00	4.00	4.00	3.40	4.00	3.81	2.00	3.75	4.00	4.00	4.00	3.33	3.00	3.44	3.60
10. Efficient Cloak Room		4.00	4.00	3.80	3.67	4.00	4.00	4.00	3.40	4.00	3.95	5.00	3.78	4.00	4.00	3.00	3.33	2.00	3.75	3.76
11. Adequate blankets		4.00	4.00	4.40	3.67	4.00	4.00	4.00	3.40	4.00	3.85	4.00	3.89	4.00	4.00	3.00	3.33	2.00	3.69	3.74
X2		3.94	3.21	3.47	3.33	4.00	4.18	3.82	3.35	3.86	3.71	3.82	3.59	4.00	3.82	3.55	3.45	2.91	3.53	3.64
Maintenance of Temples																				
1. Well maintained temples		4.00	2.67	3.40	3.00	3.00	4.00	4.00	3.20	4.00	3.60	4.00	3.22	4.00	4.00	3.00	3.33	3.00	3.36	3.49
2. Easily approachable temples		4.00	1.00	3.00	3.00	3.00	4.00	4.00	3.40	4.00	3.55	3.00	3.25	4.00	4.00	4.00	3.33	3.00	3.43	3.39
3. Well maintained Garbjoon		3.00	2.00	2.80	2.33	2.00	3.00	3.00	3.40	3.50	3.37	2.00	3.22	3.00	5.00	4.00	3.00	3.00	3.36	3.05
4. Easy darshan at Garbjoon		2.67	2.00	1.80	1.00	2.00	3.00	4.00	2.40	3.00	3.05	2.00	2.78	3.00	4.00	3.00	3.00	3.00	2.29	2.56
5. Easily approchable Bhairoghati		3.33	4.00	2.33	4.00	3.00	3.00	4.00	2.40	3.00	3.35	2.00	3.44	3.00	3.00	3.00	3.00	3.00	3.31	3.12
X3		3.40	2.33	2.67	2.67	2.60	3.40	3.40	2.96	3.50	3.38	2.60	3.18	3.40	4.00	3.40	3.13	3.00	3.15	3.12
Supervision of Shrine Board																				
1. Good behaviour of the staff		4.00	3.33	3.60	2.33	4.00	5.00	4.00	3.40	3.50	3.10	4.00	2.86	4.00	4.00	4.00	3.33	2.00	3.68	3.56
2. Fair dealing of the staff		1.00	1.00	1.50	2.00	2.00	2.00	1.00	1.80	1.50	1.67	2.00	2.00	2.00	2.00	2.00	2.00	3.00	2.32	1.82
3. Helpful staff		4.00	2.67	3.40	3.00	3.00	2.50	4.00	4.33	3.00	3.53	2.00	2.86	4.00	4.00	4.00	3.33	3.00	3.25	3.33
4. Better infrastructure		4.00	3.33	3.80	3.00	4.00	4.00	4.00	4.00	4.00	3.72	3.00	3.43	4.00	4.00	4.00	3.33	2.00	3.69	3.63
5. Feeling of safety		4.00	2.67	3.00	3.00	2.00	3.50	4.00	4.33	2.00	3.79	3.00	3.29	4.00	3.00	3.00	3.33	3.00	3.13	3.28
6. Efficient Management of Shrine		4.00	3.33	3.60	3.00	3.00	3.00	4.00	3.67	3.00	3.45	3.00	2.67	4.00	4.00	4.00	3.33	4.00	3.50	3.48
7. Curb begging practice		3.67	3.67	3.50	3.00	3.00	3.50	4.00	3.20	3.00	2.65	4.00	3.00	2.00	3.00	4.00	2.00	2.00	2.50	3.09
8. Over-all satisfactory working of Board		4.00	3.00	3.75	4.00	4.00	4.50	4.00	4.60	3.50	4.00	4.00	4.00	4.00	5.00	4.00	4.00	4.00	3.94	3.91
X4		3.58	2.88	3.27	2.92	3.13	3.50	3.63	3.67	2.94	3.24	3.00	3.01	3.50	3.75	3.63	3.08	2.88	3.25	3.26
X234		3.64	2.81	3.14	2.97	3.24	3.69	3.62	3.33	3.43	3.44	3.14	3.26	3.63	3.86	3.53	3.22	2.93	3.31	3.34

Table–7.5

Mean Score of Marketing Effectiveness Measured through Non-Local Female Non-Pilgrim Judgement w.r.t Supervisory Effectiveness of Shrine Board.

Variables	Age	Age Group-I Up to 25 Yrs.			Age Group-II 25 to 50 Yrs.				Age Group-III Above 50 Yrs.		X
	Income	Inc-1	Inc-2	Inc-3	Inc-1		Inc-2	Inc-3	Inc-2	Inc-3	
	Education	E-1	E-1	E-2	E-2	E-1	E-2	E-2	E-2	E-2	
(1)	(2)	(3)	(4)	(5)	(6)	(7)	(8)	(9)	(10)	(11)	(12)
Paid Services of Shrine Board											
1. Adequate accommodation		4.00	3.00	4.00	2.00	2.00	3.00	4.00	3.20	3.00	3.13
2. Easily available accommodation		2.00	3.00	4.00	2.00	2.00	2.00	4.00	3.00	1.00	2.56
3. Reasonable Charges		3.50	3.00	3.00	2.00	2.00	1.00	3.00	2.80	1.00	2.37
4. Hygienic food		3.00	2.00	3.00	1.60	3.50	2.00	2.00	3.43	2.50	2.56
5. Tasty & delicious food		3.00	2.00	4.00	2.60	3.00	2.00	3.00	2.86	2.50	2.77
6. Cheap rates of food		2.00	3.00	3.00	2.80	2.50	1.50	1.00	3.43	3.50	2.53
7. Food of different variety		2.67	2.00	3.00	3.60	3.50	1.50	3.00	2.80	3.50	2.84
8. Enjoyable shopping		3.33	2.00	2.00	3.60	4.00	2.50	4.00	3.20	3.50	3.13
9. Cooperative shopkeepers		3.00	2.00	2.00	1.33	3.50	2.00	4.00	2.80	4.00	2.74
10. Fair shopping		3.00	3.00	2.00	4.40	3.50	4.50	3.00	2.80	5.00	3.47
11. Fixed price at shops		2.00	1.00	2.00	3.80	2.00	3.00	2.00	2.20	3.00	2.33
X1		2.86	2.36	2.91	2.70	2.86	2.27	3.00	2.96	2.95	2.77
Non-Payment Services											
1. Telecommunication		3.33	4.00	3.00	3.20	3.00	2.50	4.00	4.29	3.00	3.37
2. Medical facility		3.33	4.00	4.00	3.20	3.00	2.50	4.00	4.00	2.50	3.39
3. Sanitation & Hygiene		3.00	4.00	2.00	2.00	2.00	2.00	4.00	3.14	2.00	2.68
4. Better roads		3.33	4.00	3.00	4.00	3.50	1.00	4.00	3.86	4.00	3.41

Contd.....

(1)	(2)	(3)	(4)	(5)	(6)	(7)	(8)	(9)	(10)	(11)	(12)
5. Provision of proper lights		3.33	4.00	4.00	4.00	3.00	2.00	4.00	3.43	3.50	3.47
6. Provision of proper sign boards		3.33	3.00	4.00	4.00	3.50	3.00	4.00	3.43	3.50	3.53
7. Stairs with railing		3.33	2.00	4.00	2.80	3.50	2.50	4.00	2.71	2.00	2.98
8. Provision of shelter sheds		3.33	2.00	4.00	4.00	3.50	2.50	4.00	4.00	3.50	3.43
9. Clean drinking water		3.33	4.00	4.00	4.00	2.50	3.00	4.00	3.14	4.00	3.55
10. Efficient Cloak Room		3.33	3.00	3.00	3.60	2.50	3.00	4.00	3.14	3.50	3.34
11. Adequate blankets		3.67	3.00	3.00	3.60	3.00	3.50	4.00	4.29	2.00	3.34
X2		3.33	3.36	3.55	3.49	3.00	2.50	4.00	3.58	3.05	3.32
Maintenance of Temples											
1. Well maintained temples		3.33	3.00	4.00	3.20	3.50	3.50	4.00	4.00	2.50	3.45
2. Easily approachable temples		3.33	1.00	4.00	3.30	3.50	3.00	4.00	4.00	2.50	3.18
3. Well maintained Garbjoon		3.67	3.00	4.00	3.60	3.00	3.50	3.00	3.20	3.00	3.33
4. Easy darshan at Garbjoon		2.33	3.00	3.00	3.00	2.00	1.50	3.00	2.00	2.50	2.48
5. Easily approchable Bhairoghati		2.00	3.00	3.00	3.00	2.00	1.50	3.00	2.40	2.00	2.43
X3		2.93	2.60	3.60	3.22	2.80	2.60	3.40	3.12	2.50	2.97
Supervision of Shrine Board											
1. Good behaviour of the staff		3.67	3.00	4.00	2.80	3.00	3.00	2.00	3.71	4.00	3.24
2. Fair dealing of the staff		1.33	2.00	3.00	1.20	1.00	1.00	1.00	1.33	2.00	1.54
3. Helpful staff		2.33	4.00	3.00	2.67	3.00	3.00	4.00	3.57	3.00	3.17
4. Better infrastructure		3.33	4.00	3.00	4.50	2.50	3.00	4.00	3.57	4.00	3.54
5. Feeling of safety		2.33	3.00	3.00	4.00	3.50	3.00	2.00	3.00	3.50	3.04
6. Efficient Management of Shrine		3.33	2.00	3.00	2.60	3.00	3.00	2.00	3.57	2.50	2.78
7. Curb begging practice		2.67	3.00	4.00	3.60	3.00	2.50	1.00	3.00	3.00	2.86
8. Over-all satisfactory working of Board		4.00	4.00	4.00	3.33	4.00	4.00	4.00	4.00	4.00	3.93
X4		2.87	3.13	3.38	3.09	2.88	2.81	2.50	3.22	3.25	3.01
X234		3.04	3.03	3.51	3.27	2.89	2.64	3.30	3.31	2.93	3.10

Table–7.6

Mean Score of Marketing Effectiveness Measured though Local Male & Female Non-Pilgrim Judgement w.r.t Supervisory Effectiveness of Shrine Board

		MALE											FEMALE
Variables	Age	Age Group-I Up to 25 Yrs.		Age Group-II 25 to 50 Yrs.					Age Group-III Above 50 Yrs.				Age Group-I Up to 25 Yrs.
	Income	Inc-1		Inc-1		Inc-2		Inc-3	Inc-1	Inc-2	Inc-3		Inc-2
	Education	E-1	E-2	E-1	E-2	E-1	E-2	E-2	E-1	E-2	E-2	X	E-2
(1)	(2)	(3)	(4)	(5)	(6)	(7)	(8)	(9)	(10)	(11)	(12)	(13)	(14)
Paid Services of Shrine Board													
1. Adequate accommodation		3.00	5.00	4.00	5.00	3.00	3.00	1.00	2.67	1.00	1.00	2.87	3.00
2. Easily available accommodation		4.00	5.00	3.00	5.00	2.30	2.00	1.00	2.11	1.00	1.00	2.64	3.00
3. Reasonable Charges		3.00	3.00	3.00	3.00	2.00	4.00	1.00	2.67	1.67	2.00	2.54	3.00
4. Hygienic food		1.00	2.00	4.00	2.00	3.00	2.50	1.00	2.33	1.67	4.00	2.35	2.00
5. Tasty & delicious food		3.00	4.00	4.00	4.00	3.00	2.50	1.00	2.56	1.67	4.00	2.97	2.00
6. Cheap rates of food		3.00	4.00	4.00	4.00	2.67	2.50	1.00	2.56	1.67	4.00	2.94	4.00
7. Food of different variety		3.00	4.00	3.00	4.00	2.67	3.00	1.00	2.67	1.67	4.00	2.90	2.00
8. Enjoyable shopping		3.00	5.00	3.00	5.00	2.67	3.50	4.00	3.33	2.67	2.00	3.42	4.00
9. Cooperative shopkeepers		4.00	3.00	4.00	5.00	2.00	3.00	4.00	3.22	2.67	2.00	3.29	3.00
10. Fair shopping		5.00	2.00	5.00	2.00	2.00	2.00	4.00	3.56	4.00	4.00	3.36	4.00
11. Fixed price at shops		2.00	3.00	2.00	3.00	3.00	2.50	2.00	2.00	2.00	2.00	2.35	3.00
X1		3.09	3.64	3.55	3.82	2.57	2.77	1.91	2.70	1.97	2.73	2.88	3.00
Non-Payment Services													
1. Telecommunication		4.00	4.00	4.00	4.00	3.67	3.50	1.00	3.00	1.67	2.00	3.08	5.00
2. Medical facility		3.00	3.00	3.00	3.00	3.67	4.00	1.00	3.00	1.67	2.00	2.73	3.00
3. Sanitation & Hygiene		4.00	2.00	4.00	2.00	3.67	3.50	1.00	3.22	3.00	4.00	3.04	2.00
4. Better roads		4.00	2.00	4.00	2.00	2.33	3.50	1.00	3.22	3.00	4.00	2.91	4.00

Contd......

(1)	(2)	(3)	(4)	(5)	(6)	(7)	(8)	(9)	(10)	(11)	(12)	(13)	(14)
5. Provision of proper lights		4.00	4.00	4.00	4.00	3.00	3.50	1.00	3.44	3.00	4.00	3.39	4.00
6. Provision of proper sign boards		4.00	4.00	4.00	4.00	2.67	3.50	1.00	3.44	3.00	4.00	3.36	4.00
7. Stairs with railing		2.00	2.00	2.00	2.00	2.67	3.00	1.00	2.33	1.67	2.00	2.07	2.00
8. Provision of shelter sheds		3.00	2.00	3.00	2.00	4.00	4.00	1.00	3.33	3.00	4.00	2.93	2.00
9. Clean drinking water		3.00	4.00	3.00	4.00	4.00	2.50	1.00	2.44	1.67	2.00	2.76	2.00
10. Efficient Cloak Room		4.00	3.00	4.00	3.00	4.00	2.50	1.00	2.44	1.67	2.00	2.76	2.00
11. Adequate blankets		4.00	3.00	4.00	3.00	4.00	4.00	1.00	3.56	3.00	4.00	3.36	4.00
X2		3.55	3.00	3.55	3.00	3.43	3.41	1.00	3.04	2.40	3.09	2.94	3.09
Maintenance of Temples													
1. Well maintained temples		3.00	3.00	3.00	3.00	4.00	4.00	2.00	3.43	2.00	3.00	3.04	4.00
2. Easily approachable temples		4.00	2.00	4.00	2.00	4.00	4.00	1.00	3.29	1.00	3.00	2.83	4.00
3. Well maintained Garbjoon		3.00	2.00	3.00	2.00	3.67	3.50	2.00	3.00	2.00	3.00	2.72	3.00
4. Easy darshan at Garbjoon		4.00	1.00	4.00	1.00	3.67	3.00	1.00	2.57	1.00	2.00	2.32	2.00
5. Easily approchable Bhairoghati		4.00	3.00	4.00	3.00	3.33	3.50	1.00	3.14	1.00	2.00	2.80	2.00
X3		3.60	2.20	3.60	2.20	3.73	3.60	1.40	3.09	1.40	2.60	2.74	3.00
Supervision of Shrine Board													
1. Good behaviour of the staff		3.00	1.00	4.00	1.00	3.67	3.00	1.00	2.89	3.00	4.00	2.66	3.00
2. Fair dealing of the staff		1.00	1.00	2.00	1.00	2.00	2.00	1.00	2.00	1.33	2.00	1.53	2.00
3. Helpful staff		3.00	4.00	1.00	4.00	3.67	3.00	1.00	2.40	1.00	3.00	2.61	2.00
4. Better infrastrucutre		1.00	4.00	3.00	4.00	4.00	3.50	1.00	3.14	1.00	2.00	2.66	4.00
5. Feeling of safety		3.00	2.00	3.00	2.00	3.33	3.50	1.00	2.86	1.00	2.00	2.37	3.00
6. Efficient Management of Shrine		4.00	2.00	4.00	2.00	3.67	4.00	1.00	3.29	1.00	2.00	2.70	4.00
7. Curb begging practice		4.00	1.00	4.00	1.00	1.67	3.00	4.00	3.88	2.33	2.00	2.69	3.00
8. Over-all satisfactory working of Board		3.00	5.00	3.00	5.00	3.33	4.50	3.00	4.11	3.67	4.00	3.86	4.00
X4		2.75	2.50	3.00	2.50	3.17	3.31	1.63	3.07	1.79	2.63	2.64	3.13
X234		3.30	2.57	3.38	2.57	3.44	3.44	1.34	3.07	1.86	2.77	2.77	3.07

Table-7.7

Over-all Marketing Orientation and Customer Judgement w.r.t Supervisory Effectiveness of Shrine Board

Local	Gender		Income	Low Education					High Education					Over-all Mean				
				A	B	C	D	X	A	B	C	D	X	A	B	C	D	X
(1)	(3)		(4)	(5)	(6)	(7)	(8)	(9)	(10)	(11)	(12)	(13)	(14)	(15)	(16)	(17)	(18)	(19)
PILGRIMS	Male		Inc-1	2.77	3.14	3.20	3.57	3.17	2.54	2.67	3.30	2.83	2.84	2.66	2.91	3.25	3.20	3.01
			Inc-2	2.32	3.55	2.90	3.07	2.96	3.01	3.48	3.32	3.30	3.28	2.67	3.52	3.11	3.19	3.12
			Inc-3	2.82	3.28	2.80	3.29	3.05						2.82	3.28	2.80	3.29	3.05
			X1	2.64	3.32	2.97	3.31	3.06	2.78	3.08	3.31	3.07	3.06	2.72	3.20	3.14	3.19	3.06
	Female		Inc-1	3.32	3.64	3.40	3.56	3.48	2.96	3.00	3.60	3.63	3.30	3.14	3.32	3.50	3.60	3.39
			Inc-2	2.91	4.00	2.80	3.00	3.18	3.48	3.75	3.45	3.38	3.52	3.20	3.88	3.13	3.19	3.35
			Inc-3															
			X2	3.12	3.82	3.10	3.28	3.33	3.22	3.38	3.53	3.51	3.41	3.17	3.60	3.32	3.40	3.37
			X12	2.88	3.57	3.04	3.30	3.20	3.00	3.23	3.42	3.29	3.24	2.95	3.40	3.23	3.30	3.22
NON-PILGRIMS	Male		Inc-1	3.11	3.38	3.43	2.94	3.22	3.73	3.00	2.20	2.50	2.86	3.42	3.19	2.82	2.72	3.04
			Inc-2	2.58	3.43	3.73	3.17	3.23	2.33	2.91	2.50	2.55	2.57	2.46	3.17	3.12	2.86	2.90
			Inc-3						2.32	2.05	2.00	2.13	2.13	2.32	2.05	2.00	2.13	2.13
			X3	2.85	3.41	3.58	3.06	3.23	2.79	2.65	2.23	2.39	2.52	2.73	2.80	2.65	2.57	2.69
	Female		Inc-1															
			Inc-2						3.00	3.09	3.00	3.13	3.06	3.00	3.09	3.00	3.13	3.06
			Inc-3															

Contd.....

(1)	(2)	(3)	(4)	(5)	(6)	(7)	(8)	(9)	(10)	(11)	(12)	(13)	(14)	(15)	(16)	(17)	(18)	(19)
	PILGRIMS	Local	X4						3.00	3.09	3.00	3.13	3.06	3.00	3.09	3.00	3.13	3.06
			X34	2.85	3.41	3.58	3.06	3.23	2.90	2.87	2.62	2.76	2.79	2.88	3.14	3.10	2.91	3.01
			X	2.87	3.49	3.31	3.18	3.21	2.95	3.05	3.02	3.03	3.01	2.91	3.27	3.17	3.11	3.12
Non-Local		Male	Inc-1	2.73	3.31	3.15	3.12	3.08	3.26	3.30	3.67	3.05	3.32	3.00	3.31	3.41	3.09	3.20
			Inc-2	2.66	3.28	2.84	2.95	2.93	2.70	3.43	3.06	3.25	3.11	2.68	3.36	2.95	3.10	3.02
			Inc-3	2.82	3.37	2.78	2.92	2.97	2.71	3.31	3.00	2.93	2.99	2.77	3.34	2.89	2.93	2.98
			X1	2.74	3.32	2.92	3.00	3.00	2.89	3.35	3.24	3.08	3.14	2.82	3.34	3.08	3.04	3.07
		Female	Inc-1	2.60	3.47	2.98	2.89	2.99	2.49	3.37	3.42	2.86	3.04	2.55	3.42	3.20	2.88	3.01
			Inc-2	2.90	3.39	2.88	3.15	3.08	2.45	3.34	2.84	2.99	2.91	2.68	3.37	2.86	3.07	3.00
			Inc-3	2.41	2.59	2.80	3.32	2.78	2.65	3.00	2.64	2.91	2.80	2.53	2.80	2.72	3.12	2.79
			X2	2.64	3.15	2.89	3.12	2.95	2.53	3.24	2.97	2.92	2.92	2.59	3.20	2.93	3.02	2.94
			X12	2.69	3.24	2.91	3.06	2.98	2.71	3.30	3.11	3.00	3.03	2.71	3.27	3.01	3.03	3.01
NON-PILGRIMS		Male	Inc-1	2.48	3.92	3.40	3.57	3.34	2.78	3.25	3.10	3.43	3.14	2.63	3.59	3.25	3.50	3.24
			Inc-2	2.93	3.63	3.19	3.28	3.26	3.08	3.50	3.06	3.08	3.18	3.01	3.57	3.13	3.18	3.22
			Inc-3	2.79	2.60	2.87	3.00	2.82	3.33	3.75	3.24	3.21	3.38	3.06	3.18	3.06	3.11	3.10
			X3	2.73	3.38	3.15	3.28	3.14	3.06	3.50	3.13	3.24	3.23	2.90	3.44	3.14	3.26	3.19
		Female	Inc-1	2.86	3.33	2.93	2.87	3.00	2.70	3.49	3.20	3.08	3.12	2.78	3.41	3.07	2.98	3.06
			Inc-2	2.61	3.18	2.60	3.00	2.85	2.62	3.04	2.86	3.02	2.89	2.62	3.11	2.73	3.01	2.87
			Inc-3						2.95	3.53	3.17	3.04	3.17	2.95	3.53	3.17	3.04	3.17
			X4	2.74	3.26	2.77	2.94	2.93	2.76	3.35	3.08	3.05	3.06	2.75	3.31	2.93	3.00	3.00
		Non-Local	X34	2.74	3.32	2.96	3.11	3.03	2.91	3.43	3.11	3.15	3.15	2.83	3.38	3.04	3.13	3.10
			X	2.72	3.28	2.94	3.09	3.01	2.81	3.37	3.11	3.08	3.09	2.77	3.33	3.03	3.09	3.06
Over-all X	Over-all		X	2.80	3.39	3.13	3.14	3.12	2.88	3.21	3.07	3.06	3.06	2.84	3.30	3.10	3.10	3.09

Table–7.8

Variable-wise Multiple Regression Coefficient Values of Pilgrim and Non-Pilgrim Visitors

	PILGRIMS		NON-PILGRIMS	
Variable	Local	Non-Local	Local	Non-local
A	0.572	0.009	-0.572	0.044
B	0.402	-0.492	1.397	0.134
C	-0.237	0.530	-1.462	0.360
D	-0.200	0.492	0.794	0.495
Constant	2.213	2.367	4.332	0.899

Table–7.9

Test of Significance Values

	PILGRIMS		NON-PILGRIMS	
Values	Local	Non-Local	Local	Non-local
R	0.555	0.293	0.775	0.397
R^2	0.308	0.086	0.600	0.157
F (CAL)	2.66854	7.97035	3.00011	5.04603
df($v^1 v^2$)	4,24	4,340	4,8	4,108
F (Tab) at 5% level	2.7763	2.3719	3.8378	2.4472

Table-7.10

Variable-wise Overall Satisfaction and Percentage of Respondents Falling Under Three Orientation Levels

Variables	OVERALL SATISFACTION										Non-Pilgrim	
	Pilgrims											
	B.Avg	% of Resp.	Avg.	% of Resp.	A.Avg.	% of resp.	B.Avg.	% of Resp.	Avg.	% of Resp.	A.Avg.	% of Resp.
(1)	(2)	(3)	(4)	(5)	(6)	(7)	(8)	(9)	(10)	(11)	(12)	(13)
Paid Services of Shrine Board												
1. Adequate accommodation	1.89	11.07	2.85	41.50	2.92	47.43	2.75	4.76	3.11	53.57	3.69	41.67
2. Easily available accommodation	2.04	11.16	2.34	42.23	2.50	46.61	2.50	4.76	2.36	53.37	2.97	41.67
3. Reasonable Charges	2.16	10.78	2.32	42.67	2.49	46.55	1.67	3.80	2.51	54.43	3.15	4.18
4. Hygienic food	2.56	11.33	2.99	39.78	3.02	48.89	2.00	7.69	3.12	42.74	3.09	49.57
5. Tasty & delecious food	2.56	11.91	2.67	39.61	2.87	48.48	2.70	8.40	2.71	42.86	3.10	48.74
6. Cheap rates of food	2.16	11.94	2.44	39.45	2.76	48.61	2.50	8.47	2.51	41.53	2.98	50.00
7. Food of different variety	2.19	11.75	2.63	39.89	2.84	48.36	2.80	8.77	2.77	41.23	3.14	50.00
8. Enjoyable shopping	2.33	8.30	3.14	44.98	3.37	46.72	2.56	7.69	3.24	43.59	3.23	48.72
9. Cooperative shopkeepers	2.44	8.74	2.80	44.76	3.05	46.50	2.11	8.26	2.92	44.04	2.81	47.70
10. Fair shopping	3.38	9.09	3.35	43.36	3.22	47.55	4.11	7.89	3.56	43.86	3.44	48.25
11. Fixed price at shops	2.00	8.45	3.13	44.93	3.12	46.62	2.75	7.02	2.70	43.86	2.80	49.12
X1		10.41		42.11		47.48		7.05		45.93		47.02
Non-Payment Services												
1. Telecommunication	2.97	10.47	3.34	40.41	3.33	49.12	3.80	8.47	3.62	44.92	3.47	46.61
2. Medical facility	2.93	12.11	3.17	40.28	3.20	47.61	3.60	8.26	3.27	42.98	3.59	48.76
3. Sanitation & Hygiene	2.30	11.53	2.45	39.68	2.69	48.79	3.50	8.00	3.07	43.20	3.08	48.80
4. Better roads	3.56	11.62	3.22	39.46	3.46	48.92	3.40	8.00	3.50	43.20	3.66	48.80
5. Provision of proper lights	3.40	11.56	3.34	39.52	3.61	48.92	3.40	7.94	3.49	43.65	3.79	48.41

Contd.....

(1)	(2)	(3)	(4)	(5)	(6)	(7)	(8)	(9)	(10)	(11)	(12)	(13)
6. Provision of proper sign boards	3.56	11.62	3.33	39.19	3.57	49.19	3.40	8.06	3.38	44.35	3.80	47.59
7. Stairs with railing	3.21	11.62	3.03	40.00	3.28	48.38	2.80	8.13	3.02	42.28	3.13	49.59
8. Provision of shelter sheds	3.20	11.56	3.42	40.05	3.75	48.39	3.60	8.26	3.69	42.98	3.61	48.76
9. Clean drinking water	3.42	11.53	3.28	39.95	3.55	48.52	3.44	7.26	3.18	44.35	3.72	48.39
10. Efficient Cloak Room	3.23	11.68	3.27	40.22	3.41	48.10	3.60	7.94	3.27	43.65	3.80	48.41
11. Adequate blankets	3.51	11.29	3.40	40.50	3.77	48.21	3.40	8.00	3.71	44.00	3.72	48.00
X2		11.51		39.93		48.56		8.03		43.60		48.27
Maintenance of Temples												
1. Well maintained temples	3.40	11.73	3.41	39.11	3.63	49.16	2.90	8.55	3.43	43.59	3.54	47.86
2. Easily approachable temples	3.26	11.76	3.32	39.78	3.54	48.46	2.60	8.85	3.44	42.48	3.49	48.67
3. Well maintained Garbjoon	3.10	11.30	3.78	40.11	3.08	48.59	3.00	7.76	3.14	43.97	3.32	48.27
4. Easy darshan Garbjoon	2.23	11.43	2.24	40.57	2.45	48.00	2.33	7.76	2.59	43.97	2.59	48.27
5. Easily approchable Bhairoghati	2.90	11.11	2.43	40.17	2.94	48.72	3.00	8.04	2.79	46.43	3.10	45.53
X3		11.47		39.95		48.58		8.19		44.09		47.72
Supervision of Shrine Board												
1. Good behaviour of the staff	3.15	10.80	3.32	40.44	3.34	48.76	3.00	8.13	3.34	43.09	3.47	48.78
2. Fair dealing of the staff	3.32	10.98	3.24	40.46	3.21	48.56	3.00	8.62	3.10	43.10	3.34	48.28
3. Helpful staff	1.64	4.42	2.98	44.58	2.94	51.00	3.33	8.49	3.20	43.40	3.27	48.11
4. Better infrastrucutre	2.57	5.49	3.59	43.53	3.59	50.98	3.38	7.34	3.57	42.20	3.76	50.46
5. Feeling of safety	2.27	4.35	2.96	44.27	3.12	51.38	3.33	8.11	3.14	39.64	3.38	52.25
6. Efficient Management of Shrine	2.00	5.14	3.38	43.87	3.35	50.99	3.11	8.18	3.37	41.82	3.27	50.00
7. Curb begging practice	1.98	11.42	2.20	40.11	2.22	48.47	2.10	8.20	2.17	43.44	2.19	46.36
8. Overall satisfactory working of Board	3.68	12.24	3.88	39.40	3.83	48.36	3.90	8.26	3.82	45.46	4.05	46.28
X3	2.76	8.11	3.02	42.08	3.17	49.81	3.01	8.17	3.14	42.77	3.33	49.06
Overall		1037.00		41.02		48.61		7.86		44.10		48.04
No %of age	44(11.76)		150(40.11)	180 (48.13)			9(7.14)		56(44.44)		61 (48.42)	

MARKETING STRATEGY FOR
PILGRIMAGE TOURISM

Background

Developing marketing strategy for pilgrimage tourism requires consolidation of research findings, summarizing them in the direction of existing research literature (Peters 1969) vis-a-vis the research in question. Such strategic guidance is required for travel tourism and leisure services (Poon 1993) because of the positive relationship between the information sought about the pilgrims and their satisfaction from the aforesaid services. This continuous exercise facilitates the regular and effective delivery of these services along with a monitoring mechanism which ensures parity between the level of satisfaction of the tourists and their expectations (Newman & Taylor 1978, Shostack 1977). The level of customer satisfaction measured in the selected services of the pilgrimage tourism provided by the different suppliers such as hoteliers, transporters, retailers and the supervisory services of Shrine Board at the pilgrimage destination of Shri Mata Vaishno Devi Shrine indicates the quality of service and accordingly efforts have been made to formulate marketing strategies for the pilgrimage tourism.

The marketing strategic actions required in the present case have come up from the level of pilgrim satisfaction in the various selected services examined separately in the proceeding chapters on the basis of first hand information/data gathered personally through a pretested questionnaire primarily structured on the five point Likert scale from the randomly selected 500 respondents of different backgrounds. The original questionnaire consisted of 50 statements within the jurisdiction of marketing orientation selected from the detailed literature survey and after a series of discussions with the experts and other researchers in the field. These statements after purification through factor analysis and several iterations finally resulted in 31 items under eight factors, viz. (food services at destination, en route supportive services, additional supportive services, transport services, food services en route to destination, shopping services, accommodation en route to destination, accommodation at destination) of MKTORIENT. These factors have been identified and named on the grouping pattern of various dimensions covered under these statements (Table-8.1).

Marketing Strategy

The nature and extent of customer satisfaction regarding the different services availed by the pilgrim and non-pilgrim visitors classified under different demographic groups and needed marketing strategy stemming up from the study has been given as under:

Food Services at the Destination

Food services at the pilgrimage destination have an important status in the pilgrimage itself as during this kind of visit customers require special food to eat, not always in various variety but it needs to be cooked and served in the way prescribed under religious norms. At '*Bhavan*', the destination of the Shrine, both pilgrim and non-pilgrim visitors expect and eat vegetarian food which is provided by the bhojanalyas managed by the supervisory staff of the Shrine Board on a 'no profit-no loss' basis and private dhabas/hotels working as per the norms specified by the Board itself. Besides two bhojanalyas there are 10 to 12 dhabas/hotels (Annexure 2&3), catering to the overall food service needed at the destination. After a long journey of thirteen kilometres mostly on foot, the visitors have meals/tea/coffee/other soft drinks, etc. at *Bhavan* and their overall satisfaction regarding the pilgrimage mostly centres around the satisfaction they obtain while availing such services. The satisfaction from this service depends upon how food was served, how much variety was available, the taste and delight and its price, etc. The providers of such services enjoy full market potential here and make their customers satisfied due to which their words of mouth work in their favour. The study provides a below average (2.69) score of overall satisfaction (Table-8.2) regarding this service. The lowest satisfaction of 1 point has been observed by three groups viz. (i) highly educated middle aged local non-pilgrim males with an above average income, (ii) highly educated old aged non-local female pilgrims with a below average income and (iii) low educated old aged non-local female pilgrims with an above average income. The highest of 4.34 score has been reflected by highly educated old aged non-local non-pilgrim males with an average income. The table reveals that most of the groups under study observe a below average satisfaction. The lowest of 2.09 score of satisfaction is shown by local non-pilgrim males regarding the hygienic condition of the food served followed by 2.16 score for the cheap rates paid for the food at *Bhavan* by non-local female pilgrims. The highest score of 4 points and 3.5 has been shown by the local female pilgrim group for taste and delight of the food served and variety in food served respectively. The food service at destination *Bhavan* explain a highest of 20.7% variance and has the highest impact on the over-all satisfaction among the extracted eight factors (Table-8.1). The four linear equations given in Exhibit-8.1 indicate both positive and negative association of this service with over-all customer/pilgrim satisfaction. It shows that all the three groups except the non-local non-pilgrims show a positive but low association with the over-all satisfaction thereby confirming the below average score of satisfaction in Table-8.2.

The level of customer satisfaction expressed by the proportion of respondents obtaining satisfaction scores between a minimum of one point and a maximum of five points on the Likert scale used indicates the weak areas which need to be targeted for formulating an appropriate marketing strategy (Table-8.13). The various dimensions covered under factor–1, viz. "food services at destination", responsible for an over-all lower satisfaction of 2.69, are given below along with the proportion of sample pilgrims and non-pilgrims obtaining below average satisfaction.

(i)   rates of food service   46.2%

(ii)   variety in food   41%

(iii) tasty & delicious food   34.8%

(iv)   hygienic food   29.2%

All this indicates the necessity of a well-planned marketing strategy for providing and maintaining better variety, fair rates, tasty and hygienic food at the pilgrimage destination.

En route Supportive Services

The factor analysis through varimax rotation has produced the various en route supportive services as the second important consideration at a pilgrimage destination by explaining 9.6% of variance after 20.7% in case of food services at the destination. These services are provided both by private agencies and the Shrine Board on a 'commercial' as well as "no profit – no loss" basis respectively. These services between Katra and *Bhavan* have to be provided keeping in consideration the hard journey on hilly track of about 13 kms. The degree of customer satisfaction worked out within the framework of expectations v/s performance in Table-8.3 reveals the scores varying between a maximum of 1.75 for safety measures by the Shrine Board and the maximum of 4.31 points for 'transport service' between both 'Katra-Banganga ' and 'Banganga-Bhavan' primarily provided by private agencies. Among all the visitor groups under study the lowest satisfaction score of 1.77 has been reflected by low educated non-local old aged male pilgrims with an average of income level followed by 1.8 points scored by highly educated local non-pilgrim old aged males with an above average income, which draws immediate attention of all the concerned to the proper and effective services as per the pilgrim requirements.

The four linear equations given in Exhibit-8.1 show a positive association of these services with the over-all satisfaction explained, especially for the non-local, non-pilgrim visitors who indicate the highest positive association. The proportion of sample pilgrims under below average, average and above average region of customer satisfaction in Table-8.13 explains that more than 77% and 65% visitors express an above average satisfaction regarding transport and shopping services respectively indicating thereby the necessity of maintaining the present quality of these services.

Additional Infrastructural Services

The visitors to the Shrine, whether they visit for pilgrim or non-pilgrim purposes, feel more satisfied if they are provided some additional supportive services during their journey. These services differ from destination to destination. At the Vaishno Devi Shrine—the pilgrimage destination with about 13 km hard-some track usually covered on foot, the visitors require drinking water, cloak rooms, adequate bedding, shelter sheds and better roads with proper sanitation and hygiene en route primarily provided by the Board. These dimensions are covered under factor-3, i.e. 'additional infrastructural services'. These services obtained an above average 3.21 score of over all satisfaction (Table-8.4) from all the groups of respondents taken together but the lowest satisfaction score of 1 point has been expressed by the highly educated middle aged local non-pilgrim males with an above average income followed by 2.33 points observed by the highly educated young local male pilgrims with a below average income. The liner equations shown in Exhibit-8.1 explaining the positive association of these services confirm the over-all above average satisfaction score but the main weak area, viz. the maintenance of sanitation and hygiene, has been identified again after proportioning the respondents between 1 and 5 points on the Likert scale where 46% visitors express dissatisfaction (Table-8.13) from this service, thereby showing a requirement for a properly planned and regularly monitored strategy leading to well maintained frequently cleaned and hygienic bathrooms, toilets and roads en route in addition to maintaining the satisfaction explained regarding other additional infrastructural services.

Transportation Services

The satisfaction evaluation process of a pilgrimage trip starts the minute a visitor boards any mode of transport and ends as the visitor boards off after returning from the journey. The transportation services available en route to the Vaishno Devi pilgrimage not only make the trip easy but also save time and attract more and more of visitors every year. As much as 7.2% variance in the over all customer satisfaction has been explained by this service (Table-8.1) under factor-4 where all the respondents taken together express a below average satisfaction score of 2.91 points. As low as 1 point score of satisfaction has been shown by the highly educated old aged local non-pilgrim males with an above average income and a low of 1.75 score by the highly young non-local female pilgrims with an above average income (Table-8.5).

Exhibit-8.1 shows that all the non-pilgrim visitors, whether they are local or non-local, are not satisfied with this service. The proportions of respondents obtaining below average satisfaction scores on the Likert scale indicating the weak areas of transport service are as:

(i)   ordinary bus service   38.2%

(ii) pony and pithu service   26.0%

(iii) luxury bus service   16.2%

(iv) taxi service   15.4%

All this suggests a well-balanced strategy for the transportation service en route to the destination with the main focus on the services of ordinary bus which are required by most of the visitors and pony and pithu service which is required for carrying luggage and children and is the only mode of hill transport available on the track.

Food Services En route to Destination

Most of the visitors reaching Katra—the base camp and continuing their journey to *Bhavan* halt at many places to have some light refreshment and other eatables en route to the track. This food service en route necessary for different segments of the visitors is required to be tasty and served hygienically. After varimax rotation the factor covered only two dimensions viz. (i) tasty and delicious food and (ii) hygienic food, as important explaining 6% of variance with the over all satisfaction (Table-8.1).

Only an average satisfaction score has been observed by all the respondent groups taken together. The lowest score of 1 point has been observed by two groups, viz. (i) the highly educated young local male pilgrims with a below average income and (ii) the highly educated middle aged non-pilgrim local males with an above average income showing dissatisfaction regarding the service. (Table-8.6)

The association of this service with over-all satisfaction of the visitors given in Exhibit-8.1 under four linear equations explain that local pilgrims show a negative association and other three groups under study show a positive but low level of association. Table-8.13 further reflects that 31.8% visitors and 30.8% visitors express a below average satisfaction regarding tasty delicious food and hygienic food respectively. A marketing strategy for providing and maintaining satisfactory food services en route to the destination primarily of better taste and hygiene would bring up the level of pilgrim satisfaction.

Retail Services

En route to the journey to the Shrine, a visitor needs to purchase various articles of daily requirement and of special importance of the pilgrimage (gift items/souvenirs) from shops in and around Katra and also from the shops en route to *Bhavan*. This service has been extracted to be the sixth factor with an explanation of 5.3% variance (Table-8.1) and negative association of non-local non-pilgrim visitors with the over all satisfaction (Exhibit-8.1). Mean scores of different pilgrim and non-pilgrim groups extracted a below average of 2.91 satisfaction score from all the respondents taken together (Table-8.7). The lowest of 1.5 score has been observed by the low educated middle aged non-local non-pilgrim males with a below average income followed by 1.75 score of satisfaction observed by four groups, viz.

(i)   low educated old aged local female pilgrims with an average income,

(ii)   highly educated old aged local male non-pilgrims with an above average income,

(iii) highly educated non-local female pilgrims with an above average income and

(iv)   low educated middle aged non-local non-pilgrim males with an average income, which identify the segments which are least satisfied with this service and are required to be targeted while formulating the required marketing strategy.

The proportion of respondents falling within the 5 points on the Likert scale indicate the weak areas with below average scores as under (Table-8.13).

(i)   cooperative shopkeepers at Katra   37.4%

(ii)   cooperative shopkeepers at *Bhavan*   29.0%

(iii) adequate shopping at Katra   24.6%

(iv)   .adequate shopping at *Bhavan*   19.6%

The concerned agencies including general shopkeepers and the Shrine Board should work out the needed changes in the light of the aforesaid findings of the study.

Accommodation at Katra and En route to the Destination

En route to the track towards *Bhavan*, the accommodation required by the visitors as per their requirements is provided both by private agencies and the Shrine Board. 4.5% variance is explained by this service in the over all satisfaction (Table-8.1) and this factor covers three dimensions among which the charges for the accommodation make 48% visitors satisfied at a below average level, 33.6% visitors are not satisfied with the maintenance of accommodation, and 31.4% experience non-availability during peak season. (Table-8.13). It is because of such a high proportion of dissatisfied pilgrims about the accommodation provided by both the aforesaid agencies that the over all value/score of pilgrim satisfaction has come down to 2.66 (Table-8.8).

Further the degree of pilgrim satisfaction has significantly declined to point 1 in case of two groups, viz. (i) low educated young female non-local pilgrims with an average income and (ii) highly educated young non-local non-pilgrim males with an average income. The linear equations given in Exhibit-8.1 also show a very low positive association of this service with the visitors' over all satisfaction and as such this accommodation service at Katra and en route to the destination need to be adequately developed and properly maintained as per the pilgrim traffic.

Accommodation at Destination

The proportion of the pilgrims who have experienced below average satisfaction with respect to the various aspects of accommodation at *Bhavan* provided by the Shrine Board has arrived at 38.4% in case of readily available, 34.8% in reasonability of charges and 23.2% in case of quality of maintenance of this service (Table-8.13). Such a significant proportion of dissatisfied pilgrims has brought down the overall level of satisfaction score to just 2.42 (Table-8.9). Only a 1 point of satisfaction score has been given by as many as four segments, viz. (i) low educated young local male pilgrims with an average income, (ii) highly educated middle aged local non-pilgrim males with an above average income and (iii) highly educated young local non-pilgrim males with an above average income and (iv) low educated young non-local female pilgrims with an average income, whereas a high of 4.33 satisfaction score has been shown only by the highly educated middle aged local non-pilgrim males with a below average income.

Similarly a low positive association of this service with the over all satisfaction has been explained in the equations given under Exhibit-8.1. This service is needed the most at the destination mostly by non-local visitors who want to halt there and need a satisfactory place to stay but this service has proved to be unsatisfactory to most of them. The Shrine Board thus needs to provide more accommodation at reasonable charges. Moreover, such accommodation is required to be properly maintained keeping in view the increasing number of pilgrims.

Conclusion

The various pilgrimage tourism services studied through the customer satisfaction approach indicate a wide range of mis-management, lack of quality services and over all supervisory effectiveness. The weak areas identified under each of these services need to be designed and delivered to the pilgrims/visitors as per their requirements. The providers of food, transport, accommodation and retailing services need to understand pilgrim requirements in terms of pilgrim profile and pilgrimage significance rather than just their market potential. In fact the market potential of these services also increases if the providers continue to maintain the quality and relevance of the services to the pilgrimage purpose, nature of journey and pilgrimage destination.

Policy Implications

The adoption of such strategies most likely calls for changes in the existing organizational structure which can be brought about by various commercial and non-commercial agencies joining hands together. Shri Mata Vaishno Devi Shrine Board which controls and manages the Shrine needs to develop more of economical & hygienic food and accommodation services at Katra and at *Bhavan*. The Board is required to open an adequate number of fixed price shops selling souvenirs and gift items at reasonable prices at important places between and around Katra and *Bhavan*. Further an economical fleet of buses in good condition keeping in consideration the road connecting Katra should be deployed from Jammu bus stand and railway station. The infrastructural facilities en route to the track should be properly managed and developed as and when required as per the pilgrimage requirements especially keeping in view the traffic influx during the peak season of pilgrimage. Moreover, the Board should from time to time evaluate/monitor the working of the different private agencies providing various pilgrim services and with the help of government body pass a legislation against profiteers and cheaters so that the visitors do not have any bad experience during their visit. The various private agencies should form an association so that they all work under the guidance of some set rules and regulations thereby having a check on each other. They can also fix some award for those providing best services and penalty for defaulters because the marketing of pilgrimage tourism services ought not to be carried on exclusively with a commercial interest but within the parameters of commercial viability, concerned religious code of conduct and also with local socio-economic relevance.

Exhibit–8.1

Linear Equations

Linear Equations

(I) $Y = 2.174 + .054(FADX1) + .109(ESSX2) + .215(AISX3) + .179(TSX4) - 0.90(FEDX5) + .301(RSX6) + .060(AEDX7) + .007(AADX8)$

(ii) $Y = 1.628 + .128(FADX1) + .0.13(ESSX2) + .0.94(AISX3) + .151(TSX4) + 1.14(FEDX5) + 2.04(RSX6) + .0.24(AEDX7) + .104(AADX8)$

(iii) $Y = 2.168 + .208(FADX1) + .190(ESSX2) + .047(AISX3).035(TSX4) + 174(FEDX5) + .110(RSX6) + .111(AEDX7) + .170(AADX8)$

(iv) $Y = 6.259 - .007(FADX1) + ..528(ESSX2) + .042(AISX4) + 0.32(FEDX5) - .750(RSX6) + 1.090(AEDX7) + .497(AADX8)$

Note:

FAD	Food at Destination
ESS	En route Supportive Services
AIS	Additional Infrastructural Services
TS	Transport Services
FED	Food En route to Destination
RS	Retail Services
AED	Accommodation en route to Destination
AAD	Accommodation at Destination

Exhibit–8.2

Grievances

Accommodation services

1. Inadequate accommodation at *Bhavan* & Adhkumari
2. Costly & unhygienic accommodation en route
3. Costly accommodation at Katra
4. Exploitation of pilgrims by hotel agents at Katra
5. Dharamshalla accommodation given on commercial basis.
6. Accommodation at *Bhavan* not managed properly.
7. Even prior booking of rooms not honoured at *Bhavan*.

Food Services

1. Food facilities not adequate for longer stays
2. Very costly & unhygienic food services

Road and Transport Services

1. Taxi fare is very high
2. En route the route to *Bhavan* ponies disrupt the yatra
3. At many places road is in bad condition
4. Track up to *Bhavan* not cleaned & maintained frequently
5. No adequate shelter shed at the track adjoining *Bhavan*
6. No proper railings provided along the stairs

Retail Services

1. Inadequate shopping items available
2. Very few fixed price shops
3. Shopkeepers cheat the pilgrims
4. Very costly items kept in special gift/souvenir shops

Shrine Board Services

1. Misbehaving staff of Shrine Board
2. Careless attitude of staff especially during rush hours
3. Proper management of services lacking

General Services

1. Unhygienic toilets and bathrooms
2. Inadequate medical facilities
3. No proper old age facilities available
4. Inadequate bathrooms at *Bhavan* & Adhkumari
5. Inadequate lighting arrangement around Bhaironghati
6. Improper water drainage system at *Bhavan*
7. Very long queues at Garbjoon & lesser time for darshan inside the cave
8. VIP treatment is the result of high donation given personally to pujaris inside the cave
9. Local people do not behave properly with visitors

Table–8.1
Summary of Results from Scale Purification, Loading & Variance Explained

Factors	Dimensions/ Statements	Factor Loading	% of variance Explained
(1)	(2)	(3)	(4)
Factor-1	**Food services at destination**		
	1. Variety in food at *Bhavan*	0.74	20.7
	2. Rate of food services at *Bhavan*	0.71	
	3. Tasty & delicious food at *Bhavan*	0.69	
	4. Hygienic food at *Bhavan*	0.58	
Factor-2	**En route Supportive services**		
	1. Satisfactory shopping	0.84	9.6
	2. Satisfactory transportation	0.64	
	3. Satisfaction from accommodation	0.68	
	4. Satisfactory safety measures	0.77	
	5. Satisfactory infrastructure	0.69	
Factor-3	**Additional Infrastructural services**		
	1. Adequate cloak room	0.81	7.9
	2. Clean drinking water	0.75	
	3. Better roads	0.66	
	4. Sanitation & hygiene	0.6	
	5. Adequate bedding	0.58	
	6. Adequate shelter sheds	0.48	

Contd.....

Factor-4	Transport services		
	1. Luxury bus service	0.68	7.2
	2. Ordinary bus service	0.68	
	3. Pony & pithu services	0.65	
	4. Taxi services	0.64	
Factor-5	Food services en route to destination		
	1. Tasty & delicious food at Katra	0.83	6
	2. Hygienic food at Katra	0.78	
Factor-6	Retail services		
	1. Cooperative shopkeepers at *Bhavan*	0.77	5.3
	2. Adequate shopping at *Bhavan*	0.75	
	3. Adequate shopping at Katra	0.75	
	4. Cooperative shopkeepers at Katra	0.72	
Factor-7	Accommodation at Katra & enroute to destination		
	1. Maintenance accommodation at Katra	0.79	4.5
	2. Availability of accommodation at Katra	0.78	
	3. Reasonable charges for accommodation at Katra	0.77	
Factor-8	Accommodation at destination		
	1. Availability of accommodation at *Bhavan*	0.76	3.6
	2. Maintenance of accommodation at *Bhavan*	0.65	
	3. Reasonable charges for accommodation at *Bhavan*	0.47	
	Total Varianace explained		64.8

Table-8.2

Mean Scores of Marketing Effectiveness Observed by Pilgrim and Non-Pilgrim Groups for Food Services at Destination

Local

Groups		Variables	Age Group-I Up to 25 Yrs.						Age Group-II 25 to 50 Yrs.							Age Group-III Above 50 Yrs.							
			Inc-1		Inc-2		Inc-3	X	Inc-1		Inc-2		Inc-3		X	Inc-1		Inc-2		Inc-3		X	X
(1)	(2) (3)	(4)	E-1 (6)	E-2 (7)	E-1 (8)	E-2 (9)	E-2 (10)	(11)	E-1 (12)	E-2 (13)	E-1 (14)	E-2 (15)	E-1 (16)	E-2 (17)	(18)	E-1 (19)	E-2 (20)	E-1 (21)	E-2 (22)	E-1 (23)	E-2 (24)	(25)	(26)
	Pilgrim Male	1. Variety in food	4.00	4.00	1.00	-	-	3.00	-	2.00	4.00	3.00	-	-	3.00	-	-	-	-	-	2.00	2.17	2.72
		2. Rates of food service	2.00	3.00	2.00	-	-	2.33	-	2.67	3.00	3.50	-	-	3.06	-	-	-	3.67	-	2.00	2.84	2.74
		3. Tasty & delicious food	2.00	3.00	2.00	-	-	2.33	-	2.33	2.00	3.50	-	-	2.61	-	-	-	2.33	-	3.00	2.67	2.54
		4. Hygienic food	3.00	3.00	3.00	-	-	3.00	-	2.33	2.00	3.50	-	-	2.61	-	-	-	3.00	-	2.00	2.50	2.70
		X1	2.75	3.25	2.00	-	-	2.67	-	2.33	2.75	3.38	-	-	2.82	-	-	-	2.83	-	2.25	2.55	2.68
	Female	1. Variety in food	-	-	-	-	-	-	-	3.00	-	3.00	-	-	3.00	-	4.00	-	-	-	4.00	3.50
		2. Rates of food service	-	-	-	-	-	-	-	4.00	-	4.00	-	-	4.00	-	1.00	-	-	-	1.00	2.50
		3. Tasty & delicious food	-	-	-	-	-	-	-	4.00	-	4.00	-	-	4.00	-	4.00	-	-	-	4.00	4.00
		4. Hygienic food	-	-	-	-	-	-	-	3.00	-	2.00	-	-	2.50	-	4.00	-	-	-	4.00	3.25
		X2	-	-	-	-	-	-	-	3.50	-	3.25	-	-	3.38	-	3.25	-	-	-	3.25	3.31
		X12	2.75	3.25	2.00	-	-	2.67	-	2.92	2.75	3.32	-	-	3.10	-	3.25	2.83	-	2.25	2.90	3.00
	Non-Pilgrim Male	1. Variety in food	-	-	-	-	-	-	-	4.00	2.67	2.33	-	1.00	2.50	-	-	-	-	-	2.00	2.00	2.25
		2. Rates of food service	-	-	-	-	-	-	-	4.00	2.67	3.33	-	1.00	2.75	-	-	-	-	-	2.00	2.00	2.38
		3. Tasty & delicious food	-	-	-	-	-	-	-	4.00	3.00	2.67	-	1.00	2.67	-	-	-	-	-	2.00	2.00	2.34
		4. Hygienic food	-	-	-	-	-	-	-	2.00	3.00	2.67	-	1.00	2.17	-	-	-	-	-	2.00	2.00	2.09
		X3	-	-	-	-	-	-	-	3.50	2.84	2.75	-	1.00	2.52	-	-	-	-	-	2.00	2.00	2.27
	Local	X	2.75	-	2.00	-	-	2.67	-	3.21	2.80	3.04	-	1.00	2.81	-	3.25	-	-	2.13	2.45	2.64

Contd.....

(1)	(2)	(3)	(4)	(5)	(6)	(7)	(8)	(9)	(10)	(11)	(12)	(13)	(14)	(15)	(16)	(17)	(18)	(19)	(20)	(21)	(22)	(23)	(24)	(25)	(26)
Non-locals	Pilgrims	Male	1. Variety in food		2.50	-	2.75	3.00	2.00	2.56	2.50	3.20	2.53	2.74	2.29	2.55	2.64	4.00		3.00	2.64	3.00	2.48	3.02	2.74
			2. Rates of food service		2.38	-	3.00	3.00	3.00	2.85	3.00	4.00	2.53	3.19	2.00	1.45	2.70	4.00		2.00	2.07	3.00	2.08	2.63	2.73
			3. Tasty & delicious food		2.50	-	3.00	2.67	3.00	2.79	2.00	3.40	2.47	2.61	2.14	2.27	2.48	4.00		3.00	2.71	2.67	2.84	3.00	2.77
			4. Hygienic food		2.75	-	3.50	3.67	3.00	3.23	2.00	3.40	2.87	2.84	2.29	2.98	2.72	4.00		3.00	3.07	2.67	3.13	3.17	3.04
			X1		2.53		3.06	3.09	2.75	2.86	2.38	3.50	2.60	2.85	2.18	2.31	2.64	4.00		2.75	2.62	2.84	2.63	2.96	2.82
		Female	1.Variety in food		2.67	4.00	2.00	-	-	2.89	2.38	2.15	-	2.60	3.00	3.00	2.63	1.60	1.00	3.67	3.00	1.00	2.42	2.12	2.55
			2. Rates of food service		2.00	4.00	1.00	-	-	2.33	2.63	2.00	-	2.60	3.00	2.00	2.45	2.20	1.00	2.33	1.50	1.00	2.25	1.71	2.16
			3. Tasty & delicious food		3.00	4.00	3.00	-	-	3.33	2.50	2.46	-	3.20	3.00	3.00	2.83	2.20	1.00	3.00	3.00	i.00	2.33	2.09	2.75
			4. Hygienic food		3.00	4.00	3.00	-	-	3.33	2.75	2.77	-	3.00	3.00	3.00	2.90	3.20	1.00	3.67	1.50	1.00	2.33	2.12	2.78
			X2		2.67	4.00	2.25		2.75	2.97	2.57	2.35	2.60	2.85	3.00	2.75	2.70	2.30	1.00	3.17	2.25	1.00	2.33	2.01	2.56
			X12		2.60	4.00	2.66	3.09	2.75	2.92	2.48	2.93	2.60	2.85	2.59	2.53	2.67	3.15	1.00	2.96	2.44	1.92	2.48	2.49	2.69
	Non-Pilgrim	Male	1. Variety in food		-	1.00	3.00	3.00	3.00	2.33	2.00	3.67	3.00	3.26	2.00	2.50	2.74	2.00	-	4.00	4.00	3.00	2.43	2.86	2.64
			2. Rates of food service		-	1.00	-	1.00	3.00	1.67	2.00	1.33	2.50	2.89	3.00	3.00	2.54	2.00	-	-	4.00	3.00	2.33	2.83	2.35
			3. Tasty & delicious food		-	4.00	3.00	3.00	3.00	3.33	3.00	2.67	2.00	2.84	3.00	2.00	2.59	4.00	-	4.00	4.67	3.00	2.27	3.49	3.14
			4. Hygienic food		-	4.00	3.00	1.00	3.00	2.67	2.00	2.67	2.00	3.21	4.00	2.50	2.73	4.00	-	4.67	4.67	3.00	3.00	3.67	3.02
			X3		-	2.50	2.00	2.00	3.00	2.50	2.25	2.59	2.50	3.05	3.00	2.50	2.65	3.00	-	4.67	4.34	3.00	2.51	3.21	2.79
		Female	1.Variety in food		2.67	-	-	-	-	2.67	-	3.60	3.50	1.50	3.00	3.00	2.90	-	-		3.00	3.00	3.50	3.25	2.94
			2. Rates of food service		2.00	-	-	-	-	2.00	-	2.80	2.50	1.50	1.00	1.00	1.95	-	-		3.33		3.50	3.42	2.46
			3. Tasty & delicious food		3.00	-	-	-	-	3.00	-	2.60	3.00	2.00	3.00	3.00	2.65	-	-		3.00		2.50	2.75	2.80
			4. Hygienic food		3.00	-	-	-	-	3.00	-	1.60	3.50	2.00	1.00	1.00	2.03	-	-		3.33		2.50	2.92	2.65
			X4		2.67					2.67		2.65	3.13	1.75	2.00	2.00	2.38				3.17		3.00	3.09	2.71
			X34		2.67	2.50	-	2.00	3.00	2.59	2.25	2.62	2.82	2.40	3.00	2.25	2.52	3.00	1.00		3.76	3.00	2.76	3.15	2.75
	Non-Locals		X		2.64	3.25	2.66	2.55	2.88	2.76	2.37	2.78	2.63	2.63	2.80	2.39	2.60	3.08	1.00	2.96	3.10	2.46	2.62	2.82	2.72
			Over-all X		2.70	3.25	2.33	2.55	2.88	2.73	2.37	3.00	2.76	2.84	2.80	1.70	2.71	3.08	1.00	3.11	2.97	2.46	2.38	2.64	2.69

Table-8.3

Mean Score of Marketing Effectiveness Observed by Pilgrim and Non-Pilgrim Groups for En route Supportive Services

Groups	Variables	Education	Age Group-I Upto 25 Yrs. Inc-1 E-1	Inc-1 E-2	Inc-2 E-1	Inc-2 E-2	Inc-3 E-1	Inc-3 E-2	X	Age Group-II 25 to 50 Yrs. Inc-1 E-1	Inc-1 E-2	Inc-2 E-1	Inc-2 E-2	Inc-3 E-1	Inc-3 E-2	X	Age Group-III Above 50 Yrs. Inc-1 E-1	Inc-1 E-2	Inc-2 E-1	Inc-2 E-2	Inc-3 E-1	Inc-3 E-2	X	X
(1)	(2)(3)	(4)	(5)	(6)	(7)	(8)	(9)	(10)	(11)	(12)	(13)	(14)	(15)	(16)	(17)	(18)	(19)	(20)	(21)	(22)	(23)	(24)	(25)	(26)
Local Pilgrm Male	Satisfaction from shopping		3.00	3.00	3.00				3.00		4.00	4.00	3.50			3.83				4.00		4.00	4.00	3.61
	Satisfaction from transport		3.00	4.00	4.00				3.67		3.67	3.00	4.25			3.64				3.80		4.00	3.90	3.74
	Satisfaction from accommodation		3.00	2.00	2.00				2.33		4.00	3.00	3.00			3.33				2.50		5.00	3.75	3.14
	Satsifaction from safety measures		3.00	3.00	1.00				2.33		3.67	4.00	3.50			3.72				4.00		3.00	3.50	3.18
	Satsifaction from infrastructure		2.00	4.00	1.00				2.33		3.00	4.00	4.25			3.75				4.00		3.00	3.50	3.19
	X1		2.80	3.20	2.20				2.73		3.67	3.60	3.70			3.65				3.66		3.80	3.73	3.37
Female	Satisfaction from shopping										1.00		3.00			2.00			4.00			4.00	4.00	3.00
	Satisfaction from transport										4.00		4.00			4.00			4.00			4.00	4.00	4.00
	Satisfaction from accommodation										4.00		4.00			4.00			4.00			4.00	4.00	4.00
	Satsifaction from safety measures										4.00		1.00			2.50			4.00			4.00	4.00	3.25
	Satsifaction from infrastructure										4.00		1.00			2.50			4.00			4.00	4.00	3.25
	X2										3.40		2.60			3.00			4.00			4.00	4.00	3.50
	X12		2.80	3.20	2.20				2.73		3.54	3.60	3.15			3.33			4.00	3.66		3.80	3.87	3.44
Non-Pilgrim Male	Satisfaction from shopping										5.00	3.67	4.00		5.00	4.42						2.00	2.00	3.21
	Satisfaction from transport										5.00	3.67	4.00		2.00	3.67						1.00	1.00	2.34
	Satisfaction from accommodation										5.00	2.67	4.00		3.00	3.67						4.00	4.00	3.84
	Satsifaction from safety measures										2.00	3.33	3.67		1.00	2.50						1.00	1.00	1.75
	Satsifaction from infrastructure										4.00	4.00	3.00		1.00	3.00						1.00	1.00	2.00
	X3										4.20	3.47	3.73		2.40	3.45						1.00	1.80	2.63
Local	X		2.80	3.20	2.20				2.73		3.87	3.54	3.44		2.40	3.39			4.00	3.66		2.80	2.84	3.03

Contd......

(1)	(2)	(3)	(4)	(5)	(6)	(7)	(8)	(9)	(10)	(11)	(12)	(13)	(14)	(15)	(16)	(17)	(18)	(19)	(20)	(21)	(22)	(23)	(24)	(25)	(26)
Non-locals	Pilgrims																								
	Male	Satisfaction from shopping		3.92		3.50	4.25		3.67	3.84	4.50	3.67	3.94	3.95	3.45	3.32	3.81	3.50		3.83	3.70	4.20	3.36	3.72	3.79
		Satisfaction from transport		3.70		3.75	3.75		4.33	3.88	4.00	3.83	3.79	4.38	3.55	3.73	3.88	4.00		2.00	3.90	4.00	3.83	3.55	3.77
		Satisfaction from accommodation		3.17		4.50	3.00		1.00	2.97	3.00	3.33	4.07	3.29	3.29	2.50	3.25	2.00		1.00	4.08	3.50	3.05	2.73	2.97
		Satisfaction from safety measures		2.60		3.25	3.00		3.00	2.96	4.00	3.50	3.40	3.14	2.00	2.57	3.10	1.00		1.00	3.50	3.00	2.58	2.21	2.76
		Satsifaction from infrastructure		3.40		3.75	4.00		3.00	3.54	4.00	3.75	3.80	3.41	3.71	3.58	3.71	3.00		1.00	3.75	3.33	2.72	2.76	3.34
		X1		3.36		3.75	3.60		3.00	3.44	3.90	3.62	3.8	3.63	3.20	3.14	3.55	2.70		1.77	3.79	3.61	3.11	2.99	3.33
	Female	Satisfaction from shopping		4.00	3.40	3.00				3.47	3.64	3.61		4.09	4.00	3.00	3.67	3.71	4.00	3.78	3.80	4.00	4.14	3.91	3.68
		Satisfaction from transport		4.00	3.80	4.00				3.93	3.82	3.50		4.27	3.00	3.50	3.62	3.57	4.00	4.00	4.20	4.00	4.00	3.96	3.84
		Satisfaction from accommodation		1.67	2.00	5.00				2.89	2.50	3.69		3.20	3.00	4.00	3.28	3.60	3.00	3.33	2.50	4.00	3.00	3.24	3.14
		Satisifaction from safety measures		1.00	1.00	1.00				1.00	2.60	2.71		3.20	4.00	4.00	3.30	1.33	1.00	3.33	4.00	3.00	2.60	2.54	2.28
		Satsifaction from infrastructure		4.00	1.00	1.00				2.00	3.40	3.29		3.40	3.00	2.00	3.02	3.00	1.00	3.67	4.00	4.00	3.58	3.21	2.74
		X2		2.93	2.24	2.80				2.66	3.19	3.36		3.63	3.40	3.30	3.38	3.04	2.60	3.62	3.70	3.80	3.46	3.37	3.14
		X12		3.15	2.24	3.28	3.60		3.00	3.05	3.55	3.49	3.80	3.63	3.30	3.22	3.47	2.87	2.69	2.70	3.75	3.71	3.29	3.18	3.24
Non-Pilgrim																									
	Male	Satisfaction from shopping			5.00	4.00	4.00		4.50	4.17	2.00	3.40	3.50	3.95	3.00	3.22	3.18	4.00			4.99	4.00	3.64	3.91	3.75
		Satisfaction from transport			4.00	3.00	3.00		5.00	4.33	4.00	4.60	3.50	4.14	4.00	4.44	4.11	4.00			4.99	4.00	4.19	4.05	4.16
		Satisfaction from accommodation			4.00	4.00	4.00		1.00	3.00	2.00	3.40	4.00	3.74	4.00	3.20	3.39	4.00			4.67	4.00	3.09	3.94	3.44
		Satisfaction from safety measures			4.00				3.00	3.33	4.00	4.33	2.00	3.88	2.00	3.40	3.27	4.00			3.33	3.00	2.91	3.31	3.30
		Satsifaction from infrastructure			4.20		1.00		4.00	3.00	4.00	4.00	4.00	3.75	4.00	3.20	3.83	4.00			3.33	2.00	3.64	3.24	3.36
		X3			4.24	3.00	3.00		3.50	3.57	3.20	3.95	3.40	3.89	3.40	3.49	3.56	4.00			4.26	3.40	3.49	3.69	3.60
	Female	Satisfaction from shopping		4.33						4.33	4.00	3.00	4.50		4.00		3.88				3.71		4.50	4.11	4.11
		Satisfaction from transport		4.33						4.33	4.40	3.00	4.50		4.00		3.98				4.71		4.50	4.51	4.31
		Satisfaction from accommodation		3.67						3.67	2.40	3.00	3.50		4.00		3.23				3.67		3.00	3.34	3.41
		Satsifaction from safety measures		2.33						2.33	4.00	3.50	1.00		2.00		2.63				3.33		3.50	3.42	2.71
		Satsifaction from infrastructure		3.33						3.33	4.50	2.50	1.00		4.00		3.00				4.99		4.00	4.00	3.44
		X		3.60						3.60	3.86	3.00	2.90		3.60		3.34				4.08		3.90	3.90	3.60
		X34		3.60	4.24				3.50	3.59	3.53	3.48	3.15	3.89	3.50	3.49	3.45	4.00	2.69	2.70	4.17	3.40	3.70	3.79	3.60
Non-Local	X			3.38	3.24	3.28	3.30		3.25	3.32	3.54	3.49	3.48	3.76	3.40	3.36	3.46	3.44	2.69	3.35	3.82	3.56	3.50	3.49	3.42
Overall	X			3.09	3.22	2.74	3.30		3.25	3.03	3.54	3.68	3.51	3.60	3.40	2.88	3.43	3.44		3.35	3.74	3.56	3.15	3.17	3.22

Table–8.4

Mean Scores of Marketing Effectiveness Observed by Pilgrim and Non-Pilgrim Groups for Additional Infrastructural Services

(1) Groups	(2)	(3)	(4) Variables	(5)	Age Group-I Upto 25 yrs							Age Group-II 25 to 50 Yrs							Age Group-III Above 50 Yrs							X
				Income	Inc-1		Inc-2		Inc-3		X	Inc-1		Inc-2		Inc-3		X	Inc-1		Inc-2		Inc-3		X	X
				Education	E-1	E-2	E-1	E-2	E-1	E-2	X	E-1	E-2	E-1	E-2	E-1	E-2	X	E-1	E-2	E-1	E-2	E-1	E-2	X	X
(1)	(2)	(3)	(4)	(5)	(6)	(7)	(8)	(9)	(10)	(11)	(12)	(13)	(14)	(15)	(16)	(17)	(18)	(19)	(20)	(21)	(22)	(23)	(24)	(25)	(26)	(27)
Local	Pilgrim	Male	Adequate cloak room		3.00	4.00	4.00				3.67	3.00	3.00	3.00	4.00			3.33			-	3.00		5.00	4.00	3.67
			Clean drinking water		2.00	1.00	4.00				2.33	3.00	2.33	3.00	3.00			2.78			-	3.67	4.00	4.00	3.84	2.98
			Better roads		3.00	4.00	4.00				3.67	3.67	3.67	2.00	4.75			3.47			-	3.60	4.00	4.00	3.80	3.65
			Sanitation & hygiene		1.00	2.00	4.00				2.33	2.33	2.33	1.00	3.00			2.11			-	2.33	1.00	1.00	1.67	2.04
			Adequate bedding		4.00	1.00	4.00				3.00	3.00	3.00	4.00	3.50			3.50			-	3.67	4.00	4.00	3.84	3.45
			Adequate shelter sheds		4.00	2.00	4.00				3.33	2.33	2.33	4.00	3.25			3.19			-	4.00	3.00	3.00	3.50	3.34
			X1		2.83	2.33	4.00				3.06	2.83	2.78	2.83	3.58			3.06		.		3.38		3.50	3.44	3.19
		Female	Adequate cloak room								-	4.00			4.00			4.00			4.00				4.00	4.00
			Clean drinking water								-	3.00			2.00			2.50			4.00				4.00	3.25
			Better roads								-	4.00			4.00			4.00			4.00				4.00	4.00
			Sanitation & hygiene								-	3.00			3.00			3.00			4.00				4.00	3.50
			Adequate bedding								-	4.00			4.00			4.00			4.00				4.00	4.00
			Adequate shelter sheds								-	4.00			2.00			3.00			4.00				3.50	3.50
			X2								-	3.67			3.17			3.42			4.00				4.00	3.71
			X12		2.83	2.33	4.00				3.06	3.23	2.78	2.83	3.38			3.24			4.00	3.38		3.50	3.72	3.44
	Non-Pilgrim	Male	Adequate cloak room									3.00		4.00	2.00		1.00	2.50				2.00			2.00	2.25

Contd.....

(1)	(2)	(3)	(4)	(5)	(6)	(7)	(8)	(9)	(10)	(11)	(12)	(13)	(14)	(15)	(16)	(17)	(18)	(19)	(20)	(21)	(22)	(23)	(24)	(25)	(26)	(27)
		Pilgrim	Clean drinking water		-	-	-				-	-	4.00	4.00	1.67		1.00	2.67			-	-	-	2.00	2.00	2.34
			Better roads		-	-	-				-		2.00	4.00	4.00		1.00	2.75			-	-	-	1.00	1.00	1.87
			Sanitation & hygiene		-	-	-				-		2.00	3.67	4.00		1.00	2.67			-	-	-	4.00	4.00	3.34
			Adequate bedding		-	-	-				-		3.00	4.00	4.00		1.00	3.00			-	-		4.00	4.00	3.50
			Adequate shelter sheds		-	-	-				-		2.00	4.00	3.67		1.00	2.67			-	-	-	4.00	4.00	3.34
			X3		2.83								2.67	3.95	3.22		1.00	2.71						2.83	2.83	2.77
		Locals	X			2.33	4.00				3.06		2.95	3.39	3.30		1.00	2.98			4.00	3.38		3.17	3.28	3.11
Non-Local		Male	Adequate cloak room			-	2.50	3.75		5.00	3.72	5.00	4.00	3.67	3.58	3.00	3.71	3.83	4.00		3.00	3.40	4.00	3.00	3.48	3.68
			Clean drinking water				3.50	3.75		3.00	3.50	2.50	2.60	3.13	3.32	3.43	3.62	3.10	4.00		3.00	3.47	4.00	2.60	3.41	3.34
			Better roads		3.45		2.75	3.67		3.67	3.39	4.00	3.50	3.23	3.58	2.73	3.33	3.40	3.50		3.17	3.30	3.50	3.06	3.31	3.37
			Sanitation & hygiene		2.13		2.50	3.67		3.00	2.83	1.00	2.80	2.40	2.90	2.00	2.43	2.26	4.00		2.00	3.07	3.00	3.26	3.07	2.74
			Adequate bedding		3.75		3.50	3.50		5.00	3.94	4.50	4.00	3.26	3.71	3.29	3.07	3.64	4.00		3.00	3.33	3.75	2.32	3.28	3.62
			Adequate shelter sheds		3.75		3.50	3.50		3.00	3.44	1.50	3.80	3.47	3.77	3.14	3.08	3.13	4.00		4.00	3.40	4.00	3.08	3.70	3.42
			X1		3.41		3.04	3.64		3.78	3.47	3.08	3.45	3.19	3.48	2.93	3.21	3.23	3.92	4.00	3.03	3.33	3.71	2.89	3.38	3.36
		Female	Adequate cloak room		4.00	3.00	3.00	-			3.33	3.63	3.54	-	2.80	4.00	4.00	3.59	4.00	4.00	3.67	3.00	3.00	3.42	3.52	3.48
			Clean drinking water		4.00	3.00	4.00	-		-	3.67	3.50	3.38	-	3.20	3.00	3.00	3.22	3.40	4.00	4.00	4.00	3.00	3.08	3.58	3.49
			Better roads		3.67	3.20	4.00			-	3.62	3.36	3.53		3.56	4.00	2.50	3.39	3.14	4.00	3.50	3.40	3.00	3.50	3.42	3.48
			Sanitation & hygiene		4.00	4.00	1.00	-		-	3.00	2.38	2.54		2.40	2.00	2.00	2.26	2.20	2.00	2.67	1.50	1.00	2.17	1.92	2.39
			Adequate bedding		4.00	3.00	3.00	-		-	3.33	3.38	3.31		3.60	3.00	4.00	3.46	3.80	4.00	3.67	3.50	3.00	3.42	3.57	3.45
			Adequate shelter sheds		4.00	3.00	3.00	-		-	3.33	3.13	3.54		3.60	2.00	3.00	3.05	3.00	4.00	3.67	2.50	3.00	2.75	3.15	3.18
			X2		3.95	3.20	3.02				3.38	3.23	3.31	3.19	3.19	3.00	3.08	3.16	3.26	3.67	3.53	2.98	2.67	3.06	3.19	3.25
			X12		3.68	3.20	3.64			3.78	3.43	3.16	3.38	3.19	3.34	2.97	3.15	3.20	3.59	3.67	3.28	3.16	3.19	2.98	3.29	3.31

Table–8.5

Mean Scores of Marketing Effectiveness Observed by Pilgrim and Non-Pilgrim Groups for Transport Services

Groups (1)	(2)	(3)	Variables (4)	Age Group-I Up to 25 yrs. — Inc-1 E-1 (6)	Inc-1 E-2 (7)	Inc-2 E-1 (8)	Inc-2 E-2 (9)	Inc-3 E-1 (10)	Inc-3 E-2 (11)	X (12)	Age Group-II 25 to 50 Yrs. — Inc-1 E-1 (13)	Inc-1 E-2 (14)	Inc-2 E-1 (15)	Inc-2 E-2 (16)	Inc-3 E-1 (17)	Inc-3 E-2 (18)	X (19)	Age Group-III Above 50 Yrs. — Inc-1 E-1 (20)	Inc-1 E-2 (21)	Inc-2 E-1 (22)	Inc-2 E-2 (23)	Inc-3 E-1 (24)	Inc-3 E-2 (25)	X (26)	X (27)
Local	PILGRIM	Male	Luxury bus service	2.00	3.00	4.00	-			3.00		2.67	4.00	3.50	3.00	-	3.29				3.25		4.00	3.63	3.31
			Ordinary bus service	2.00	2.00	2.00				2.00		2.33	3.00	3.25	3.00	-	2.90				2.40		3.50	2.95	2.62
			Pony & pithu service	2.00	2.00	1.00				1.67		3.67	3.00	4.00	3.00	-	3.42				2.60		3.00	2.80	2.63
			Taxi services	2.00	3.00	3.00				2.67		2.67	4.00	3.50	3.00	-	3.29				3.40		3.50	3.45	3.14
			X1	2.00	2.50	2.50				2.34		2.84	3.50	3.56	3.00	-	3.23				2.91		3.50	3.21	2.93
		Female	Luxury bus service	-	-							3.00	-	2.00	-	3.50	2.83	4.00	4.00	4.00	4.00		-	4.00	3.42
			Ordinary bus service	-	-							3.00	-	2.00	-	3.00	2.67	4.00	4.00	4.00	4.00		-	4.00	3.34
			Pony & pithu service	-	-							3.00	-	3.50	-	4.00	3.50	4.00	4.00	4.00	4.00		-	4.00	3.75
			Taxi services	-	-							3.00	-	2.00	-	3.50	2.83	4.00	4.00	4.00	4.00		-	4.00	3.42
			X2	-	-							3.00	-	2.38	-	3.50	2.96	4.00	4.00	4.00	4.00		-	4.00	3.48
			X12	2.00	2.50	2.50				2.34		2.92	3.50	2.97	3.00	3.50	3.10		4.00	4.00	3.46		3.50	3.61	3.21
	NON-PILGRIM	Male	Luxury bus service									3.00	3.00	4.00	-	2.00	3.00				-		1.00	1.00	2.00
			Ordinary bus service									5.00	2.67	3.00	2.00	2.00	3.17				-		1.00	1.00	2.09
			Pony & pithu service									5.00	3.67	4.00	-	3.00	3.92				-		1.00	1.00	2.46
			Taxi services									5.00	2.67	4.00	3.00	3.00	3.67				-		1.00	1.00	2.34
			X3									4.50	3.00	3.75	3.00	2.50	3.44				-		1.00	1.00	2.22
	Locals		X	2.00	2.50	2.50				2.34		3.71	3.25	3.36	3.00	3.00	3.27	4.00	4.00	4.00	3.46		2.25	2.31	2.72

Contd......

(1)	(2)	(3)	(4)	(5)	(6)	(7)	(8)	(9)	(10)	(11)	(12)	(13)	(14)	(15)	(16)	(17)	(18)	(19)	(20)	(21)	(22)	(23)	(24)	(25)	(26)	(27)
Non-Local	PILGRIM	Male	Luxury bus service		3.42	2.75	2.50	4.00	4.00	4.00	3.45	4.00	3.67	3.32	3.61	3.36	3.06	3.50	3.00	-	3.50	3.11	3.60	2.93	3.23	3.39
			Ordinary bus service		2.80	2.50	2.50	3.00	3.80	3.50	3.02	1.50	2.50	2.65	2.80	1.91	2.53	2.32	2.00	-	3.50	2.63	3.00	2.30	2.69	2.68
			Pony & pithu service		2.80	2.50	3.75	1.00	3.50	3.50	2.84	3.00	2.40	2.96	3.06	2.78	2.72	2.82	2.00	-	3.00	2.78	2.50	2.97	2.65	2.72
			Taxi services		2.57	3.00	3.25	1.00	4.00	5.00	3.14	4.00	3.25	3.04	3.40	3.09	3.14	3.32	2.14	-	3.00	3.30	3.00	3.45	2.98	3.09
			X1		2.90	2.69	3.00	2.25	3.83	4.00	3.11	3.13	2.96	2.99	3.22	2.79	2.86	2.99	2.29	-	3.25	2.96	3.03	2.91	2.89	2.97
		Female	Luxury bus service		4.00	3.20	2.00	-		4.00	3.30	2.64	3.33	5.00	3.33	4.00	3.00	3.55	3.00	3.00	3.14	3.33	4.00	3.50	3.33	3.39
			Ordinary bus service		3.00	2.40	3.00	-		1.00	2.35	2.09	2.78	1.00	2.80	2.00	2.00	2.12	3.00	3.00	3.25	2.40	4.00	2.92	3.10	2.58
			Pony & pithu service		3.00	2.00	3.00	-		1.00	2.25	2.11	2.88	5.00	2.88	2.00	3.50	3.06	3.40	1.00	3.50	2.50	3.00	2.57	2.66	2.66
			Taxi services		3.00	2.33	2.00	-		1.00	2.08	2.55	2.75	1.00	2.17	4.00	3.00	2.58	3.40	3.00	3.29	2.50	1.00	3.42	2.77	2.48
			X2		3.25	2.48	2.50	-		1.75	2.50	2.35	2.94	3.00	2.80	3.00	2.88	2.83	3.20	2.50	3.30	2.68	3.00	3.10	2.97	2.78
			X12		3.08	2.59	2.75	2.25	3.83	2.58	2.81	2.74	2.95	3.00	3.01	2.90	2.87	2.91	2.75	2.50	3.28	2.82	3.02	3.01	2.93	2.88
	NON PILGRIM	Male	Luxury bus service		-	4.00	-	2.33		4.50	3.61	3.00	3.00	3.50	3.61	4.00	4.00	3.52	4.00	4.00	4.00	3.33	4.00	3.43	3.79	3.64
			Ordinary bus service		-	4.00	-	2.33		4.50	3.61	3.00	1.80	3.00	3.26	3.00	3.43	2.92	3.00	4.00	2.00	3.00	3.00	3.00	3.00	3.18
			Pony & pithu service		-	4.00	-	2.67		4.00	3.56	1.00	3.60	3.00	3.16	3.00	3.00	2.79	4.00	4.00	4.00	3.33	4.00	3.57	3.82	3.39
			Taxi services		-	1.00	-	3.00		4.50	2.83	1.00	2.40	3.00	2.76	3.00	3.57	2.63	3.00	4.00	4.00	3.00	3.00	2.94	3.32	2.93
			X3		-	3.25	-	2.58		4.38	3.40	2.00	2.70	3.13	3.20	3.25	3.50	2.97	3.50	4.00	3.50	3.17	3.50	3.24	3.48	3.29
		Female	Luxury bus service		4.00	-	-				4.00		3.20	4.00	3.00	-	4.00	3.55	-	-	-	3.86	-	3.00	3.43	3.66
			Ordinary bus service		3.33	-	-				3.33		3.20	3.50	2.50	-	4.00	3.30	-	-	2.86	2.86	-	3.00	2.93	3.19
			Pony & pithu service		3.33	-	-				3.33		3.20	4.00	3.00	-	2.00	3.05	-	-	2.71	2.71	-	4.00	3.36	3.25
			Taxi services		3.00	-	-				3.00		3.60	4.00	2.50	-	2.00	3.03	-	-	2.71	2.71	-	4.00	3.36	3.13
			X4		3.42						3.42		3.30	3.88	2.75		3.00	3.23		4.00		3.04		3.50	3.27	3.31
			X34		3.42	3.25	-	2.58	3.83	4.38	3.41	2.00	3.00	3.51	2.98	3.25	3.25	3.00	3.50	4.00	3.50	3.11	3.50	3.37	3.38	3.30
		Non-Local	X		3.25	2.92	2.75	2.42	3.83	3.63	3.11	2.37	2.98	3.26	3.00	3.08	3.06	3.01	3.13	3.25	3.39	2.97	3.26	3.19	3.16	3.09
		Overall	X		2.63	2.71	2.63	2.42	3.83	3.63	2.73	2.37	3.35	3.26	3.18	3.04	3.03	3.14	3.13	3.63	3.70	3.22	3.26	2.72	2.74	2.91

Table-8.6

Mean Scores of Marketing Effectiveness Observed by Pilgrim and Non- Pilgrim Groups for Food Services En route to Destination

(1)	Groups (2)	(3)	Variables (4)	Education (5)	Age Group-I Up to 25 yrs.							Age Group-II 25 to 50 Yrs.							Age Group-III Above 50 Yrs.							(27)
					Inc-1		Inc-2		Inc-3			Inc-1		Inc-2		Inc-3			Inc-1		Inc-2		Inc-3			
					E-1	E-2	E-1	E-2	E-1	E-2	X	E-1	E-2	E-1	E-2	E-1	E-2	X	E-1	E-2	E-1	E-2	E-1	E-2	X	X
					(6)	(7)	(8)	(9)	(10)	(11)	(12)	(13)	(14)	(15)	(16)	(17)	(18)	(19)	(20)	(21)	(22)	(23)	(24)	(25)	(26)	(27)
Local	PILGRIM	Male	Tasty & delicious food		1.00	1.00	2.00	-			1.33		1.67	3.00	3.50			2.72			-	2.00	4.00	4.00	3.00	2.35
			Hygienic food		2.00	1.00	3.00	-			2.00		1.67	3.00	3.25			2.64			-	3.00	4.00	4.00	3.50	2.71
			X1		1.50	1.00	2.50	-			1.67		1.67	3.00	3.38			2.68			-	2.50	4.00	4.00	3.25	2.53
		Female	Tasty & delicious food		-	-	-	-			-		4.00	-	3.00			3.50			4.00	-	-	-	4.00	3.75
			Hygienic food		-	-	-	-			-		3.00	-	1.00			2.00			4.00	-	-	-	4.00	3.00
			X2		-	-	-	-			-		3.50	-	2.00			2.75			4.00	-	-	-	4.00	3.38
			X12		1.50	1.00	2.50				1.67		2.59	3.00	2.69			2.72			4.00	2.50	4.00	4.00	3.63	2.96
	NON-PILGRIM	Male	Tasty & delicious food		-						-		2.00	3.33	2.33		1.00	2.17			-		4.00	4.00	4.00	3.09
			Hygienic food										2.00	3.33	3.00		1.00	2.33			-		4.00	4.00	4.00	3.17
			X3										2.00	3.33	2.67		1.00	2.25			-		4.00	4.00	4.00	3.13
		Local	X		1.50	1.00	2.50				1.67		2.30	3.17	2.68		1.00	2.49			4.00	2.50	4.00	4.00	3.82	3.06

Contd......

(1)	(2)	(3)	(4)	(5)	(6)	(7)	(8)	(9)	(10)	(11)	(12)	(13)	(14)	(15)	(16)	(17)	(18)	(19)	(20)	(21)	(22)	(23)	(24)	(25)	(26)	(27)
Non-locals	PILGRIM	Male	Tasty & delicious food		3.13	-	3.50	3.25		2.00	2.97	2.50	3.40	2.53	2.84	2.86	3.07	2.87	4.00		3.00	2.08	3.75	2.88	3.14	2.99
			Hygienic food		3.00	-	3.50	3.25		3.00	3.19	2.50	3.00	2.67	2.81	2.29	2.67	2.66	4.00		3.00	2.23	3.50	2.87	3.12	2.99
			X1		3.07	-	3.50	3.25		2.50	3.08	2.50	3.20	2.60	2.83	2.58	2.87	2.77	4.00		3.00	2.16	3.63	2.88	3.13	2.99
		Female	Tasty & delicious food		3.33	3.00	3.00	-		-	3.11	2.88	2.31	-	3.20	2.00	2.00	2.48	2.80	2.00	3.00	2.00	4.00	2.58	2.73	2.77
			Hygienic food		3.33	3.00	3.00	-		-	3.11	2.63	2.71	-	3.00	2.00	1.00	2.27	2.60	2.00	3.00	2.50	4.00	2.42	2.75	2.71
			X2		3.33	3.00	3.00	-		-	3.11	2.76	2.51	-	3.10	2.00	1.50	2.38	2.70	2.00	3.00	2.25	4.00	2.50	2.74	2.74
			X12		3.20	3.00	3.25	3.25		2.50	3.10	2.63	2.86	2.60	2.97	2.29	2.19	2.58	3.35	2.00	3.00	2.21	3.82	2.69	2.94	2.87
	NON-PILGRIM	Male	Tasty & delicious food		-	4.00	-	3.00		3.00	3.33	3.00	3.00	2.00	3.79	2.00	3.00	2.80	4.00			4.67	3.00	3.00	3.67	3.27
			Hygienic food		-	4.00	-	1.00		3.00	2.67	3.00	1.67	2.00	3.95	2.00	2.80	2.57	4.00			4.67	3.00	2.91	3.65	2.96
			X3		-	4.00	-	2.00		3.00	3.00	3.00	2.34	2.00	3.87	2.00	2.90	2.69	4.00			4.67	3.00	2.96	3.66	3.12
		Female	Tasty & delicious food		3.00	-	-	-		-	3.00	-	3.00	3.00	2.00	-	3.00	2.75	-			3.00	-	3.50	3.25	3.00
			Hygienic food		3.00	-	-	-		-	3.00	-	2.00	3.00	2.00	-	1.00	2.00	-		3.50	3.50	-	3.00	3.25	2.75
			X4		3.00	4.00	-	2.00		3.00	3.00	2.50	2.50	3.00	2.00	2.00	2.00	2.38	-			3.25	-	3.25	3.25	2.88
			X34		3.00	3.50	-	2.00		3.00	3.00	3.00	2.42	2.50	2.94	2.00	2.45	2.54	4.00			3.96	3.00	3.11	3.46	3.00
	Non-Local X				3.10	2.25	3.25	2.63		2.75	3.05	2.82	2.64	2.55	2.96	2.15	2.32	2.56	3.68	2.00	3.00	3.09	3.41	2.90	3.20	2.94
	Overall	X			2.30	2.25	2.88	2.63		2.75	2.36	2.82	2.47	2.86	2.82	2.15	1.66	2.53	3.68	2.00	3.50	2.80	3.41	3.45	3.51	3.00

Table–8.7

Mean Scores of Marketing Effectiveness Observed by Pilgrim and Non-Pilgrim Groups for Retail Services En route to Destination

Groups		Age	Variables	Income	Age Group-I Upto 25 yrs.							Age Group-II 25 to 50 Yrs.							Age Group-III Above 50 Yrs.							X
					Inc-1		Inc-2		Inc-3		X	Inc-1		Inc-2		Inc-3		X	Inc-1		Inc-2		Inc-3		X	
				Education	E-1	E-2	E-1	E-2	E-1	E-2		E-1	E-2	E-1	E-2	E-1	E-2		E-1	E-2	E-1	E-2	E-1	E-2		X
(1)	(2)	(3)	(4)	(5)	(6)	(7)	(8)	(9)	(10)	(11)	(12)	(13)	(14)	(15)	(16)	(17)	(18)	(19)	(20)	(21)	(22)	(23)	(24)	(25)	(26)	(27)
Local	PILGRIMS	Male	Cooperative shop-keepers at *Bhavan*		4.00	5.00	2.00	-	-	-	3.67	-	2.00	4.00	3.33	4.00	4.00	3.47				3.20		4.00	3.60	3.58
			Adequate shop-ping at *Bhavan*		4.00	3.00	2.00	-	-	-	3.00	-	3.33	4.00	4.00	3.00	4.00	3.67				3.40		4.00	3.70	3.46
			Cooperative shop-keepers at *Katra*		2.00	3.00	3.00	-	-	-	2.67	-	3.00	2.00	4.00	2.00	4.00	3.00				2.80		3.50	3.15	2.94
			Adequate shop-keepers at *Katra*		1.00	2.00	2.00	-	-	-	1.67	-	1.67	2.00	3.33	2.00	4.00	2.60				2.20		2.50	2.35	2.21
			X1		2.75	3.25	2.25				2.75		2.50	3.00	3.67	2.75	4.00	3.19				2.90		3.50	3.20	3.05
		Female	Cooperative shop-keepers at *Bhavan*		-	-	-	-	-	-	-	-	3.00	-	3.00	-	4.00	3.33	-	1.00	1.00	5.00	-	-	2.33	2.83
			Adequate shop-ping at *Bhavan*		-	-	-	-	-	-	-	-	3.00	-	3.50	-	4.00	3.50	-	4.00	4.00	4.00	-	-	4.00	3.75
			Cooperative shop-keepers at *Katra*		-	-	-	-	-	-	-	-	3.00	-	3.00	-	4.00	3.33	-	4.00	1.00	5.00	-	-	3.33	3.33
			Adequate shop-keepers at *Katra*		-	-	-	-	-	-	-	-	3.00	-	2.00	-	4.00	3.00	-	4.00	1.00	4.00	-	-	3.00	3.00
			X2										3.00		2.88		4.00	3.29		3.25	1.75	4.50			3.17	3.23

Contd......

(1)	(2)	(3)	(4)	(5)	(6)	(7)	(8)	(9)	(10)	(11)	(12)	(13)	(14)	(15)	(16)	(17)	(18)	(19)	(20)	(21)	(22)	(23)	(24)	(25)	(26)	(27)
Non-Pilgrim		Male	X12		2.75	3.25	2.25	-	-		2.75		2.75	3.00	3.28	2.76	4.00	3.24		3.25	1.75	3.70		3.50	3.19	3.14
			Cooperative shop-keepers at *Bhavan*		-	-	-	-	-			4.00	5.00	2.00	3.00	-	4.00	3.60		-	-	-		2.00	2.00	2.88
			Adequate shop-ping at *Bhavan*			-	-	-	-			3.00	5.00	2.67	3.50	-	4.00	3.63		-	-	-		2.00	2.00	2.82
			Cooperative shop-keepers at Katra			-	-	-	-			3.00	5.00	3.33	3.00	-	4.00	3.67		-	-	-		1.00	1.00	2.34
			Adequate shop-keepers at Katra			-	-	-	-			4.00	5.00	3.33	3.00	-	4.00	3.87		-	-	-		2.00	2.00	2.94
			X3		-	-	-	-	-		-	3.50	5.00	2.83	3.13	-	4.00	3.69		-	-	-		1.75	1.75	2.73
		Local	X		2.75	3.25	2.25	-	-		2.75	3.50	3.80	2.92	3.21	2.75	4.00	3.47		3.25	1.75	3.70		2.63	2.47	2.94
Non-Locals	PILGRIM	Male	Cooperative shop-keepers at *Bhavan*		3.38	3.67	2.75	3.50	2.50	3.50	3.22	3.00	2.00	3.24	2.93	3.27	2.76	2.87	2.00	-	3.00	3.00	2.86	2.71	2.71	2.93
			Adequate shop-ping at *Bhavan*		3.38	3.00	2.50	3.33	3.25	4.50	3.33	3.00	2.33	3.45	3.31	3.09	3.42	3.10	2.00	-	2.00	2.85	3.14	2.90	2.58	3.00
			Cooperative shop-keepers at Katra		2.91	3.33	3.00	3.50	3.83	3.67	3.37	2.00	2.50	3.33	3.24	2.91	3.50	2.90	3.00	-	3.33	2.94	3.14	2.91	3.06	3.11
			Adequate shop-keepers at Katra		3.27	3.33	2.50	3.50	3.50	3.33	3.24	2.00	2.75	2.85	2.97	2.45	2.41	2.57	2.00	-	3.00	2.22	2.57	2.74	2.51	2.77
			X1		3.24	3.33	2.69	3.46	3.27	3.75	3.29	2.50	2.40	3.22	3.11	2.93	3.02	2.86	2.25		2.83	2.75	2.93	2.82	2.72	2.95
		Female	Cooperative shop-keepers at *Bhavan*		2.00	2.00	4.00	-	-	2.00	2.50	2.60	2.64	4.00	2.82	2.00	3.00	2.84.	3.33	3.00	2.71	1.67	3.00	2.17	2.65	2.66
			Adequate shop-ping at *Bhavan*		2.00	2.00	3.00	-	-	2.00	2.25	2.40	3.27	4.00	2.90	4.00	3.50	3.35	3.33	3.00	3.29	2.67	4.00	3.25	3.26	2.95
			Cooperative shop-keepers at Katra		3.33	3.60	4.00	-	-	1.00	2.98	2.45	3.29	5.00	3.09	4.00	3.50	3.56	3.00	3.00	1.88	3.20	4.00	2.71	2.97	3.17

Contd.....

(1)	(2)	(3)	(4)	(5)	(6)	(7)	(8)	(9)	(10)	(11)	(12)	(13)	(14)	(15)	(16)	(17)	(18)	(19)	(20)	(21)	(22)	(23)	(24)	(25)	(26)	(27)
			Adequate shop-keepers at Katra		3.00	3.40	2.00	-	-	2.00	2.60	2.18	2.53	4.00	2.73	2.00	2.50	2.66	2.71	3.00	1.75	2.80	3.00	2.57	2.64	2.63
			X2		2.58	2.75	3.25			1.75	2.58	2.41	2.93	4.25	2.89	3.00	3.13	3.10	3.09	3.00	2.41	2.59	3.50	2.68	2.88	2.85
			X12		2.91	3.04	2.97	3.46	3.27	2.75	2.94	2.46	2.67	3.74	3.00	2.97	3.08	2.98	2.67	3.00	2.62	2.67	3.22	2.75	2.80	2.91
	NON-PILGRIM	Male	Cooperative shop-keepers at Bhavan		3.20	1.67	-	2.33	-	4.00	2.80	2.00	4.00	1.00	2.55	3.00	3.25	2.63	2.00	4.00	3.00	2.67	2.00	2.08	2.63	2.69
			Adequate shopping at Bhavan		3.40	2.00	-	3.00	-	4.50	3.23	1.00	3.20	2.00	3.00	3.00	4.00	2.70	2.00	4.00	3.00	2.67	2.00	2.71	2.73	2.89
			Cooperative shop-keepers at Katra		2.00	4.00	-	2.33	-	4.50	3.21	1.00	3.40	2.00	3.10	2.00	3.25	2.46	2.00	4.00	4.00	2.67	2.00	2.64	2.89	2.85
			Adequate shop-keepers at Katra		2.50	2.67	-	1.67	-	4.00	2.71	2.00	3.80	2.00	2.75	2.00	2.78	2.56	2.00	4.00	4.00	2.67	2.00	2.36	2.84	2.70
			X3		2.78	2.59	-	2.33	-	4.25	2.99	1.50	3.60	1.75	2.85	2.50	3.32	2.59	2.00	4.00	3.50	2.67	2.00	2.45	2.77	2.78
		Female	Cooperative shop-keepers at Bhavan		3.00	-	2.00	-	-	-	2.50	2.00	1.33	3.50	2.00	-	4.00	2.57	-	-	2.80	2.80	-	4.00	3.40	2.82
			Adequate shopping at Bhavan		3.33	-	3.00	-	-	-	3.17	3.00	3.60	4.00	2.50	-	4.00	3.42	-	-	3.20	3.20	-	3.50	3.35	3.31
			Cooperative shop-keepers at Katra		2.67	-	1.00	-	-	-	1.84	3.00	1.60	3.00	2.00	-	4.00	2.72	-	-	2.60	2.60	-	2.00	2.30	2.29
			Adequate shop-keepers at Katra		3.67	-	3.00	-	-	-	3.34	4.00	2.40	4.00	2.50	-	4.00	3.38	-	-	3.00	3.00	-	2.00	2.50	3.07
			X4		3.17	-	2.25	-	-	-	2.71	3.00	2.23	3.63	2.25	-	4.00	3.02	-	-	2.90	2.90	-	2.88	2.89	2.87
			X34		2.98	2.82	2.61	2.90	3.27	3.50	2.85	2.25	2.92	2.69	2.55	2.74	3.66	2.81	2.55	3.50	3.06	2.79	2.61	2.67	2.83	2.83
		Non-Local	X		2.95	-	-	-	3.27	3.50	2.90	2.36	2.80	3.22	2.78	-	3.37	2.90	2.55	-	2.41	2.73	2.61	2.71	2.82	2.87
		Overall	X		2.85	3.04	2.43	2.90	3.27	3.50	2.83	2.93	3.34	3.07	3.00	2.75	3.69	3.19	2.55	3.38	2.41	3.22	2.61	2.67	2.65	2.91

Table–8.8

Mean Scores of Marketing Effectiveness Observed by Pilgrim and Non-Pilgrim Groups for Accommodation Services at Katra & En route to Destination

Column key — Age Groups: **I** = Age Group-I Up to 25 yrs.; **II** = Age Group-II 25 to 50 Yrs.; **III** = Age Group-III Above 50 Yrs. Each Age Group has Income bands **Inc-1, Inc-2, Inc-3** (each with Education levels **E-1, E-2**) and a mean **X**.

(1) Groups	(2)	(3) Variables	(4) Income / Education	(5) I Inc-1 E-1	(6) I Inc-1 E-2	(7) I Inc-2 E-1	(8) I Inc-2 E-2	(9) I Inc-3 E-1	(10) I Inc-3 E-2	(11) I X	(12) II Inc-1 E-1	(13) II Inc-1 E-2	(14) II Inc-2 E-1	(15) II Inc-2 E-2	(16) II Inc-3 E-1	(17) II Inc-3 E-2	(18) II X	(19) III Inc-1 E-1	(20) III Inc-1 E-2	(21) III Inc-2 E-1	(22) III Inc-2 E-2	(23) III Inc-3 E-1	(24) III Inc-3 E-2	(25) III X	(26) X
Local Pilgrim	Pilgrims Male	Maintenance of accommodation at Katra		4.00	4.00	4.00				4.00		2.67	3.00	4.00			3.22				3.00		3.00	3.00	3.41
		Easily available accommodation at Katra		3.00	3.00	2.00				2.67		2.33	1.00	3.00			2.11				2.33		1.00	1.67	2.15
		Reasonable charges for accommodation		3.00	1.00	2.00				2.00		1.67	2.00	3.50			2.39				3.00		1.00	2.00	2.13
		X1		3.33	2.67	2.67				2.89		2.22	2.00	3.50			2.57				2.78	0.00	1.67	2.22	2.56
	Female	Maintenance of accommodation at Katra		-	-	-				-		4.00	-	4.00			4.00				-	-	-		4.00
		Easily available accommodation at Katra		-	-	-				-		3.00	-	1.00			2.00				-	-	-		2.00
		Reasonable charges for accommodation		-	-	-				-		3.00	-	1.00			2.00				-	-	-		2.00
		X2		-	-	-				-		3.33	-	2.00			2.67				-	-	-		2.67
		X12		3.33	2.67	2.67				2.89		2.78	2.00	2.75			2.62				2.78		1.67	2.22	2.62
Local Non-Pilgrim	Male	Maintenance of accommodation at Katra		-	-	-				-		5.00	3.33	3.67		4.00	3.84				-	-	2.00	2.00	2.92
		Easily available accommodation at Katra		-	-	-				-		4.00	3.33	2.67		1.00	2.75				-	-	2.00	2.00	2.38
		Reasonable charges for accommodation		-	-	-				-		4.00	2.67	3.00		1.00	2.67				-	-	1.00	1.00	1.84
		X3		-	-	-				-		4.33	2.89	3.11		2.00	3.09				-	-	1.67	1.67	2.38
Local	X			3.33	2.67	2.67				2.89		3.56	2.45	2.93		2.00	2.86				2.78		1.67	1.96	2.50

Contd.....

(1)	(2)	(3)	(4)	(5)	(6)	(7)	(8)	(9)	(10)	(11)	(12)	(13)	(14)	(15)	(16)	(17)	(18)	(19)	(20)	(21)	(22)	(23)	(24)	(25)	(26)
Non-Local Pilgrims	Male	Maintenance of accommodation at Katra		2.63	-	3.75	3.67		4.00	3.51	2.00	3.00	3.08	2.35	2.43	2.92	2.63	4.00			3.73	3.50	2.78	3.50	3.21
		Easily available accommodation at Katra		2.88	-	2.50	2.33		4.00	2.93	3.00	2.20	3.15	2.96	2.71	3.71	2.96	4.00			3.64	3.25	3.12	3.50	3.13
		Reasonable charges for accommodation		2.25	-	2.75	3.00		4.00	3.00	3.00	2.20	2.54	2.27	2.43	2.64	2.51	4.00			2.55	3.25	2.36	3.04	2.85
		X1		2.59		3.00	3.00		4.00	3.15	2.67	2.47	2.92	2.53	2.52	3.09	2.70	4.00			3.31	3.33	2.75	3.35	3.06
	Female	Maintenance of accommodation at Katra		1.00	4.00	1.00	-		-	2.00	2.50	2.55	-	2.60	4.00	3.00	2.93	2.00		2.00	2.50	3.00	2.55	2.41	2.45
		Easily available accommodation at Katra		3.00	2.00	1.00	-		-	2.00	2.50	2.91	-	2.00	3.00	4.00	2.88	2.33		2.50	3.00	1.00	2.18	2.20	2.36
		Reasonable charges for accommodation		1.00	2.00	1.00	-		-	1.33	2.00	2.18	-	2.40	2.00	3.00	2.32	1.00		1.50	3.50	1.00	2.18	1.84	1.83
		X2		1.67	2.67	1.00				1.78	2.33	2.55		2.33	3.00	3.33	2.71	1.78		2.00	3.00	1.67	2.30	2.15	2.21
		X12		2.13	2.67	2.00	3.00		4.00	2.47	2.51	2.55	2.92	2.43	2.76	3.21	2.71	2.89		1.00	3.16	2.50	2.53	2.75	2.64
Non-Local Non-Pilgrims	Male	Maintenance of accommodation at Katra		-	3.00	-	1.00		5.00	3.00	1.00	2.50	2.00	2.73	3.00	3.20	2.41	4.00			4.00	2.00	3.33	3.33	2.91
		Easily available accommodation at Katra		-	3.00	-	1.00		5.00	3.00	2.00	2.00	4.00	3.00	1.00	3.60	2.60	4.00			3.33	2.00	3.22	3.14	2.91
		Reasonable charges for accommodation		-	3.00	-	1.00		5.00	3.00	2.00	3.50	2.00	2.33	2.00	3.20	2.51	2.00			2.67	3.00	2.71	2.60	2.70
		X3		-	3.00		1.00		5.00	3.00	1.67	2.67	2.67	2.69	2.00	3.33	2.51	3.33			3.33	2.33	3.09	3.02	2.84
	Female	Maintenance of accommodation at Katra		4.00		-	-		-	4.00	-	2.00	2.00	2.00	-	1.00	1.75	-			2.67	-	2.00	2.34	2.70
		Easily available accommodation at Katra		4.00		-	-		-	4.00	-	1.60	2.00	2.50	-	4.00	2.53	-			2.67	-	1.00	1.84	2.79
		Reasonable charges for accommodation		3.50		-	-		-	3.50	-	1.60	2.00	1.00	-	4.00	2.15	-			2.67	-	1.00	1.84	2.50
		X4		3.83	0.00	0.00	0.00			3.83		1.73	2.00	1.83	3.00	3.00	2.14						1.33	2.01	2.66
		X34		3.83	3.00	5.00	1.00		5.00	3.42	1.67	2.20	2.34	2.26	2.00	3.17	2.33	3.33			3.00	2.33	2.21	2.51	2.75
Non-Local		X		2.98	2.84	2.00	2.00		4.50	2.25	2.09	2.36	2.63	2.35	2.38	3.19	2.52	3.11		1.00	3.08	2.42	2.37	2.63	2.70
Overall		X		3.16	2.76	2.34	2.00		4.50	2.92	2.09	2.57	2.32	2.55	2.38	3.19	2.57	3.11		1.00	2.93	2.42	2.02	2.43	2.66

Table–8.9

Mean Scores of Marketing Effectiveness Observed by Pilgrim and Non-Pilgrim Groups for Accommodation Services at Destination

Groups		Variables	Age / Income / Education	Age Group-I Upto 25 yrs							Age Group-II 25 to 50 Yrs							Age Group-III Above 50 Yrs							
				Inc-1		Inc-2		Inc-3		X	Inc-1		Inc-2		Inc-3		X	Inc-1		Inc-2		Inc-3		X	X
(1)	(2)	(3)	(4)	E-1	E-2	E-1	E-2	E-1	E-2		E-1	E-2	E-1	E-2	E-1	E-2		E-1	E-2	E-1	E-2	E-1	E-2		
			Education	Ed-1	Ed-2	Ed-1	Ed-2	Ed-1	Ed-2	X	Ed-1	Ed-2	Ed-1	Ed-2	Ed-1	Ed-2	X	Ed-1	Ed-2	Ed-1	Ed-2	Ed-1	Ed-2	X	X
	(2)	(3)	(4)	(5)	(6)	(7)	(8)	(9)	(10)	(11)	(12)	(13)	(14)	(15)	(16)	(17)	(18)	(19)	(20)	(21)	(22)	(23)	(24)	(25)	(26)
Local Pilgrims	Male	Easily available accommodation		1.00	3.00	1.00				1.67		2.00	2.00	3.00			2.33				2.00		3.00	2.50	2.17
		Maintenance of accommodation		2.00	1.00	1.00				1.33		1.00	3.00	4.00			2.67				3.00		4.00	3.50	2.50
		Reasonable charges		1.00	1.00	1.00				1.00		2.50	2.00	3.25			2.58				1.50		3.00	2.25	1.94
		X1		1.33	1.67	1.00				1.33		1.83	2.33	3.42			2.53				2.17		3.33	2.75	2.20
	Female	Easily available accommodation										3.00		4.00			3.50			4.00				4.00	3.75
		Maintenance of accommodation										4.00		1.00			2.50			4.00				4.00	3.25
		Reasonable charges										3.00		1.00			2.00			3.00				3.00	2.50
		X2										3.33		2.00			2.67			3.67				3.67	3.17
		X12		1.33	1.67	1.00				1.33		2.58	2.33	2.71			2.60			3.67	2.17		3.33	3.21	2.69
Non-Local Pilgrims	Male	Easily available accommodation										5.00	3.00	4.00		1.00	3.25						1.00	1.00	2.13
		Maintenance of accommodation										5.00	2.33	2.33		1.00	2.67						1.00	1.00	1.84
		Reasonable charges										3.00	2.00	4.00		1.00	2.50						2.00	2.00	2.25
		X3										4.33	2.44	3.44		1.00	2.81						1.33	1.33	2.07
		X		1.33	1.67	1.00				1.33		3.46	2.39	3.08		1.00	2.71			3.67	2.17		2.33	2.27	2.38

Contd.....

(1)	(2)	(3)	(4)	(5)	(6)	(7)	(8)	(9)	(10)	(11)	(12)	(13)	(14)	(15)	(16)	(17)	(18)	(19)	(20)	(21)	(22)	(23)	(24)	(25)	(26)
Non-Local PILGRIM	Male	Easily available accommodation		2.00	-	2.50	2.00		1.00	1.88	3.00	3.33	2.92	2.84	1.14	2.55	2.63				2.38	3.00	2.22	2.53	2.35
		Maintenance of accommodation		2.29	-	2.50	2.00		1.00	1.95	2.50	3.33	3.23	3.26	2.86	3.09	3.05				3.25	3.50	2.48	3.08	2.69
		Reasonable charges		2.00	-	2.00	2.00		1.00	1.75	2.00	3.33	2.54	3.00	2.43	2.82	2.69				2.50	3.50	1.91	2.64	2.36
		X1		2.10	-	2.33	2.00		1.00	1.86	2.50	3.33	2.90	3.03	2.14	2.82	2.79			3.33	2.71	3.33	2.20	2.75	2.47
	Female	Easily available accommodation		1.00		1.00	-		-	1.00	2.25	1.78	-	1.60	2.00	1.00	1.73	3.00			1.00	1.00	2.08	2.08	1.60
		Maintenance of accommodation		3.00		1.00	-		-	2.00	2.38	2.89	-	2.60	3.00	2.00	2.57	3.33		3.67	1.00	4.00	2.58	2.92	2.50
		Reasonable charges		1.00		1.00	-			1.00	2.13	2.56	-	2.00	2.00	1.00	1.94	2.33		2.00	3.00	1.00	2.17	2.10	1.68
		X2		1.67		1.00				1.33	2.25	2.41		2.07	2.33	1.33	2.08	2.89		3.00	1.67	2.00	2.28	2.37	1.93
		X12		1.89		1.67	2.00		1.00	1.60	2.38	2.87	2.90	2.55	2.24	2.08	2.44	2.89		3.00	2.19	2.67	2.24	2.56	2.20
Non-Local Pilgrims	Male	Easily available accommodation		-	3.00	-	-			3.00		1.00	2.00	3.13	2.00	2.50	2.13	2.00			2.00	2.00	2.86	2.22	2.45
		Maintenance of accommodation		-	3.00	-	-			3.00		3.50	3.00	3.60	3.00	4.00	3.42	4.00			4.00	2.00	2.86	3.22	3.21
		Reasonable charges		-	3.00	-	-			3.00		2.50	2.00	3.07	2.00	3.50	2.61	2.00			2.67	3.00	2.86	2.63	2.75
		X3		-	3.00	-	-			3.00		2.33	2.33	3.27	2.33	3.33	2.72	2.67			2.89	2.33	2.86	2.69	2.80
	Female	Easily available accommodation		2.00	-	-	-		-	2.00	-	2.00	2.00	2.00	-	4.00	2.50			3.00	3.00	-	1.00	2.00	2.17
		Maintenance of accommodation		4.00	-	-	-		-	4.00	-	2.00	2.00	3.00	-	4.00	2.75				3.00	-	3.00	3.00	3.25
		Reasonable charges		3.50		-	-		-	3.50	-	2.00	2.00	1.00	-	3.00	2.00				3.00	-	1.00	2.00	2.50
		X4		3.17						3.17		2.00	2.00	2.00	2.33	3.67	2.42				3.00	2.33	1.67	2.33	2.64
		X34		3.17	3.00	-				3.09		2.17	2.17	2.64	2.33	3.50	2.57	2.67			2.95	2.33	2.27	2.51	2.72
Non-Local		X		2.53	3.00	1.67	2.00		1.00	2.35	2.38	2.52	2.54	2.60	2.29	2.79	2.51	2.78		3.00	2.57	2.50	2.26	2.54	2.46
Overall		X		1.93	2.54	1.34	2.00		1.00	1.84	2.38	2.99	2.47	2.84	2.29	1.90	2.61	2.78		3.34	2.37	2.50	2.30	3.41	2.42

Table–8.10

Overall Marketing Orientation before Scale Purification

Gender	Income	Hotel Services				Transport Services				Retail Services				Shrine Board Services					Overall
		A	B	C	X	A	B	C	X	A	B	C	X	A	B	C	D	X	X
(1)	(2)	(3)	(4)	(5)	(6)	(7)	(8)	(9)	(10)	(11)	(12)	(13)	(14)	(15)	(16)	(17)	(18)	(19)	(20)
Local Pilgrim Male	Inc-1	2.2	2.26	2.73	2.40	2.69	2.92	3.1	2.90	1.95	3.53	3.53	3.00	2.66	2.91	3.25	3.2	3.01	2.83
	Inc-2	2.88	2.52	3.64	3.01	3.43	3	3.02	3.15	2.4	2.93	3.35	2.89	2.67	3.52	3.11	3.19	3.12	3.04
	Inc-3	2.59	2.92	4	3.17	2.94	3.25	3.35	3.18	2.38	3.34	3.54	3.09	2.82	3.28	2.8	3.29	3.05	3.12
	X1	2.55	2.44	3.37	2.79	3.02	3.06	3.16	3.08	2.24	3.27	3.47	2.99	2.72	3.2	3.14	3.19	3.06	2.98
Female	Inc-1	3.42	3.42	3.75	3.53	3.5	3.75	3.9	3.72	· 1.5	1.5	1.57	1.52	3.14	3.32	3.5	3.6	3.39	3.04
	Inc-2	1.75	3.38	3.5	2.88	3.63	3.94	3.7	3.76	2.17	2.84	4.04	3.02	3.2	3.88	3.13	3.19	3.35	3.25
	Inc-3				0.00	3.5	4	4	3.83	1.84	1.84	1.82	1.83						2.83
	X2	2.05	3.55	3.69	3.10	3.71	3.94	3.75	3.80	2.28	2.95	3.89	3.04	3.17	3.6	3.32	3.4	3.37	3.33
	X12	2.3	3	3.53	2.94	3.37	3.5	3.46	3.44	2.26	3.11	3.69	3.02	2.95	3.4	3.23	3.3	3.22	3.16
Local Non-Pilgrim Male	Inc-1	3.17	4.17	3	3.45	3.75	3.5	3.8	3.68	3.5	3.34	4	3.61	3.42	3.19	2.82	2.72	3.04	3.45
	Inc-2	3.01	2.83	3.42	3.09	3.15	3.92	3.49	3.52	2.69	2.53	3.53	2.92	2.46	3.17	3.12	2.86	2.90	3.11
	Inc-3	2.17	1.25	2	1.81	1.5	1.25	1.3	1.35	1.09	1.17	1.84	1.37	2.32	2.05	2	2.13	2.13	1.67
	X3	2.88	2.77	3.31	2.99	2.82	3.38	3.17.	3.12	2.91	2.76	3.73	3.13	2.73	2.8	2.65	2.57	2.69	3.03
Female	Inc-1					1.75	3.5	3.4	2.88	1.17	1.34	1.5	1.34						2.11
	Inc-2													3	3.09	3	3.13	3.06	3.06
	Inc-3																		
	X4					1.75	3.5	3.4	2.88	1.17	1.34	1.5	1.34	3	3.09	3	3.13	3.06	2.43

Contd.....

(1)	(2)	(3)	(4)	(5)	(6)	(7)	(8)	(9)	(10)	(11)	(12)	(13)	(14)	(15)	(16)	(17)	(18)	(19)	(20)
	X34	2.88	2.77	3.31	2.99	2.52	3.53	3.31	3.12	2.75	2.66	3.52	2.98	2.88	2.14	3.1	2.91	2.76	3.03
Local	X	2.59	2.89	3.42	2.97	2.95	3.52	3.39	3.29	2.51	2.89	3.61	3.00	2.91	3.27	3.17	3.11	3.12	3.09
Non-Local Pilgrim Male	Inc-1	2.95	2.81	3.65	3.14	3.03	3.12	3.46	3.20	2.74	2.6	3.4	2.91	3	3.31	3.41	3.09	3.20	3.11
	Inc-2	2.59	2.57	3.42	2.86	3.05	2.94	3.38	3.12	2.86	2.87	3.67	3.13	2.68	3.36	2.95	3.1	3.02	3.03
	Inc-3	2.93	2.43	3.48	2.95	3.29	3.15	3.25	3.23	2.92	3	3.52	3.15	2.77	3.34	2.89	2.93	2.98	3.08
	X1	2.82	2.6	3.51	2.98	3.12	3.07	3.37	3.19	2.84	2.83	3.53	3.07	2.82	3.34	3.08	3.04	3.07	3.08
Female	Inc-1	2.14	2.09	3.57	2.60	3.05	2.95	2.77	2.92	2.51	2.31	3.39	2.74	2.55	3.42	3.2	2.88	3.01	2.82
	Inc-2	2.27	2.4	3.39	2.69	2.82	3.13	2.91	2.95	2.53	2.58	3.53	2.88	2.68	3.37	2.86	3.07	3.00	2.88
	Inc-3	2.51	2.28	3.17	2.65	2.71	2.84	3.03	2.86	2.3	2.51	3.6	2.80	2.53	2.8	2.72	3.12	2.79	2.78
	X2	2.31	2.25	3.38	2.65	2.86	2.98	2.9	2.91	2.44	2.47	3.51	2.81	2.59	3.2	2.93	3.02	2.94	2.83
	X12	2.57	2.43	3.45	2.82	3	3.02	3.14	3.05	2.65	2.65	3.52	2.94	2.71	3.27	3.01	3.03	3.01	2.96
Non-Pilgrim Male	Inc-1	2.8	2.5	3.6	2.97	2.89	3.17	3.57	3.21	2.37	2.26	3.36	2.66	2.63	3.59	3.25	3.5	3.24	3.02
	Inc-2	2.51	2.54	3.58	2.88	3.05	3.47	3.19	3.24	2.36	2.63	3.27	2.75	3.01	3.57	3.13	3.18	3.22	3.02
	Inc-3	2.91	2.49	3.23	2.88	3.41	3.4	3.38	3.40	2.27	2.88	3.25	2.80	3.06	3.18	3.06	3.11	3.10	3.04
	X3	2.74	2.51	3.47	2.91	3.12	3.34	3.38	3.28	2.34	2.59	3.29	2.74	2.9	3.44	3.14	3.26	3.19	3.03
	Inc-1	2.75	2.63	3.61	3.00	3.29	3.27	3.4	3.32	2.26	2.3	3.29	2.62	2.78	3.41	3.07	2.98	3.06	3
Female	Inc-2	2.54	2.65	3.09	2.76	3.28	3.47	2.95	3.23	2.11	2.35	3.46	2.64	2.62	3.11	2.73	3.01	2.87	2.88
	Inc-3	1.82	2.54	3.63	2.66	3.29	3.13	3.35	3.26	1.17	1.54	1.71	1.47	2.95	3.53	3.17	3.04	3.17	2.64
	X4	2.57	2.65	3.36	2.86	3.32	3.36	3.21	3.30	2.27	2.49	3.4	2.72	2.75	3.31	2.93	3	3.00	2.97
	X34	2.66	2.58	3.42	2.89	3.22	3.35	3.29	3.29	2.31	2.54	3.25	2.70	2.83	3.38	3.04	3.13	3.10	3
Non-Local	X	2.62	2.51	3.43	2.85	3.12	3.19	3.22	3.18	2.48	2.6	3.44	2.84	2.77	3.33	3.03	3.09	3.06	2.98
Overall	X	2.61	2.7	3.43	2.91	3.03	3.36	3.31	3.23	2.5	2.75	3.53	2.93	2.84	3.3	3.1	3.1	3.09	3.04

Table–8.11

Variable-wise Multiple Regression Coefficient
Values of Pilgrim and Non-Pilgrim Visitors

Variable	PILGRIMS		NON-PILGRIMS	
	Local	Non-Local	Local	Non-local
A	0.540	0.128	0.208	-0.0070
B	0.109	0.013	0.190	0.5280
C	0.215	0.094	0.047	
D	1.790	0.151	-0.035	0.0420
E	-0.090	0.114	0.174	0.0320
F	0.301	0.204	0.110	-0.7500
G	0.060	0.024	0.111	1.0900
H	0.007	0.104	0.170	0.4970
Constant	2.174	1.628	2.168	6.259

Table–8.12

Test of Signifiance values

Variables	PILGRIMS		NON-PILGRIMS	
	Local	Non-Local	Local	Non-local
R	0.773	0.415	0.52	1
R^2	0.598	0.172	0.72	1
F(Cal.)	65.968	9.22	16.359	4.537
df(V^1V^2) at 5% level	11,488	11,488	11,488	11,488

Table-8.13

Variable-wise Frequency Distribution

Variables	| Frequency Distribution													
(1)	(2)	(3)	(4)	(5)	(6)	(7)	(8)	(9)	(10)	(11)	(12)	(13)	(14)	(15)
	1	%	2	%	3	%	4	%	5	%	NR	%	X	Total
Food Services at destination														
1. Variety in food	48	9.6	157	31.4	149	29.8	121	24.2	5	1	20	4	2.72	500
2. Rates of food Services	82	16.4	149	29.8	127	25.4	115	23	5	1	22	4.4	2.52	500
3. Tasty & delight of food	44	8.8	130	26	196	39.2	102	20.4	8	1.6	20	4	2.82	500
4. Hygienic food	29	5.8	117	23.4	181	36.2	144	28.8	8	1.6	21	4.2	2.65	500
En route supportive services													2.68	
1. Satisfactory Shopping	3	0.6	13	2.6	147	29.4	261	52.2	66	13.2	10	2	3.5	500
2. Satisfactory Transport	0	0	0	0	108	21.6	283	56.6	105	21	4	0.8	4	500
3. Satisfactory Accommodation	15	3	122	24.4	119	23.8	173	34.6	48	9.6	23	4.6	3.1	500
4. Satisfactory safety measures	19	3.8	70	14	140	28	128	25.6	7	1.4	136	27.2	2.5	500
5. Satisfactory Infrastructure	8	1.6	21	4.2	111	22.2	204	40.8	20	4	136	27.2	2.45	500
Additional Infrastructural services													3.11	
1. Adequate cloak room	17	3.4	43	8.6	112	22.4	289	57.8	33	6.6	6	1.2	3.38	500
2. Clean drinking water	17	3.4	48	9.6	149	29.8	269	53.8	14	2.8	3	0.6	3.14	500
3. Better roads	22	4.4	52	10.4	135	27	226	45.2	20	4	45	9	3	500
4. Sanitation & hygiene	105	21	125	25.2	98	19.6	160	32	10	2	2	0.4	2.72	500
5. Adequate bedding	13	2.6	21	4.2	140	28	282	56.4	30	6	14	2.8	3.49	500
6. Adequate shelter sheds	20	4	67	13.4	107	21.4	289	57.8	10	2	7	1.4	3.33	500

Contd.....

(1)	(2)	3)	(4)	(5)	(6)	(7)	(8)	(9)	(10)	(11)	(12)	(13)	(14)	(15)
Transportation services													3.18	
1. Luxury Bus service	7	1.4	74	14.8	111	22.2	232	46.4	10	2	66	13.2	2.97	500
2. Ordinary Bus service	31	6.2	160	32	145	29	106	21.2	7	1.4	51	10.2	2.98	500
3. Pony & pithu service	12	2.4	118	23.6	149	29.8	121	24.2	12	2.4	88	17.6	3.23	500
4. Taxi service	7	1.4	70	14	171	34.2	109	21.8	12	2.4	131	26.2	2.77	500
Food service en route destination													2.9	
1. Tasty & delicious food	36	7.2	118	23.6	176	35.2	145	29	11	2.2	14	2.8	2.98	500
2. Hygienic food	42	8.4	117	23.4	182	36.4	127	25.4	10	2	22	4.4	2.97	500
Retail Services													2.98	
1. Cooperative shopkeepers at *Bhavan*	28	5.6	117	23.4	140	28	101	20.2	9	1.8	105	21	2.9	500
2. Adequate shopping at *Bhavan*	15	3	83	16.6	134	26.8	162	32.4	12	2.4	94	18.8	3	500
3. Adequate shopping at Katra	34	6.8	89	17.8	143	28.6	164	32.8	12	2.4	58	11.6	3	500
4. Cooperative shopkeepers at Katra	39	7.8	148	29.6	181	36.2	71	14.2	7	1.4	54	10.8	2.75	500
Accommodation at Katra & en route destination													2.91	
1. Maintaince of accommodation	57	11.4	111	22.2	127	25.4	136	27.2	9	1.8	60	12	2.6	500
2. Availability of accommodation	45	9	112	22.4	132	26.4	147	29.4	9	1.8	55	11	2.45	500
3. Reasonable charges	94	18.8	146	29.2	93	18.6	103	20.6	5	1	59	11.8	2.13	500
Accommodation at destination													2.39	
1. Maintaince of accommodation	37	7.4	79	15.8	102	20.4	114	22.8	5	1	163	32.6	2	500
2. Availability of accommodation	66	13.2	126	25.2	79	15.8	58	11.6	6	1.2	165	33	2.65	500
3. Reasonable charges	49	9.8	125	25	83	16.6	48	9.6	6	1.2	189	37.8	2.06	500

Table-8.14

Frequency Distribution of Visitors Grievances

Services	GRIEVANCES	PILGRIMS												NON-PILGRIMS							
		Locals					Non-Locals					Locals					Non-locals			
		Male		Females			Males		Females			Male		Female			Male		Female	
	S.No	No	%	No	%	N.R	No	%	No	%	N.R	No	%	No	%	N.R	No	%	No	%
(1)	(2)	(3)	(4)	(5)	(6)	(7)	(8)	(9)	(10)	(11)	(12)	(13)	(14)	(15)	(16)	(17)	(18)	(19)	(20)	(21)
Accommodation	1	10	76.92	7	46.67		221	97.36	108	90.76		5	71.43	3	60		76	95	29	85.29
service	2	12	92.31	13	86.67		219	96.48	112			4		3			77		24	
	3	8	61.54	0	0		222	97.8	100			2		0			71		25	
	4	71	53.85	2	13.33		201	88.55	93			4		0			70		22	
	5	6	46.15	0	0		208	91.63	0			0		0			43		0	
	6	4	30.77	3	20		197	86.78	83			5		2			57		13	
	7	2	15.38	0	0		171	75.33	14			0		0			28		4	
Food service	8	5	38.46	8	53.33		204	89.87	113			2		2			35		26	
	9	7	53.85	8	53.33		219	96.48	113			4		2			71		29	
Road & transport	10	0	0	0	0		182	80.18	71			0		0			33		11	
service	11	5	38.46	7	46.67		123	54.19	44			2		1			24		7	
	12	1	7.69	4	26.67		100	44.05	33			0		3			45		13	

Contd.....

(1)	(2)	(3)	(4)	(5)	(6)	(7)	(8)	(9)	(10)	(11)	(12)	(13)	(14)	(15)	(16)	(17)	(18)	(19)	(20)	(21)
	13	0	0	0	0		73	32.16	24			3		0			32		8	
	14	4	30.77	2	13.33		109	48.02	88			0		0			62		10	
	15	11	84.62	0	0		189	83.26	39			4		0			56		7	
	16	0	0	0	0		173	76.21	72			0		0			23		30	
Shopping	17	0	0	0	0		203	89.43	103			0		0			64		24	
service	18	0	0	0	0		118	51.98	46			3		0			18		10	
	19	5	38.46	7	46.67		92	40.53	86			3		2			32		20	
Shrine Board	20	0	0	0	0		76	33.48	34			0		0			63		13	
service	21	0	0	8	53.33		133	58.59	71			2		0			43		9	
	22	3	23.08	4	26.67		111	48.9	65			2		0			38		7	
General service	23	2	15.38	8	53.33		182	80.18	92			3		1			63		18	
	24	0	0	0	0.		79	34.8	63			3		0			23		8	
	25	0	0	0	0		13	5.73	20			0		0			34		11	
	26	7	53.85	5	33.33		108	47.58	75			2		3			51		14	
	27	0	0	0	0		80	35.24	16			0		0			48		10	
	28	5	38.46	3	20		132	58.15	67			2		1			36		8	
	29	6	46.15	8	53.33		179	78.85	83			2		2			55		15	
	30	0	0	0	0		86	37.89	0			0		0			38		12	
	31	0	0	0	0		113	49.78	38			3		0			51		21	

References

Newman, Joseph, W. Westbrook Roberts & James, R Tylor (1978) "Satisfaction/Dissatisfaction in the Purchase Decision Process". Journal of Marketing Vol 42 (October), 54-60.

Peters, M. (1969). International Tourism—The Economics & Development of Internal Tourism Trade, Hutchinson; London, 20-33.

Poon, Auliana (1993) Tourism Technology and Competitive Strategies, C.A.B., International; U.K., 3-61.

Shostack, G. Lynn (1977) "Breaking free From Product Marketing", Journal of Marketing, Vol., 41 (April), 7-80.

Marketing Strategy for Pilgrimage Tourism 205

ANNEXURES

1. QUESTIONNAIRE

Topic: Marketing Strategy for Pilgrimage Tourism—A Case Study of Shri Mata Vaishno Devi Shrine

Note: Information collected herewith shall be strictly used for research purposes only.

1. **General Information (Kindly specify)**
    (a) S. no   _____
    (b) Gender   _____
    (c) Educational qualification   _____
    (d) Marital Status   _____ .
    (e) Occupation   _____
    (f) Income per month (in Rs.)   _____
    (g) State to which you belong   _____
    (h) Purpose of visits to this state   _____
    (i) Date of entry in Jammu city   _____
    (j) Proposed date of leaving Jammu city   _____
    (k) Appropriate reason for your visit to the Shrine   _____
    (l) Source from which you got information about the Shrine   _____

2. **Mode of Travel (Kindly specify)**
    (a) Place of origin to Jammu city   _____
    (b) Jammu Railway Station to Bus Stand   _____
    (c) Katra to Ban Ganga   _____
    (d) Ban Ganga to *Bhavan*   _____
    (e) *Bhavan* to Bhairo Ghati   _____

3. **Composition of Visitors : You Travel; (Kindly tick mark)**
    (a) Individually   _____
    (b) With relatives   _____

(c) With friends _____

(d) In a package tour _____

Note : Kindly tick mark the statements according to your satisfaction

Abbreviations used :

SA= Strongly Agree   N= Neutral   SD= Strongly Disagree

A=   Agree   DA= Disagree   NR= No Response

1. **Transportation Services**	SA	A	N	DA	SD	NR
A) Services from Jammu to Katra						
a) Satisfactory luxury bus service	—	—	—	—	—	—
b) Satisfactory ordinary bus service	—	—	—	—	—	—
c) Satisfactory taxi services	—	—	—	—	—	—
d) Quality of Road from Jammu to Katra	—	—	—	—	—	—
B) Services from Katra to *Bhavan*						
a) Satisfactory pony/pithu services	—	—	—	—	—	—
b) Quality of road from Katra to *Bhavan*	—	—	—	—	—	—
C) Common Services						
a) Safe transport	—	—	—	—	—	—
b) Fixed fare for transport	—	—	—	—	—	—
c) High fare for transport	—	—	—	—	—	—
d) Significant sign boards	—	—	—	—	—	—
e) Adequate transport available	—	—	—	—	—	—
2) Retail Services						
A) Services at Katra						
a) Adequate shopping items	—	—	—	—	—	—
b) Cooperative shopkeepers	—	—	—	—	—	—
c) Fair shopping	—	—	—	—	—	—
B) Services at *Bhavan*						
a) Adequate shopping items	—	—	—	—	—	—
b) Cooperative shopkeepers	—	—	—	—	—	—
c) Fair shopping	—	—	—	—	—	—

C) Other Retail Services

a) Prices are fixed   —   —   —   —   —   —

b) Quality of souvenirs purchased   —   —   —   —   —   —

c) Shopping was satisfactory   —   —   —   —   —   —

d) What else do you like to purchase ?   _____

3) Accommodation Services

A) Services at Katra

a) At Katra you stayed at   —   —   —   —   —   —

b) Well maintained accommodation   —   —   —   —   —   —

c) Accommodation is easily available   —   —   —   —   —   —

d) High charges for accommodation   —   —   —   —   —   —

B) Services at *Bhavan*

a) At *Bhavan* you stayed   _____

b) Well maintained accommodation   —   —   —   —   —   —

c) Accommodation is easily available   —   —   —   —   —   —

d) High charges for accommodation   —   —   —   —   —   —

C) Over-all services

a) Satisfactory sanitation & hygiene   —   —   —   —   —   —

b) Proper lights and ventilation   —   —   —   —   —   —

c) Feeling of safety   —   —   —   —   —   —

d) Clean drinking water   —   —   —   —   —   —

e) Cloak room and security   —   —   —   —   —   —

f) Adequate bedding   —   —   —   —   —   —

g) Adequate accommodation   —   —   —   —   —   —

h) Better infrastructure   —   —   —   —   —   —

i) You prefer accommodation outside Katra   —   —   —   —   —   —

4) Food Services

A) Services at Katra

a) Hygienic food   —   —   —   —   —   —

b) Tasty and delicious food   —   —   —   —   —   —

c) Cheap rates for food   —   —   —   —   —   —

d) Variety in food services   —   —   —   —   —   —

B) Services at *Bhavan*

a) Hygienic food   —   —   —   —   —   —

b) Tasty and delicious food   —   —   —   —   —   —

c) Cheap rates for food   —   —   —   —   —   —

d) Variety in food services   —   —   —   —   —   —

5) Non-Payment Services Provided by
    Shrine Board

A) General Services

a) Efficient telecommunication   —   —   —   —   —   —

b) Adequate medical facility   —   —   —   —   —   —

c) Satisfactory Sanitation & Hygiene   —   —   —   —   —   —

d) Better maintained roads   —   —   —   —   —   —

e) Proper lights en route   —   —   —   —   —   —

f) Proper sign boards en route   —   —   —   —   —   —

g) Railings at stairs   —   —   —   —   —   —

h) Adequate shelter sheds   —   —   —   —   —   —

i) Clean drinking water   —   —   —   —   —   —

j) Efficient cloak room   —   —   —   —   —   —

k) Adequate blankets   —   —   —   —   —   —

B) Maintenance of Temples

a) Well maintained temples en route   —   —   —   —   —   —

b) Easily approachable temples   —   —   —   —   —   —

c) Well maintained Garbjoon   —   —   —   —   —   —

d) Easy Darshan at Garbjoon   —   —   —   —   —   —

e) Easily approachable Bhairoghati   —   —   —   —   —   —

C) Supervision of Shrine Board

a) Good behaviour of staff   —   —   —   —   —   —

b) Fair dealing of staff   —   —   —   —   —   —

c) Helpful staff   —   —   —   —   —   —

d) Better infrastructure maintained   —   —   —   —   —   —

e) Feeling of safety   —   —   —   —   —   —

f) Efficient management of Shrine   —   —   —   —   —   —

g) Curb begging practice   —   —   —   —   —   —

h) Satisfactory working of Board   —   —   —   —   —   —

6)   Over-all satisfaction from various services

a)   Transportation services   —   —   —   —   —   —

b)   Shopping services   —   —   —   —   —   —

c)   Food services   —   —   —   —   —   —

d)   Accommodation services   —   —   —   —   —   —

e)   Reasonable charges   —   —   —   —   —   —

f)   Well managed temples   —   —   —   —   —   —

g)   Efficient working of Shrine Board   —   —   —   —   —

h)   Satisfactory Darshan   —   —   —   —   —   —

7)   Other Social Aspects reflect that

a)   Behaviour of local people is good   —   —   —   —   —   —

b)   Living standard of locals is high   —   —   —   —   —   —

c)   Local people cheat pilgrims   —   —   —   —   —   —

d)   Efficient guides are required   —   —   —   —   —   —

e)   Accommodation outside Katra
     preferred   —   —   —   —   —   —

8) Some other aspects (Kindly specify/ Tick mark your response)

a) Have you ever waited in a queue during the trip? Yes/ No

b) If yes, Specify the purpose   _____

c) Does it give a bad impression? Yes/ No

d) What alternative do you suggest to reduce these queues ?

e) Do you like to visit any other Shrine ? Yes/ No

f) If yes, name the Shrine   _____

g) What is lacking at this Shrine as
   compared to any other Shrine ?   _____

h) Would you like to come again? Yes/ No

i) Any other grievances or complaints,
    kindly specify.   _____

9) Address

_____

Thank you for you cooperation.

2. DEVELOPMENT REPORT

Prior to September 1986, the management of the Shrine and the complex at *Bhavan* and Adhkumari left much to be desired. The track from Katra to *Bhavan* was kacha and stonelittered and nagging beggars could be seen everywhere. There were no shelters against sun or rain on the track and the sanitary arrangements were almost non-existant. Water was in acute shortage and lighting arrangements inadequate.

An act to provide for the better management, administration and governance of Shri Mata Vaishno Devi Shrine and its endowments including the land and buildings attached or appurtenant to the Shrine beginning from Katra up to the Holy Cave and the adjoining hillocks was enacted on 30th August 1986 which was ratified by the State Legislature in 1988.

Under the provision of the Act the management-administration and control of Shri Mata Vaishno Devi Shrine fund was entrusted to the Shri Mata Vaishno Devi Shrine Board with the object of providing proper facilities to the pilgrims and channelising the resources for development and philanthropic purposes. Thus came into existence on 30th August 1986 a statutory Board named the Shri Mata Vaishno Devi Shrine Board.

Ever since its inception, the Shrine Board has been discharging the following functions and duties in conformity with the provisions enshrined in the Act :

1. arrange for the proper conduct of Puja at the Shrine;

2. provide facilities for the proper performance of worship by the pilgrims;

3. Make arrangements for the safe custody of the funds; valuables and jewellry and for the preservation of the Shrine funds;

4. to undertake for the benefit of worship and pilgrims"

   a) construction of buildings for their accommodation;

   b) construction of sanitary works;

   c) improvement in means of communication; and

   d) to ensure safety and fulfilling of pilgrimage including insurance of each pilgrim under Personal Accident Benefit Policy for Rs. 1.00 lakh, entire premium being paid by the Shrine Board.

5. to undertake the development activities concerning the area of the Shrine and its surroundings;

6. to make suitable arrangements for the imparting of religious instruction and general education;

7. to make provision for medical relief for worshippers and pilgrims;

8. to make provision for the payment of suitable emoluments to salaried staff;

9. to do all such things as may be incidental and conducive to the efficient management, maintenance and administration of the Shrine fund and the convenience of the pilgrims.

Yatra

Word of mouth publicity of the facilities and services provided and the improvement in mangement of the yatra since taken over by the Board has resulted in an unprecedented increase in the number of pilgrims visiting the Shri Mata Vaishno Devi Shrine.

The figures of pilgrims over the previous years are presented below which shows an ever-increasing trend over the last one decade:

Year	Pilgrims (in Lacs)
1986	13.96
1987	18.53
1988	19.93
1989	23.12
1990	21.87
1991	31.15
1992	35.16
1993	33.69
1994	37.05
1995	40.12
1996	43.35
1997	44.34
1998	46.22
1999	46.70
2000	51.92
2001	50.57
2002	44.32
2003	54.00

Facilities for the Yatris

The Board, during the last one-decade has been successful in providing the following facilities to the pilgrims :

i)   Track from Katra to *Bhavan*

a)   Entire 16.2 kms. track (including Bhairo Ghati) has been laid with tiles widened and made pacca and smoothened, parpets have been constructed on the valley side and retaining wall/breast walls provided to prevent landslide and slips.

b) Rain-cum-sun shelter sheds viewpoints cum cafeterias and drinking water stand posts/water coolers have been set up.

c) Powerful sodium vapour lamps have been installed along the entire track.

d) Medical units function at Katra, Banaganga and Sanjichatt.

e) Green cover with flowerbed and Shrubs and Orchards have been created.

ii) Sanitation

An adequate number of public convenience, both on the track and in the complexes has been constructed. More than 450 safaikaramcharis engaged to maintain sanitation on the track and the public conveniences. A sufficient number of cleaning pumps, vacuum cleaners, fogging and spray machines and disinfectants have been provided. New set bathing rooms for general public with accompanying facilities have been constructed.

iii) Accommodation

The old buildings have been remodeled, extensively repaired, refloored and rewired. The Board has constructed additional rooms and huts at *Bhavan* and Adhkumari to accommodate the ever-increasing influx of pilgrims.

At Katra, Niharika Vishram Ghar complex provides accommodation to pilgrims.

At Jammu, a multistoreyed complex namely Vaishnavi Dham caters to about one thousand pilgrims and among others, provides accommodation at a cost as reasonable as Rs. 10.00 per bed/day.

A complex namely Gouri Bavan is ready for operation at Mata Ka Bagh, *Bhavan*. Another complex namely Manokamana Bhavan coming up at *Bhavan* when commissioned will provide accommodation to thousands of pilgrims.

iv) Hygienic Food

The Board has set up Bhojanalyas at *Bhavan*, Sanjichatt, Adhkumari, Katra and Jammu where wholesome vegetarian food, cooked with modern machines and hot/cold drinks are available. Also 13 cafeterias are functioning all along the track from Katra to *Bhavan* which serve cold and hot drinks and light refreshments. The sales at all the eating places are being made on a no-profit no-loss basis. To eliminate environmental pollution, LPG has been introduced at all the eating places managed by the Board and private shopkeepers. These outlets also ensure a check on the prices of the eatables being sold by the private shopkeepers.

v) Audio/ Video Programs

TV sets, supported by centralized control over the display of Video Cassettes, have been installed in all the buildings at *Bhavan* to enable the yatris to spend their waiting time gainfully by viewing well known religious films. Popular devotional songs are also played through Audio control systems.

vi) Social and Philanthropic Activities

i)   School blocks in and around Katra have been constructed by the Board such as School building at Nomain, Agharjitto, Higher Secondary School, Katra, Girls School Katra, School building at Nangal, Arli, Moori, Serla Bhaga, Kotli Bhagha, Bathera, Panthal, etc.

ii)   To promote study of Indian Culture, a number of fellowships have been awarded to scholars under the guidance of Jammu University

iii)   With the objectives of providing work to poor women, two Mahila Mandals have been started by the Board.

iv)   The religious/historical places of importance such as Baba Agharjitto, Kot Kandoli (Nagrota), Deva Mai Jai temple, Baba Dhansar, Bhim Ghar Fort Reasi have been extensively renovated by the Shrine Board.

v)   On occasion, the Board has provided free uniforms and hunter shoes to pony owners, desks and jersises to school children and Shringar Chunnies, Cholas and Desi Ghee to various temples in and around Katra.

vi)   The Shrine Board has made a major contribution to the improvement of Katra town by widening the arterial road from the entrance of Katra town to Bus stand, Katra and improving the road condition upto the place from where the yatra (pilgrimage) begins.

vii) Activities for Staff Welfare

i)   Introduction of Contributory Provident Fund Scheme and Gratuity Scheme.

ii)   Introduction of Janta Personal Accident Benefit Policy.

iii)   Construction of staff quarters at *Bhavan*.

iv)   Construction of accommodation for safaikaramcharis at Katra, Charan Padhuka, Adhkumari, Sanjichatt and *Bhavan*.

v)   Residential accommodation for staff at Vishram Ghar, Katra.

vi)   Provision of summer as well as winter uniform and shoes to all categories of ministerial staff.

vii)   Provision of staff messes at *Bhavan*, Sanjichatt, Adhkumari and Katra.

viii) Environmental Friendly Activities

A massive afforestation programme is under way and over 10 lakh plants have since been planted under the prestigious Trikuta Afforestation Project. Under this scheme, sponsored by the National Wasteland Development Board, Government of India, 31 lakh plants would be planted for greening the Trikuta Hills and to provide ecological stability.

Apart from the above, a number of Vatikas en route to Banganga to *Bhavan* have been developed to provide green cover to the area and a soothing feeling to the pilgrims.

ix) Other Activities undertaken by Shrine Board are:

i) Construction of shopping complex at *Bhavan*, Bhairo temple, Sanjichatt, Hathi-matha, Adhkumari and Banganga.

ii) Construction of Pony sheds at Banganga, Adhkumari and *Bhavan*.

iii) Additional Cloak room facilities. *Bhavan* and Adhkumari to meet the ever increasing demand of Yatris. Recently at Jammu also Cloakroom facility has been provided.

iv) The number system for streamlining the procedure for engaging of ponies has been started.

v) An in-house newsletter for providing authentic information to the employees/public has been started which contains information on yatra, other related activities and message from the desk of Additional Chief Executive Officer.

vi) Considerable progress has been made in covering highly vulnerable stretches between Sanjichatt and *Bhavan*. Besides, a very large covered area has been constructed opposite the new shopping complex at *Bhavan* in order to provide shelter from Sun, rain and snow to the pilgrims.

x) Certain Upcoming Projects of Shrine Board are :

1. Setting up of Shri Mata Vaishno Devi Shrine University: Shri Mata Vaishno Devi Shrine Board has decided to set up a multi disciplinary university for which a separate fund amounting to Rs. 5 crores has been kept aside.

2. Construction of alternate track from Adkumari to *Bhavan* : In order to reduce the traffic pressure on the main track, an alternative track from Adhkumari to *Bhavan* is under construction. Considerable progress has been made as both the ends have been constructed. Now the track is being made negotiable by improving the gradient and adequate widening.

3. Queue complex at *Bhavan* : An ambitious project of construction of queue complex at *Bhavan* on the lines of Trimula Tirupati Devasthanam has been taken up. M/S. Larsen and Toubro have been engaged as consultants for the projects and survey work has begun, whereafter the project will be taken up. It will not only improve the amenities but also give a beautiful new look to the *Bhavan*, accommodating a very large number of pilgrims.

4. Sewage Treatment Plant at *Bhavan*.

5. Construction of Manokamana Bhavan at Darbar Mata Vaishno Devi Ji.

6. Construction of staff colony near Panchhi View Point for accommodation of staff working at *Bhavan*.

7. Construction of Bathing Ghat at Banganga.

8. Construction of Hospital building at Adhkumari.

9. Construction of Incinerators.

10.   Construction of Sarai building at Katra (Niharika Phase II).

11.   Construction of additional space for Stores at Katra.

12.   Yatrika Phase-II near Vaishnavi Dham, Jammu.

13.   Renovation of Raghunath Temple at Katra.

14.   Construction of pony stand near the start of the pilgrimage to reduce substantially pollution of Banganga.

3. Shrine Board Undertakes Massive Development Works

As a part of its continuous endeavor to provide better facilities and amenities for the visiting pilgrims, Shri Mata Vaishno Devi Shrine Board has undertaken a large number of developmental works during the year 1999-2000. Some of them are enumerated below :

Shri Mata Vaishno Devi University

The preliminary work for establishing Shri Mata Vaishno Devi University has been begun. The six members committee, which was constituted for the selection of a site, visited a number of places and has identified an ideal location for the said University situated at village Chambaserli near Katra. The State Cabinet has approved the site for the Shrine varisty. This University which will be purely a technical one, will have streams like information technology, hotel management, tourism, etc.

Alternative Track between Adhkumari & *Bhavan*

An alternate track between Adhkumari and *Bhavan* was inaugurated by the Chairman, Shri Mata Vaishno Devi Shrine Board (His Excellency the Governor of J&K) on 15.12. 1999. Constructed at a cost of Rs. 6.5 Crores, the new track has a length of 5.5 kms. It has not only decongested the existing track but is also shorter by 750 mtrs. The new track has eight toilet blocks, a number of portable water point, three view points-cum-cafeterias including one named "Himkoti" located mid-way with a beautiful small lake under construction. Besides, 255 sodium vapour lights and a number of rain shelters have been provided along the track.

Launching of Web Site on Internet

Shri Mata Vaishno Devi Shrine Board formally launched its Web Site on Internet on 22nd December, 1999. This site is to be accessible from any part of the world under web address, *http:/ www.maavaishnodevi.org*. The basic objective of the site is to provide the latest and most authentic information to prospective pilgrims. The site, besides gives yatra-related information, the legend/story of Shri Mata Vaishno Devi Ji. This is the first step of the Shrine Board towards making its global presence on information technology super high way. Subsequently the services like online room booking, acceptance of donations, etc., will be incorporated for the facility of the pilgrims the world over.

Operationalization of Manokamana Bhavan at Darbar Vaishno Devi Ji

Manokamana Yatri Niwas at *Bhavan* was operationalized on 19th October 1999. Constructed at a cost of Rs. 1.80 crores, Manokamana Bhavan has 21 dormitories which accommodate about 500 persons a day. Moreover the building has a Bhojanalya offering puri chana, rice rajmah, snacks and hot/cold beverages. Ideally located near a shopping complex/pony stand this building is owned by Shri Mata Vaishno Devi Shrine Board.

Operationalization of additional block of Niharika Yatrika Niwas

An additional block of Niharika Yatrika Niwas was operationalized on 16th October 1999. Constructed at a cost of Rs. 2.5 crores this modern building has 50 air-conditioned rooms and 4 dormitories, which will accommodate about 200 pilgrims a day. Apart from this, the building has common toilets on each floor, a cloak room and a catering outlet offering snacks and hot/cold beverages. This is yet another effort of the Shrine Board as a part of its constant endeavour to provide more and more yatris facilities to the visiting devotees. Ideally located near the bus stand in the heart of the town, this expansion of Niharika will contribute towards meeting the ever-increasing demand of accommodation at Katra.

Operationalization of New Yatra Registration Counter

A new Yatra registration counter was thrown open and made functional by the Shri Mata Vaishno Devi Shrine Board at Katra on 01.05.1999. Ideally located adjacent to the main bus stand at Katra, this modernized, sophisticated, designed yatra counter will go a long way towards meeting the long-felt need of yatris at Katra. People do not have to stand now in long queues to get the yatra slips before starting their pilgrimage. With the commissioning of the new yatra counter, the waiting period in very peak rush would get reduced to less than half an hour. The new yatra registration counter consists of two spacious halls on two floors consisting of six counters on each floor. It also has toilet, drinking water and refreshment facilities for the convenience of the pilgrims.

Commissioning of Computerized Reservation Counter

As a part of the constant endeavor of the Shri Mata Vaisno Devi Shrine Board to facilitate smooth pilgrimage to the Holy cave, a modernized railway reservation counter has been opened and made functional at Katra. Located in Vishram Ghar near the main bus stand, this computerized railway reservation counter will go a long way towards meeting the long-felt need of the yatris at Katra. The online service has enabled the yatris to get reservation/cancellation instantly for any part of the country. The building remodeled at a cost of Rs. 5 lacs. has been provided by the Shrine Board for this purpose.

Vaishnavi Dham Pase-II

Encouraged by the over-whelming response to Vaishnavi Dham Jammu by various sections of pilgrims, the Board has decided to construct another building called Vaishnavi Dham Pase-II on the adjacent plot measuring 3.5 kanals. The construction of this five-storeyed building was taken up in November 1999 and was expected to be completed by January 2001. The building is expected to cost Rs. 315 lacs and will have 30 dormitories accommodating about 400 persons a day.

Commissioning of Helipad at Katra

The helipad for copter services from Jammu-Katra-Sanjichatt was commissioned on 09.04.2000 when the Helicopter services was inaugurated. The helipad which is situated at about 1 km from Katra at Serli Village on the Katra Panthal road has been constructed at a cost of about 35 lakhs. This service would meet the needs of those pilgrims who face difficulty in doing the arduous climb.

Construction of Sewage treatment plant at *Bhavan*

Yet as another endeavor for better development of the Shrine area, the Board has undertaken construction of 3.2 MLD sewage treatment plant at *Bhavan*. Estimated at a cost of about 225 lakhs, the project was expected to be completed by June 2002.

Construction of Shankaracharya Temple at Katra

The construction of Shankaracharya Temple at Katra has also been taken up by the Board as its constant endeavor for social development in the area. Expected to be completed within a period of two years, the project shall cost about 80 lacs.

Construction of Sarai Building at Katra

For providing additional accommodation to the yatris visiting the holy Shrine, a Sarai building is being constructed at Katra. Estimated at a cost of about 400 lacs, this five storeyed structure shall endeavor to provide dormitory accommodation to about 500 persons at a time.

BIBLIOGRAPHY

Ahmed, Zafar U. (1992). "Islamic Pilgrimage (Hajj) to Kaaba in Makkah (Saudi Arabia): An Important International Tourism Activity", *The Journal of Tourism Studies*, Vol. 3(1), 35-43.

Ahuja, S.P. & S.R. Sarna (1990). *Tourism in India – A Perspective to 1990*, The Institute of Economics & Market Research; New Delhi, 70-85.

Alavi, Jafar & Mahmoud M.Yasin (2000) "A Systematic Approach to Tourism Policy", *Journal of Business Research*, Vol. 48,147-156

Bagri, S.C. (1996). "Domestic Tourism in India; Analyzing Tourist Destinations and Policies for Sustainable Tourism, Article submitted at National Seminar on Domestic Tourism, Jan 17-19, 1996. Department of Tourism Management, Kurukshetra University, Kurukshetra.

Baker, M.J. (1978) "Limited Options for Marketing Strategists" *Marketing*, June 1978, 23-27.

Baker, A. Dwayne & John I. Crompton (1999) "Quality Satisfaction & Behavioural Intentions", *Annals of Tourism Research*, Vol.27 (3) 785-803.

Barbara, G. Taba, Chnick, Linda, S. Fidell (1983). *Using Multivariate Statistics*, Harper & Row Publishers; New York, 388-411.

Bonoma, T.V (1984). "Making your Marketing Strategy work," *Harvard Business Review*, March-April, 69-76.

Bramwell, Bill (1998). "User Satisfaction and Product Development in Urban Tourism", *Tourism Management* , Vol. 19 (1), 35-47.

Briggs, Susan (1997). " *Successful Tourism Marketing – A Practical Handbook*", Kogan Page Ltd., 43-90.

Brooksbank, Roger W. (1991). " Successful Marketing Practice: A Literature Review and Checklist for Marketing Practitioners," *European Journal of Marketing*, Vol. 25, (5), 20-29.

Bryden, John M. (1973). *Tourism & Development—A Case Study of Commonwealth Caribbean*, Cambridge University Press, 195-220.

Burkart, A. J. & S. Medlik (1981). *Tourism: Past, Present and Future*, IInd ed., Heinemann, London, 192-219.

Burton, Rosemary (1995), *Travel Geography*, IInd ed., Pitman: London , 61-138.

Carmichael, B. (1992). *Using Conjoint Modeling Choice and Demand in Tourism*, Mansell Publishing: England, 93-98.

Chacko, Harsha E. (1995). " Positioning a Tourism Destination to Gain a Competitive Edge", *Asia Pacific Journal of Tourism Research*, Vol 1 (1), 69-75.

Chakraborty, B.K. (1981). *A Technical Guide to Hotel Operations*, A.P.H. Publishing, New Delhi 7-27.

Chang, Y.N. & Campo, Flores F (1980). Business Policy and Strategy, *Santa-Monica*, Good Year Publishing, 15-30.

Chopra, Suhita (1991). *Tourism & Development of India*, Ashish Publications; New Delhi, 20-27.

Crawford, I.M. & R.A. Lomas (1980). "Factor Analysis—A Tool for Data Reduction", *European Journal of Marketing*, Vol. 14, (7), 414-421.

Cronin, Jr., J. Joseph & A. Taylor (1992)." Measuring Service Quality: A Re-examination & Extension", *Journal of Marketing*, Vol. 56, 55-68.

Cronin, Jr., J. Joseph & A. Taylor. (1994)." SERVPREF versus SERVQUAL, Reconciling Performance Based and Perceptions minus Expectations Measurement of Service Quality", *Journal of Marketing*, Vol. 58, 125-131.

Czepial, John A. & Rosenberg, Larry J. (1987). " Customer Satisfaction: Concepts & Measurements" in Bellur, V.V. & H.W. Berkwar (ed.), *Readings in Marketing Management*, Himalayan Publishing House, Bombay.

Danaher, Peter J. & Jan Mattsson (1994). " Customer Satisfaction During the Service Delivery Process", *European Journal of Marketing*, Vol. 28 (5), 5-16.

Desh Bandhu (1983). "Income and Employment Effect of Tourism—A Case Study of J&K State", A Thesis Submitted at University of Jammu, 142-150, 180-185.

Deshmukh, S.B. & A.M. Navale (1996). "Impact of Pilgrimage Tourism on Host Population of Pandharpur," *Tourism Recreation Research*, Vol. 166-175.

Deshmukh, S.B.& A.M. Navale (1989). "A View on Pilgrimage Tourism – A Study in Human Geography", *The National Geographic Journal of India*, Vol. 35 (1), March, 23-36.

Doren, Carlton S. & Sam A. Lollar (1985). " The Consequences of Forty Years of Tourism Growth", *Annals of Tourism Research*, Vol. 12, 467-489.

Doyle, Peter (1995). " Marketing in the New Millennium", *European Journal of Marketing*, Vol. 29 (13), 23-41.

Dutta, Dev Malya (1994). "Application of Modern Societal Marketing Strategy—Concept for Sustainable Tourism Development in India', *Tourism Recreation Research*, 134-141.

Endris, A. Thabet & A. Meidan (1990). "On the Reliability of Psychographic Research: Encouraging Signs of Measurement Accuracy & Methodology in Consumer Research", *European Journal of Marketing*, Vol. 24, No.3, 23-27.

Etzel, M. & R. Wahlers (1985). "The Use of Requested Promotional Material by Pleasure Travellers", *Journal of Travel Research*, Vol. 23 (4), 2-6.

Gandhi, Indira (1980), *Eternal India*, B.I. Publications; India, 20-25.

Geva, Aviva & Arieh Goldman (1989). "Changes in the Perception of a Service During its Consumption: A Case of Organized Tours", *European Journal of Marketing*, Vol. 23 (12), 44-51.

Gordon, E. Greenlay & Allan S. Matcham (1983). "Problems in Marketing Services: The Case of Incoming Tourism", *European Journal of Marketing*,Vol. 17 (6) 57-64.

Gronross, C. (1978)."A Service-Oriented Approach to Marketing of Services"; *European Journal of Marketing*, Vol. 12 (8), 588-601.

Gronross, C. (1984). "A Service Quality Model and its Marketing Implications", *European Journal of Marketing*, Vol. 18 (4), 36-44

Gronross, C. (1989). "Defining Marketing: A Market-Oriented Approach," *European Journal of Marketing*, Vol.23 (1), 52-59.

Gronross, C. (1980). "Designing a Long Range Marketing Strategy for Services", *Long Range Planning*, Vol. 13, 36-42.

Gunn, Clare, A. (1994). "Tourism Planning: Basic Concepts and Cases, III ed., Taylor & Franics, 30-35.

Hartley, Keith & Nicholas Hooper (1992). "Tourism Policy: Market Failure & Public Choice", in Peter Johnson & Barry Thomas (ed.), *Perspective on Tourism policy*, Durham, 15-27.

Heath, Erine & Geoffrey Well (1992). *Marketing Tourism Destination*, John Wiley & Sons, 3-25.

Hooley, G.J. (1980). "The Multivariate Jungle: The Academics Playground but the Managers Minefield", *European Journal of Marketing*, Vol. 14 (7), 379-386.

Hotelling, H. (1983). "Analysis of a Complex of Statistical Variables into Principal Components", *Journal of Educational Psychology*, Vol. 24, 417-441 & 498-520.

Jafari, Jaffar, (1982). "The Tourism Market – A Basket of Goods and Services" in Tej Vir Singh's (ed)., *Studies in Tourism and Wildlife, Parks and Conservation*, Metropolitan" India , 1-3.

Jain, R.K. (1986). "Tourism Marketing: Issues and Strategies" Article Submitted at National Seminar on Domestic Tourism, Jan 17-19,1996, Department of Tourism Management, Kurukshetra University, Kurukshetra.

Jha, S.M. (1995). *Tourism Marketing*, Himalayan Publishing House, New Delhi, 32-70, 119-127

Kamra, K.K. (1996). "Domestic Tourism : A Force to Reckon with" Article submitted at National Seminar on Domestic Tourism, Jan 17-19,1996 Department of Tourism Management, Kurukshetra University, Kurukshetra.

Kandampully, J. (1993). *Total Quality Management Through Continuous Improvement in Service Industries*, Unpublished Doctoral Thesis, University of Exeter.

Kaul, R.N. (1985). *Dynamics of Tourism—A Trilogy-Transportation*. Sterling Publishers; New Delhi.3-25.

Ibid., 91-115.

Kaur, Jagdish (1996). "Badrinath—A Study in Himalayan Pilgrimage"In Tej Vir Singh's *Tourism Wildlife Parks and Conservation*, Metropolitan; New Delhi, 101-114.

Kaur, Jagdish (1986). "Pilgrim Progress to Himalayan Shrines- Studying the Phenomenon of Religious Tourism", in Tej Vir Singh's (ed.), *Tourism Wildlife Parks and Conservation*, Metropolitan; New Delhi, 224-273.

Keyser, Rik De & Norbert Van Hove (1997). "Tourism Quality Plan: An Effective Tourism Policy Tool", *The Tourist Review*, Vol. 3, 32-39.

Kotler, Philip (1989). Principles of Marketing, Prentice-Hall of India (P) Ltd., New Delhi, 15-40.

Kotler, Philip, John Bowen & James Makens (1996). *Marketing of Hospitality and Tourism*, Prentice-Hall of India (P) Ltd; New Delhi, 15-40.

Krippendorf, J. (1971). *Marketing of Tourism*, Berne, Lag. 46-50.

Lailajainen, Risto (1981)."The Unfamiliar Tourist Destination—A Marketing Challenge", *European Journal of Marketing*, Vol. 15 (7), 69-79.

Laws, Eric (1992). Tourism Marketing—Service and Quality Management Perspective, Stanley Thornes Publishers, 76-130.

Leppard, M. John, W. Malcolm, HB McDonald (1986). *How to Sell a Service-Guidelines for Effective Selling in Service Business*, Heinemann, London, 12-35.

Lilin, Gary I. & Arvind Rangaswamy (1998). *Marketing Engineering : Computer Assisted Marketing Analysis & Planning.* Addison-Wesley, Longman ; New York, 108-112.

Lovelock, C.H. (1983). "Classifying Services to Gain Strategic Marketing Insight", *Journal of Marketing*, Vol. 47, 9-20.

Luck, D.J. & O.C. Farrell (1979). *Marketing Strategy and Plans*, Prentice-Hall; Englewood Cliffs.

March, Roger (1994). "Tourism Marketing Myopia", *Tourism Management*, Vol. 15 (6), 411-415.

Mathieson, Alister & Geoffery Walls (1982). *Tourism—Economic, Physical and Social Impacts*, Longman Publisher; London 1-49, 88-91.

McCarthy, E.J. & William D. Perreautt, Jr., (1985). *Essentials of Marketing*, 3rd ed., Richard O. Irwin; USA, 116-119, 465-480.

McCollough, Michael A. (2000). " The Effect of Perceived Justice and Attributions Regarding Service Failure & Recovery on Post Recovery Customer Satisfaction and Service Quality Attitudes", *Journal of Hospitality and Tourism Research*, Vol. 24 (4), 423-447.

McIntosh, R.W. (1972). *Tourism—Principles, Practices, Philosophies*, Grid. Inc.; Columbus, 20-40.

McKeena, Regis (1995). "Real Time Marketing; A Market Oriented Approach", *European Journal of Marketing*, Vol. 23 (1), 52-59.

McQueen, J. & K. Miller (1985) . "Target Market Selection of Tourists : A Comparison of Approaches", *Journal of Travel Research*, Vol. 24 (1), 2-6.

McVey, Michael & Brian King (2000)." A Profile of India's Hotel Sector: Is a Giant Finally Awakening?" *Tourism Recreation Research*, Vol. 25 (2), 97-100.

Meidan, Arthur (1985). "The Marketing of Tourism" in Gordon Foxalls (ed.), *Marketing in Service Industry*, Frank Cass Publishers :England , 166-185.

Michie, D (1986). "Family Travel Behaviour & its Importance for Tourism Management", *Tourism Management*, Vol. 7 (1), 8-20.

Middleton, Victor T. C. & Rebecca Hawkins (1995). *Sustainable Tourism—A Marketing Perspective*, Butterworth, Heinemann, Oxford, 118-130.

Middleton, Victor T. C. (1994). *Marketing in Travel and Tourism*, IInd. ed., Butterworth, Heinemann: Oxford, 4-20.

Mill, Robert Christie & A.M. Morisson (1985). *The Tourism System—An Introductory*, Prentice-Hall Inc., 356-366.

Miline, David Frank, M.G.O & Lorne J.R. Whittles (1992). "Communities as Destination: A Marketing Taxonomy for the Effective Implementation of the Tourism Action Plan", *Journal of Travel Research*, Spring 31-37.

Moutinho, Luiz (1987). "Customer Behaviour in Tourism," *European Journal of Marketing*, Vol. 21 (10), 5-44.

Nash, Dannison (1992). "A Research Agenda on Variability of Tourism", In Valence, L. Smith's (ed.), *Tourism Alternatives*, 216-225.

Newman, Joseph, W. Westbrook Roberts & James, R. Tylor (1978). "Satisfaction/ Dissatisfaction in the Purchase Decision Process". *Journal of Marketing*, Vol 42 (October), 54-60.

Negi, Jagmohan (1982). *Tourism & Hotellering—A World Wide Industry*, Gitanjali Publishers, New Delhi., 108-131, 318-347.

Negi, Jagmohan (1990). *Tourism and Travel Concepts and Principles*, Gitanjali Publishers, New Delhi. 100-153.

Nicoulaud, B (1989). " Problems and Strategies in the International Marketing of Services", *European Journal of Marketing*, Vol. 23 (6), 55-65.

Norman, R. (1984). *Service Management : Strategy and Leadership in Service Business*, John Wiley & Sons; New York.

Otto, Julie E. & J.R. Brent Ritchie (1996). " The Service Experience in Tourism", *Tourism Management*, Vol. 17 (3), 165-174.

Page, Stephen (1995). *Urban Tourism*, Routledge; London, 3-8.

Papadapulos, Socrates I. (1989). " A Conceptual Tourism Marketing Planning Model: Part-1", *European Journal of Marketing*, Vol. 23 (1), 31-40.

Papadopoulos, S.I. (1989). : Strategy Development and Implementation of Tourism Marketing Plans: Part-2", *European Journal of Marketing*, Vol. 23 (3), 37-47.

Papadopoulos, S.I. (1986). " The Tourism Phenomenon: An Examination of Important Theories & Concepts", *Tourist Review*, Vol. 3, 2-11.

Parasuraman, A., Zeithamal, V. and Berry, L. (1985). "Conceptual Model of Service Quality and Its Implications for Future Research," *Journal of Marketing*, Vol. 49 (4), 41-50.

Pearce, D.G. (1981). *Tourism Development—Topics in Applied Geography*, Longman, U.K., 6-13.

Peters, M. (1969) *International Tourism—The Economics & Development of Internal Tourism Trade*, Hutchinson; London, 114-161, 218-268.

Poon, Auliana (1993). *Tourism Technology and Competitive Strategies*, C.A.B., International; U.K., 53-58.

Poon, Auliana (1994). "The New Tourism Revolution", *Tourism Management*, Vol. 15 (2), 91-92.

Pope, N.W. (1979). "More Micky Mouse Marketing", *American Banker*, Sept 12.

Qu, Hailin & Elsa Wong Yee Ping (1999). "A Service Performance Mode of Hong Kong Cruise Travellers Motivation Factors and Satisfaction", *Tourism Management*, Vol. 20, 237-244.

Raaij, W. Fred Van (1986). " Consumer Research on Tourism Mental and Behavioural Constructs" *Annals of Tourism Research*, Vol. 13,1-9.

Raghuram, G. & T. Madhavan (2000). " Issues in Handling Pilgrim Population at Tirumala", in Delivering Service Quality—Managerial Challenges for 21st Century by M Raghavachari & K.V. Ramani, McMillan; India, 541-551.

Rai, Lajipathi H. & J. S. Kumar (1988). " Poverty & Prosperity through Tourism in Third World", *Southern Economist*.

Rao, Vithala R. & Joel H. Steckel (1998). *Analysis for Strategic Marketing*, Addison-Wesley, Longman Inc., New York, 67-69.

Rebello, Andrey (1991). *Societal Response to Consumer Marketing*, Government, C.E.R.C. Publication, Ahmedabad.

Reicheal, Aric , Oded Lowengart & Ady Milman (2000). "Rural Tourism in Israel: Service Quality and Orientation", *Tourism Management*, Vol. 21,451-459.

Robinson, H. (1976). *A Geography of Tourism*, McDonald & Evans, London, 3-18.

Ronkainen, I.A. & A.G. Woodside (1978). " Cross Cultural Analysis of Market Profiles of Domestic & Foreign Travellers", *European Journal of Marketing*, Vol. 12 (8), 579-587.

Russell, Paul (1999). " Religious Travel in the New Millennium", *Travel & Tourist Analyst*, Vol. (5), 39-68.

Ruston; M. Angela & David J. Carson (1989). "The Marketing of Services; Managing the Intangibles", *European Journal of Marketing*, Vol. 23 (8), 23-44.

Ryan, Chris (1995). *Researching Tourist Satisfaction: Issues Concepts & Problems*, Routledge, London 40-61.

Seaton, A.V. & M. M. Bennett (1996). *Marketing Tourism Products Concepts,* Issues, *Cases;* International Thomson Business Press, 23-27.

Sivers, Angelika (1987). "The Significance of Pilgrimage Tourism in Sri Lanka (Ceylon)", *National Geographical Journal of India,* Vol. 33 (4), 430-445.

Sharma, R.D., Desh Bandhu & Sushma (2000). "Marketing Strategy for Pilgrimage Tourism—A Case Study of Hotel Services at Katra & Bhavan, "*Co-Operator's Bulletin,* Vol. 43 (9-10), 14-21.

Shaw, Gerath & Allan, M. Williams (1989). *Tourism & Economic Development, Western European Experience,* London, 2-8.

Shostack, G. Lynn (1977). "Breaking Free From Service Marketing", *Journal of Marketing,* Vol. 41, 73-80.

Singh, L.G. (1991). "Tourism Marketing in India—Problems & Prospectus", *Southern Economist,* January 1991, 17-19.

Singh, Rattan Deep (2000). *Tourism Marketing : Principles, Practices, and Strategies,* Kanishka Publishers: New Delhi, 114-164,385-450.

Singh, J.D. (1994). Management and Marketing of Tourism in India: The Challenge in P.K. Sinha & S.C. Sahoo's (ed.), *Services Marketing—Text & Readings,* Himalayan Publishing: New Delhi, 140-163.

Smith, L.J.S. (1989). *Tourism Analysis – A Handbook,* Longman Scientific and Technical, U.K, 5-13.

Stanley, Wolpart (1991). *An Introduction to India,* Viking Penguin: India, 70-78.

Subramanya, K.N. (1995). " Rejuvenating India's Tourism Industry", *Southern Economist,* 1-3.

Tewari, S.P. (1994). *Tourism Dimensions;* Atma Ram & Sons, New Delhi, 181-205.

Teye, B.Victor & Denis Leclerc (1998), " Product & Service Delivering Satisfaction Among North American Cruise Passengers," *Tourism Management,* Vol. 19 (2), 153-160.

Tribe, John & Tim Snaith (1998) "From SERVQUAL TO HOLSAT: Holiday Satisfaction in Varadero, Cuba", *Tourism Management,* Vol. 19 (1), 25-34.

Tull, Donald, S. & Del I. Hawkins (1980). *Marketing Research; Measurement & Methods – A Text with Cases,* IInd ed., McMillan, New York, 467-499.

Ugur, Yavas (1987). "Foregin Travel Behaviour in a Growing Vacation Market: Implications for Tourism Markets", *European Journal of Marketing,* Vol. 21 (5), 57-68.

Upchurch, Randell S. & Una Teivane (2000). "Resident Perceptions of Tourism Development in Riga Latvia", *Tourism Management,* Vol. 21, 499-507.

Usha Bala (1990). *Tourism in India—Policy and Perspectives,* Aarushi Prakashan, New Delhi, 40-49, 113-225.

Vieira, Walter E. (1994). "Marketing Services—The Challenges in India: in P.K. Sinha & S.C Sahoo's (ed.) *Services Marketing–Text Readings,* Himalayan Publishing House, N. Delhi, 242-253.

Vukonic, Boris (1996). *Tourism and Religion*, Pergamon, 53-60, 117-142.

Wahab. S.E. A. (1975). Wahab on Tourism Management, Tourism International Press, London, 5-15.

Walle, Alf H. (1996). "Quantitative versus Qualitative Tourism Research", European Journal of Marketing, Vol. 24 (3), 524-536.

Witt, S.F. & Luiz Moutinho (1994). *Tourism Marketing and Management – A Handbook*, Prentice-Hall; London, 279-284.

Witt, S.F. (1992). *The Management of International Tourism*, Routledge, 23-39.

GLOSSARY

Adhkumari	Major halt point at Shri Mata Vaishno Devi Shrine
Ajwain	A kind of aromatic spice
Almond	A kind of dry fruit
Amlok	A kind of dry fruit
Ampapad	Dry mangoes
Anardana	Dry pomegranate
Anzinalla	A stream flowing in Trikuta hills
Arti	Devotional activity
Autos	A Three wheeler means of transport
Baba Agar jitto	Place of religious value situated near Katra
Baba Dhansar	Place of religious value situated near Katra
Ban Ganga	A stream flowing at the foot of Trikuta hills
Bathera	A place near Katra
Bathing Ghat	A place for taking bath for pilgrims at the Shrine
Bazaar	Market/shopping center
Bhavan	The last halt point and actual place of worship at the Shrine
Bhim Ghar Fort	A Fort near Katra
Bhojanalaya	A place to take food and refreshment
Bhaironghati	A place of worship at the Shrine
Board	Shri Mata Vaishno Devi Shrine Board
Cashewnut	A kind of dry fruit
Charan Paduka	A halt place at the pilgrimage
Cholas	Special robe of divine goddess
Coated saunf	An Aromatic spice
Crival bag	Embroidered ethnic bag
Darbar	The actual diety worship place

(227)

Darbar Vaishno Devi	Darbar of Godess
Darshan	A glimpse of goddess
Darshani Darwaza	The first entrance to the pilgrimage
Desi Ghee	Pure vegetarian fat
Deva Mai Temple	A worship spot of goddess
Dhaba	An eating place
Dharamshala	Free of cost accommodation
Garbjoon	A worship place at a halt point during pilgrimage
Gurus	Religious gurus/heads
Hathi Matha	A halt point like elephant's forehead
Himkoti	A view point at the hills
Janta	General public
Jhajjar Nalla	A stream along the hills
JKTDC	Jammu & Kashmir Tourist Development Corporation
Katcha Track	Non-metallic road
Kanals	Measurement of land
Katra	The base camp of the Shrine
Kol Kandoli	Name of a temple
Kotli Baga	Place near Katra
Kishmish	Dry grapes
LPG	Liquified Petroleum Gas
Local	People belonging to J & K State
Lux	Luxury
MVD	Mata Vaishno Devi
MVD Shrine Act	Mata Vaishno Devi Shrine Act
Maha Kali	The Goddess named Kali
Maha Lakshmi	The Goddess named Lakshmi
Mahatmas	The great saints
Mahila Mandal	Names of a women association
Manokamna Bhavan	Names of an accommodation structure
Mata ka Bagh	Garden maintained at Shrine
Mata Saraswati	The Goddess named Saraswati
Matador	A kind of Mini bus
Moori	Place near Katra
Namda	A kind of woollen flooring

Glossary

Nangal	Place near Katra
Navratras	Nine Puja Days of the Goddess
Niharika Yatri Niwas	Name of an accommodation structure
Nomain	Place near Katra
Ord.	Ordinary
Pacca Track	Metallic Road
Painalla	A stream flowing at hills
Panchi view point	Name of a view point at hills
Panthal	Place near Katra
Pashmina	Variety of a fine woollen texture
Pirs	Saints
Pithu	Labour employed for carrying small children and luggage
Ponies	Horses and mules used for carrying luggage and people
Puja	Worship
Puja Pilgrim	Pilgrims visiting during Navratras
Puri Chana	A kind of delicacy of northern India
Raghunath Temple	Temple of Shri Ram
Rajmash	A kind of cereal/gram
SMVDSB	Shri Mata Vaishno Devi Shrine Board
SPSS	Statistical Package for Social Science
SRTC	State Road Transport Corporation
Safai Karamchari	People/staff employed for dusting and cleaning
Saffron	A kind of flower
Sanji Chatt	A halt point at hills
Sankarant	Special worship day and fasting day
Sarai	Free accommodation
Serla Bhaga	Place near Katra
Shringar Chunis	A special robe of goddess
Soveniers	A special item taken as gift
Tirthatna	Pilgrimage
Trikuta Bhagwati	Name of a goddess
Triumala Tirupati	A place of pilgrimage in Southern India
Vaishnavi Dham Jammu	Accommodation structure at Jammu
Vatika	A kind of Garden
Vishram Ghar Katra	Accommodation structure at Katra

Walnut	A kind of dry fruit
Yatra Registration Counter	A counter where pilgrims are registered and slips are issued
Yatra slip	Slips with names of Pilgrims
Yatri Niwas	Name of an accommodation structure
Yatrika Phase-II	Accommodation structure at Jammu
Yatris	Pilgrims

INDEX

❑ ❑ ❑